Moreton Morrell Site

Qualitative Marketing Research

Moreton Morrell Site

INTRODUCING QUALITATIVE METHODS provides a series of volumes which introduce qualitative research to the student and beginning researcher. The approach is interdisciplinary and international. A distinctive feature of these volumes is the helpful student exercises.

One stream of the series provides texts on the key methodologies used in qualitative research. The other stream contains books on qualitative research for different disciplines or occupations. Both streams cover the basic literature in a clear and accessible style, but also cover the 'cutting edge' issues in the area.

SERIES EDITOR
David Silverman (Goldsmiths College)

Qualitative Marketing Research
A Cultural Approach

Johanna Moisander and Anu Valtonen

SAGE Publications
London • Thousand Oaks • New Delhi

SAGE Publications Ltd
1 Oliver's Yard
55 City Road
London EC1Y 1SP

SAGE Publications Inc.
2455 Teller Road
Thousand Oaks, California 91320

SAGE Publications India Pvt Ltd
B-42, Panchsheel Enclave
Post Box 4109
New Delhi 110 017

British Library Cataloguing in Publication data

A catalogue record for this book is available from the British Library

ISBN10 1 4129 0380 7   ISBN13 978 1 4129 0380 6
ISBN10 1 4129 0381 5 (pbk)   ISBN13 978 1 4129 0381 3 (pbk)

Library of Congress Control Number 2005933780

Typeset by C&M Digitals (P) Ltd, Chennai, India
Printed on paper from sustainable resources
Printed in Great Britain by The Cromwell Press Ltd, Trowbridge Wiltshire

Contents

Preface

The general purpose of this book is to introduce and elaborate on the cultural approach to qualitative marketing research. Inspired and informed by recent developments in the field of marketing and consumer research, we set out to outline and discuss a methodological perspective and a set of methods that we see as particularly well suited for studying the cultural dynamics of consumption and marketplace interaction. Our discussion is premised upon the methodological principle that research methods are primarily ways of expressing theoretical positions; and that theory and methodology are two inextricably linked aspects of a particular philosophical perspective to social inquiry. Therefore, throughout the book we emphasize the close link between theory and methods as well as the importance of considering ontological and epistemological questions. As qualitative methods are comprehended and used differently within different philosophical and methodological frameworks, it makes sense to discuss them as research methods only in the context of specific philosophical and conceptual frameworks.

Most of the methodological textbooks on marketing research tend to take a very general approach to qualitative research methods, as the 'non-quantitative', softer, interpretive or naturalistic alternative for or complement to the established quantitative methods. In these accounts qualitative research is often treated as a single, clearly defined approach to empirical research, and qualitative methods are discussed as if they were some sort of tools in the 'qualitative toolbox'. We argue, however, that currently what these books call 'qualitative research' is in fact a heterogenous methodological field, consisting of a wide range of different approaches, which are all grounded on more or less different epistemological, ontological and methodological commitments. Even a casual review of recent journals of marketing and consumer research would seem to illustrate the great variety of methods and methodologies that are currently in use.

Therefore, we believe that it is practically impossible to cover the entire field of qualitative marketing research in a single textbook in a way that adds value to the intended readers. To be able to provide valuable knowledge on how to carry out high quality research, a textbook on qualitative research methods needs to focus on a more homogenous set of methodologies, which share – to a sufficient degree at least – a common philosophical background. In this book, the focus is particularly on a fairly new methodological perspective to marketing and consumer research, which has taken form mainly in the 1990s, and which draws extensively from cultural studies and poststructuralist thought. Here we refer to this perspective as 'the cultural approach' and the literature that reflects this approach as *cultural marketing and consumer research*.

To our knowledge, there are few available marketing-related textbooks that focus particularly on qualitative methods suitable for studying culture and cultural practice in the marketplace, for example, consumer culture, products as cultural artifacts and marketers (including product designers and advertisers) as cultural mediators. There are books that are based on various psychodynamic and cognitive approaches to social psychology, which aim to introduce qualitative methods for revealing the workings of the 'unconscious mind' or the personal, psychological meanings, emotions and experiential knowledge that guide consumers' buying behavior and brand preferences (e.g., Zaltman, 2003). But these books generally overlook the cultural dynamics of consumption, and thus fail to provide knowledge on methods for studying cultural meanings (for example, cultural narratives and myths that help consumers to make sense of their everyday life).

The book is primarily aimed at graduate and undergraduate students majoring in business administration (for example, in marketing, consumer behavior, or management and organization studies) and in other fields of social sciences (media studies, sociology and communication) who are interested in cultural approaches to economic and social theory. We have written this book for people who already have a basic knowledge of social scientific research methods and who are interested in the emerging cultural approach in the field of marketing and consumer research. For them, the book offers an account of the cultural approach to studying marketplace phenomena, and hopefully a sound and extensive comprehension of the methodological principles that should guide the process of designing and carrying out a study from such a cultural perspective. The book provides methodological tools particularly for marketing and consumer research but it also offers means and ways of tackling the close link between culture and economy in contemporary society, as well as the many related topics such as power and representation in the business context.

The book also provides insights for MBA students and other business professionals who work in the field of marketing, advertising, media planning and qualitative market research. The book offers these readers methodological resources for keeping their professional skills up to date, thereby helping them to buy, design and conduct relevant and skillful market research, which is sensitive to the cultural dynamics of the marketplace behavior.

Most of the literature we draw from and many of the examples we use in this book deal with consumer marketing, but the ideas and methodologies we discuss may equally fruitfully be applied in many other fields of marketing research, such as relationship marketing, services marketing, or marketing networks. In this book, we focus on consumer marketing primarily for the simple fact that most of the published, scholarly research on the cultural aspects of the marketplace, to date, has been conducted by consumer researchers (but cf. Brown et al., 2001; Peñaloza, 2000; Peñaloza and Gilly, 1999). As a characteristically multidisciplinary area of research, consumer inquiry has traditionally been more open to the influence of the contemporary philosophical and methodological debates in social sciences, which have largely informed the research on the cultural dynamics of consumption and marketplace activity.

The contents of the book are organized in five sections. Part 1 discusses the emerging 'cultural approach' in marketing and consumer research, and elaborates on the methodological perspective that informs and guides our discussion on qualitative methods in the book. We call this perspective *analytics of cultural practice* (*ACP*). We map out the basic assumptions of ACP and elaborate on the evaluative criteria that we see fit for this approach. We postpone the more detailed – and more scholarly – discussion on the philosophical assumptions and commitments of this approach to the very end of the book. Part 2 then concentrates on discussing and elaborating on a range of empirical materials and methods for studying the marketplace from this cultural perspective. We take up ethnography, cultural texts and talk, as well as visual materials and methods. Part 3, in turn, discusses the interpretation and analysis of cultural data, and finally, Part 4 takes up the question of writing in cultural research, also offering advice for writing up the research report or paper. In Part 5 we conclude the book by discussing the more scholarly, philosophical questions about ACP and cultural research in general, which may be raised by reviewers and members of PhD committees for example. We discuss the basic assumptions of ACP, drawing attention to theoretical legacies that have contributed to our understanding of consumer culture. We also make an attempt to historicize the cultural turn in marketing and consumer research. Our discussion is organized around a number of questions and answers. We hope they are also helpful for responding to the often misplaced critical questions that students who do cultural research sometimes encounter in research seminars and conferences where the audience is not entirely familiar with the basic assumptions of the cultural approach.

In the course of writing this book we have received support and advice from a large number of people. In particular, we are grateful for the comments and critique that we have received from Fuat A. Firat, University of Texas Pan American; Annamma Joy, Concordia University, Montreal; Lisa Peñaloza, University of Colorado at Boulder; Kristina Rolin, Helsinki School of Economics and Business Administration; Soile Veijola, University of Lapland; Maria Suokannas, Swedish School of Economics; and Kirsi Eräranta, University of Helsinki. Moreover, we wish to express our gratitude to students at Helsinki School of Economics who have participated in our courses on qualitative research and methods. Their comments have greatly contributed to this book. Financially, the writing task has been partly supported by a grant from the Finnish Foundation of Economic Education. Finally, we also would like to thank the editors of this book, Professor David Silverman and Patrick Brindle, for their continuous support and encouragement, and particularly for their most valuable comments and advice throughout the process of writing this book.

Part 1

Cultural Approach to Markets and Methods

'Hi! I'd like to buy a new mobile phone,' says a customer at the service counter of a home electronics store.

'Do you have any particular brand in mind or any particular features that you consider essential?' asks the sales person.

'Well, hmmm ... not really. I just want to get a new phone, a new model, it has to look cool, some well-known brand of course, not too expensive – and not too complicated!' the customer replies. The sales person starts to talk about the phones, explaining their features and benefits, frequently resorting to techno-jargon. The customer listens, asks a few additional questions, and finally buys a phone and walks out the door.

Later, at home, when the phone is ready to be used, the customer makes a call: 'Hi Dad, I just bought a new mobile phone.'

'Again? You just bought one a few months ago, didn't you?'

'Well, they had these cool new models on sale! You should get one too.'

'Yes, that's what you keep telling me. But I'll never get a mobile phone – you know that!'

How should we interpret this story? How can we gain insight into the everyday behavior of marketplace actors? If we interpret the little story on the basis of the knowledge we have learned from the classic textbooks on marketing management, it represents a successful market exchange. The customer's needs are satisfied, a profit is made and the shareholders are kept happy. Supply meets Demand. The story also displays different customers – different market segments and customer groups. There is the ideal customer who regularly updates the mobile device, and the non-customer, perhaps a late follower who is reluctant to accept new products, such as new technological devices.

However, if we re-read the same little story from a cultural perspective we notice that the above market-exchange interpretation ignores a range of points and issues that are relevant both from marketing and societal perspectives. The cultural approach to marketing and consumer research draws attention, for instance, to the ways in which people use particular products and services for creating and sustaining social relations. It also draws attention to the ways in which even the most ordinary market-place activities – such as buying and using mobile phones – may involve cultural contestation and even political struggle. The act of not-buying particular products may represent a form of resistance against particular forms of life and identity. A cultural approach to marketing and consumer research, hence, views marketplace interaction not only in terms of economic transactions but also as a cultural form, closely related to other cultural forms, institutions, representations and practices that make up our lifestyles and daily routines. The focus is therefore not on how people respond to marketing incentives or behave in a passively inherited culture. The cultural approach is rather concerned with the processes and practices through which different market actors produce and make use of products and services as *cultural artifacts*. The idea is to produce *cultural knowledge of the marketplace*, to study how cultural, social and materials realities are constructed through marketplace processes both for consumers and marketers. In other words, we take the view that analyzing the marketplace provides insight into the workings of contemporary culture. The objective of this book is to provide conceptual and methodological tools for such analysis.

Here in Part 1 we specify the theoretical background and the interpretive framework that informs the discussion of qualitative marketing research in this book. Chapter 1 introduces cultural marketing and consumer research and the methodological perspective that guides the discussion of qualitative methods in this book. A more detailed discussion on the historical, conceptual and philosophical foundations of this framework is postponed to the very end of the book, to Part 5. Chapter 2 then focuses specifically on evaluation, questions of validity, reliability and generalization.

1

The 'Cultural Turn' in Marketing and Consumer Research

CHAPTER SUMMARY

This chapter introduces the perspective to qualitative marketing and consumer research that is adopted in the book. The objective is to:

- introduce cultural marketing and consumer research and the methodological perspective from which qualitative research methods are discussed and elaborated on in this book;
- illustrate the conceptual, interpretive framework that informs this methodological perspective by discussing the ways in which core marketing constructs – consumers, marketers and products – may be comprehended in studies that adopt this perspective; and to
- illustrate the practical relevance of obtaining cultural knowledge on marketplace phenomena from this perspective.

Introduction

Recently, in the field of marketing and consumer research there has been a growing interest in studying marketplace phenomena from new cultural and postmodern perspectives. This increasing interest – informed by the so called 'cultural turn' in social sciences – may be seen as a response to an alleged crisis of relevance in academic marketing research. Alternative 'interpretive' and 'heretical' approaches to theorizing and empirical research have been proposed and discussed in an attempt to improve both the social and the practical pertinence of academic research. Many critics of mainstream marketing thought have argued that new perspectives and methods are needed to gain a better understanding of the cultural complexity of the increasingly multicultural and globalized market environments.

As a result, new academic journals have been established (for example, *Journal of Consumer Culture* and *Consumption Markets & Culture*), and the number of scholarly articles published in the established mainstream journals focusing on cultural aspects of consumption and market phenomena has been growing steadily. Informed by poststructuralism and contemporary cultural studies, the cultural approach to marketing and consumer research has tended to study 'the imbricated layers of cultural meaning that structure consumer actions in a given social context' (Thompson and Troester, 2002: 550). Many of the published studies manifesting such an approach have focused on topics such as the cultural construction of consumer values and lifestyles (e.g., Holt, 1997; Thompson and Troester, 2002), construction of consumer identity and self (e.g., Thompson and Haytko, 1997; Thompson and Hirschman, 1995), as well as on the ways in which historically established cultural discourses and cultural myths are appropriated, negotiated and resisted in the marketplace (e.g., Holt and Thompson, 2004; Thompson, 2004; Peñaloza, 2000, 2001). Some scholars have also focused on the ways in which different market actors, such as marketers and consumers, and market phenomena, such as exchange relationships, have been represented or constructed in marketing literature (Bristor and Fischer, 1993; Fischer and Bristor, 1994; Hirschman, 1993).

The cultural approach to marketing and consumer behavior has evolved over the past twenty years among the 'radical' marketing scholars who have contested the constitutive values of mainstream marketing thought by doing critical, experiential, feminist, interpretive, postpositivist, poststructural and postmodern marketing and consumer research. These alternative approaches have typically been based on the use of interpretive qualitative research methods and have thus often been lumped together and labeled as 'interpretive' marketing or consumer research (Beckman and Elliot, 2000; Hirschman, 1989; Sherry, 1991).

The gradual institutionalization of the interpretive and thus also the cultural marketing and consumer research began, perhaps, from a research project that has come to be known as the *Consumer Behavior Odyssey* (see Belk, 1991; Kassarjian, 1987). In the summer of 1986 about two dozen academic consumer researchers traveled across the United States, from coast to coast, in a recreation vehicle (RV) conducting qualitative research on American consumption. Working from the RV, the scholars employed 'naturalistic' methods to document various buyer and consumer behaviors, by means of videotaped in-situ consumer interviews, largely unobtrusive still photos and impressionistic journals, for example. The aim was to obtain an archive of records to be used later for various sorts of pedagogical and research purposes. Russell Belk (1991) characterizes Consumer Behavior Odyssey as an epic journey that opposed traditions in the field and sought fresh ways of acquiring knowledge about the domain and nature of consumer behavior. The project generated numerous published papers and stimulated discussion and debate on philosophy of science and methodology, and thus contributed significantly to the development of qualitative – interpretive – research in the field of marketing and consumer research.

Later, the *Heretical Consumer Research* (HCR) conference organized in association with the yearly Association for Consumer Research (ACR) conferences, as well as the ACR-sponsored conference on *Gender Marketing and Consumer Behavior,* both in Europe and in the United States, have been important discussion forums and institutions for scholars interested in the more qualitative and also critical 'interpretive' work in the field. *Consumption, Markets & Culture,* a journal established by Fuat Firat, Nikhilesh Dholakia and Alladi Venkatesh, has functioned as an important discussion forum among the scholars participating in these conferences. The journal aims to promote cultural research that is cross-disciplinary or multi-perspectival. As Firat (1997) has pointed out, to study complex cultural phenomena it is necessary to draw upon and cross the discourses of a number of different disciplines.

Concurrently, the practitioner-oriented literature on the topic has proliferated (e.g., Solomon, 2003). In the field of advertising and brand management, for example, there has been a growing interest in meanings, symbolism and postmodern forms of affinity (for example, virtual and brand communities; tribal marketing, see Kozinets, 2002b; Cova and Cova, 2002). It seems that advertising and marketing professionals are ever more readily recognizing the need to leverage cultural knowledge and creativity to induce consumers to form deeper relationships with products, for example by building powerful 'iconic brands' (Holt, 2003).

Particularly in brand management, there seems to be a shift under way, in strategic thinking, from the traditional 'features and benefits mentality' to strategies based on understanding 'what a product or service offers and how it affects customers' lives', as Michael Solomon (2003) puts it. Echoing the concerns of many contemporary scholars and practitioners, he emphasizes that it is important to consider what the brand stands for, not only how the brand performs. Particularly for products of the 'lifestyle categories', such as food, clothing, alcohol and automobiles, this would seem to be crucial for survival.

Douglas Holt (2003), for example, has recently argued in *Harvard Business Review* that Nike, Harley–Davidson and many other powerful brands maintain a firm hold in the marketplace mainly because they have become cultural icons. They do not succeed primarily because they offer distinctive benefits, trustworthy service or innovative technology but rather because they forge a deep connection with culture. They invoke powerful cultural narratives and myths, citing culturally shared meanings, norms and values, and thus give people a sense of structure and security in their life. Therefore, these brands continue to add value to their customers, year after year.

All in all then, a new research orientation with a novel way of thinking about marketing and consumption as inherently cultural phenomena seems to be emerging and taking form both in academic research and in marketing practice. The most important cognitive goal that characterizes this orientation is, perhaps, the goal of gaining a better understanding of the cultural contingency and complexity of marketplace phenomena, established on shared cultural meanings and social relations. In this book, we discuss methods and methodologies for attaining such an understanding and for obtaining cultural knowledge of the marketplace in general. We do this from a particular methodological perspective that we have labeled elsewhere as analytics of cultural practice (ACP) (Moisander and Valtonen, 2005). This perspective focuses specifically on culture and cultural practices.

ACP can be distinguished from the various forms of typically psychologically oriented interpretive marketing research that focus on the individual. In these perspectives, the importance of culture and cultural contexts of consumption is usually explicitly acknowledged but the focus of interest and empirical research is nevertheless on the individual consumers and their personal meanings, motives, perceptions and intentions. We acknowledge that this type of psychological research on personal meanings and values, for example, may well be relevant and useful for various marketing purposes. But intra-personal psychological constructs in all forms remain outside the scope of the cultural perspective that we discuss in this book. In Part 5 we discuss the conceptual and methodological foundations of this perspective in more detail.

Box 1.1   The cultural turn in marketing management

We live in a cultural economy of signs, as Robert Goldman and Stephen Papson, authors of *Nike Culture*, point out. Our everyday environment is thoroughly embedded with commercial signs: they are present in the clothing products we use, the social spaces we occupy, the media we watch and in the language we use. In this sort of economy, brands may become important cultural icons – think of brands such as Nike or Harley–Davidson – (and acquire an impressive market power), but they are, nevertheless, built according to principles entirely different from those of conventional marketing. Now, companies' success depends heavily on understanding, managing and appropriating cultural signs and symbols, and especially, the particular value-adding logic and process of a sign economy.

As widely discussed in the marketing literature, the product value has less to do with the material properties of the product than with its symbolic properties. In the Nike value chain, for instance, the production and appropriation of cultural meanings has become the key source of value, not just an addendum. Advertising constitutes, obviously, a key system for producing sign values. In comparing, for instance, Nike's annualized growth curves of total revenue with advertising and promotion expenditures there can be seen a remarkable correspondence, as Goldman and Papson point out (2004: 13).

Importantly, however, it is not merely the amount of advertising, but the content, that counts: what sorts of cultural meanings are to be linked to the product through advertising? How may it become an icon? Douglas Holt (2003) has argued that successful commercial symbols touch on key cultural contradictions and ambiguities; they help people to deal with and resolve tensions people feel in their lives. This means that powerful symbols are loaded with ambiguities: people love them and love to hate them. Accordingly, Nike advertising does not merely sell commodities, but it gives voice to important

(Continued)

cultural contradictions that define our era. Nike advertisements touch on, for instance, the issues of race and gender, and poverty and inequality. Moreover, the underlying philosophy of Nike challenges viewers to confront and to overcome barriers in their everyday life. In doing so, it leans on the powerful myth of rebellion and, above all, on the myth of individual achievement.

Yet, acknowledging that these myths of rebellion and individual achievement are widely appropriated by other marketers as well, we must ask: Why does Nike's advertising stand out? The answer lies, according to Goldman and Papson, in the domain of aesthetic style and expression. Nike is not just doing it, but carefully considering how to do it. In its advertising, Nike presents, first of all, a creative recombination of athlete culture and popular culture, and secondly, it expresses itself with a photographic style and tone that makes the difference. Actually, managing the aesthetic power of images becomes a crucial marketing task in a sign economy.

Moreover, besides the advertising, the way Nike's products are distributed plays a key role in the value-adding process. NIKETOWNs are spaces not merely for selling products, but for telling stories, for displaying company values and thereby adding value to the brand. Actually, more than stores, they have become significant tourist destinations. This phenomenon, in turn, is a typical characteristic of a sign economy: commercial signs have the power to attract us in the same vein as Niagara Falls.

Source: Goldman and Papson (2004); Holt (2003)

Taking the cultural perspective to marketing and consumer research

The cultural approach to marketing and consumer behavior that we specify here is based on the basic assumption that we live in a culturally constituted world, and that in contemporary Western society this constitution largely takes place in and through the market. The generic research problem that characterizes the cultural approach therefore is: *how* are social reality and social order produced, maintained, contested, negotiated and transformed in the market?

We take the view that the marketplace is a joint cultural production of marketers and consumers (Peñaloza, 2000, 2001). From this perspective, the focus of interest is thus on the ways in which *both* marketers *and* consumers play a part in producing the cultural world, as well as on the institutional forms and practices through which this takes place. The market is not necessarily studied *either* from the marketers' *or* the consumers' perspective, as it is typically studied in the field of marketing. As Lisa Peñaloza has pointed out:

[I]n carving out the study of consumer behavior as a separate field of inquiry independent of marketing activities, consumer researchers may be losing sight of the ways in which consumers and marketers negotiate cultural meanings in relation to each other in the marketplace. The many contrasts and overlaps between consumer cultures and market cultures here create a prime setting for exploring the mediating roles of cultural meanings for consumers in relation to market agents and institutions. (Peñaloza, 2001: 394)

We also acknowledge that marketing academics have an important role in producing the cultural world. Anthropological and ethnographic literature has highlighted well the mutually constitutive relationship between academic disciplines and people's life-worlds (Appadurai, 1996; Clifford and Marcus, 1986). Therefore, we also wish to draw attention to the ways in which *marketing discipline* and *marketing knowledge* take part in the construction of social reality. It is our contention that marketing researchers not only discover facts, theories and representations but also construct them, as Fuat Firat and Alladi Venkatesh (1995: 258–9) point out. Much of this construction takes place through the discipline's core constructs, which always carry a particular view of social reality, implicitly or explicitly.

We now turn to discuss briefly the assumptions upon which core constructs such as consumer, marketer and market rely in the cultural approach we discuss in this book, and how they differ from mainstream definitions. A fundamental premise in our approach is that none of these constructs can be taken as a given. From this vantage point, concepts such as economy and consumer are not necessarily accepted as received, but rather the ways in which they come into being are taken under investigation (Firat, 1999). We begin the discussion by elaborating on the key concept of cultural approach, namely culture.

Culture

Culture is a complex concept, which can be defined in a number of different ways depending on the research paradigm and theoretical perspective taken. In the cultural perspective that we discuss here, culture refers to the systems of representation through which people make sense of their everyday life. It includes the culturally standardized or institutionalized discourses (cultural discourses) that constitute the conditions of possibility for people to think, talk and act. It also includes the everyday discursive, social and material practices (everyday cultural practices) through which meaning and cultural artifacts are produced, and through which people express themselves, interpret each other and exert power on others in social life. Through everyday cultural practices institutional discourses are also produced, transformed, negotiated and contested.

In this line of thinking, culture is not an objectified thing or self-enclosed, coherent, patterned field of meaning, which is often the everyday meaning of the term 'culture', particularly in the talk about cultural differences between nation-states. Culture is not a socially integrating system of norms and values that produces social order. Rather, it is produced, transformed and contested in social interaction. Therefore, culture is not seen as something to be reduced to a fixed locality or entity such as nationality or ethnicity. Neither is it a factor external to individual actors or groups of actors that guides action through exerting an impact on actors' motivation or intentions. It is not a force that is more or less the same for all members of a culture or a subculture – and thus something that can be reduced to a variable or a set of variables accounting for cultural variation in the survey data. Nor is culture necessarily something that can be engineered at will (Frow and Morris, 2003). In management literature, for example, culture is sometimes seen as a plastic medium that can be managed, reworked and remolded to change and challenge employees' everyday working practices (for example, service culture, corporate culture). And finally, culture is not merely a detached domain for playing games of social distinction and good taste.

Culture refers, instead, to the whole way of life of a social group as it is structured by representation and by power. It is something that is constantly produced, reproduced, contested and negotiated in the everyday practices of the members of the culture. It thus gets variable interpretations and takes different forms in different social and institutional situations and contexts. As John Frow and Meaghan Morris (2003: 491) put it, 'it is a network of embedded practices and representations (texts, images, talk, codes of behavior and the narrative structures organizing these) that shapes every aspect of social life'. Culture permeates all of society.

On the one hand, culture is produced in the communication and interaction processes and practices of everyday life where meanings are continuously being reproduced, contested, negotiated and changed. On the other hand, it constitutes an archive of shared meanings, a whole system of representation (Hall, 1997a) and a matrix of intelligibility (Butler, 1990) that guides and constrains the ways in which people interact and make sense of themselves, others and their being in the world. Culture thus organizes and orients social life through narratives, myths, taken-for-granted categorizations, role expectations and social practices, and in particular, through the implicit values, norms and relations of power they involve (Mackay, 1997).

In contemporary Western society, economy and the world of business play a significant role in the production of culture. In the modern consumer society, culturally shared meanings and practices are produced, reproduced and transformed in the market, through the symbolic processes and practices of production and consumption. The role of marketing in the birth and growth of the consumer society as well as in the formation of consumer culture in specific markets has been extensively discussed (e.g., Firat and Venkatesh, 1995; Peñaloza, 1994). As participants in a culture, consumers and marketers give meaning to people, objects and events by the different ways in which they *represent* them in text, talk, images and signifying practices (Hall, 1997a). Marketers, for example, construct meanings by creating images and by weaving narratives and fantasies – with particular morals – around brands and products, among other things. Consumers, in turn, engage in the production of cultural meanings when they make use of, appropriate and give value to these brands and products, and to the symbolic meanings attached to them, in the rituals and practices of their everyday life. From this perspective, both consumption and marketing can be viewed as production: as production of meaning in the 'circuit of culture' (du Gay et al., 1997). They are signifying practices, parts of the systems of representation where social reality is produced and takes form. Meanings are thus not only assumed to animate marketplace behavior, but consumption and production, including marketing, are viewed as essentially cultural phenomena.

Marketers

One way of looking at marketers is to view them as 'new cultural intermediaries' (Negus, 2002; see also McCracken, 1986) of some sort. Producing and circulating symbolic forms, goods and services, producers and marketing practitioners play a critical role in connecting production to consumption. On the one hand, they shape products and services according to market expectations, feeding the preferences and practices of consumers back into the design and marketing processes. On the other hand, they also function as significant shapers of taste, inducing and giving birth to new wants, needs and consumption-oriented lifestyles, exerting power and authority from their position within important cultural institutions.

Marketers and advertisers, then, can be understood as cultural mediators both accommodating their consumers and working to alter their consumption patterns to bring them in line with their own strategies and policies (Peñaloza and Gilly, 1999; Peñaloza, 2000, 2001). However, this is not always the case. The link between consumers and marketers can be missing for a number of reasons (Negus, 2002). First of all, marketing and consumer intelligence are not always effective. Marketers are not necessarily able to gain a sufficiently good understanding of their target customers. Moreover, much of the work of marketing practitioners is habitual. They rely on symbolic material that is constructed as a result of well-established routines that require little effort and sourcing, such as updating old marketing concepts, re-writing old advertising narratives, and re-packaging old products. And finally, sometimes through the use of imagery, words and symbols that marketers construct and circulate, they deliberately offer only an illusion of a link between consumers and marketers.

Products and brands

Products and brands in this framework can be viewed and analyzed as cultural artifacts, as resources and carriers of meanings, produced and consumed in and through processes and practices of representation. The same is also true, obviously, of services and servicescapes, where signs, symbols and artifacts are particularly important in creating service concepts (Bitner, 1992; Sherry, 1998).

Throughout the history of consumer research, one of the most dominant ways of conceptualizing product symbolism has been to consider brands and products as social markers that communicate and express the social status or preferable lifestyle of a consumer. In this line of thinking, products and brands function as symbolic goods and signs that are used to signify status, prestige and social standing. We would like to emphasize, however, that products and brands are not merely symbolic markers of social status or tools for image management. As Arjun Appadurai (1996: 67) points out, '[t]he fact that consumption may sometimes be conspicuous and imitative should not tempt us to regard it as always being so'. People do not use brands and products just to 'keep up with the Joneses'.

Neither are brands and products merely symbolic tools for constructing and re-constructing identity, as many contemporary psychologically oriented scholars seem to assume. In consumer behavior textbooks, products are often discussed as part of the *extended self* (Belk, 1988) or as means of closing the gap between their *actual* and *desired* or *ideal selves*. In these accounts, the focus of interest is usually on the psychological processes or personal structures of meaning that are theorized to motivate consumers' use of products and brands. It is thought, for example, that consumers buy, use and display particular products to close the gap between the real and the ideal self or to try on a new – younger, sexier and more 'cool' – selves as well as to symbolize self-change (Arnould et al., 2002). This is an interesting stream of research but, in focusing on individual experience, it tends to downplay the cultural dynamics and social complexity of consumption and social behavior in general (Moisander and Valtonen, 2005; Oksala, 2004; Scott, 1992).

The dynamics of consumption is much more complex. As Solomon (2003: 33) has pointed out, products and brands are 'inextricably woven into the fabric of our cultural universe'. As gifts, products may play important roles in interpersonal relationships for example (Joy, 2001). Brands can function as cultural icons and as encapsulated myths (Holt, 2003; Holt and Thompson, 2004). People buy them because they deliver powerful cultural myths in a tangible form. The myths that these brands embody prescribe an ideology with moral imperatives and a vision for the community to aspire to, thus giving people a sense of structure in life.

To further illustrate, several consumption activities play a significant role in giving people a sense of time. A set of common consumption practices takes on the function of structuring temporal rhythm, and thereby creating regimes of periodicity. Think of, for instance, the ways in which season-based cycles of fashion – summer fashion and winter fashion collections – play a role in giving some form of seasonality. Actually, consumption periodicities may even constitute the principal significance of these 'natural' events instead of simply marking them in some loose, 'symbolic' manner, as Appadurai (1996: 69) points out. Moreover, acts of consumption that surround routine rites of passage – the ways to transfer from one sphere of life to another – enter into the creation of different temporal categories, such as free time and work time. People have a cup of coffee or smoke a cigarette when they take a break from work, for example, or have a bottle of beer after work to create an end for the work day and to liberate themselves from work-related matters. As these sorts of products are commonly used to produce the sort of time we tend to call and understand as *free* time, they also come to embody and reproduce the Western myth of freedom (Valtonen, 2004a).

Consumers

Consumers, in the cultural framework we wish to elaborate on here, are seen as active players, perpetually re-working the meaning that they consume. In using and domesticating products and technologies, for example, consumers often transform, customize and re-configure the products they buy (Mackay, 1997; D. Miller, 1997). In this process they also invest meanings in these products and technologies, re-accenting and re-articulating the meanings that marketers or producers attach to them. Importantly, therefore, meaning is not just inscribed on products through design, advertising and marketing. It is also produced by consumers through the use to which they put these products in the practice of their everyday lives. While producers try to commodify meaning, encoding images and symbols into things that can be sold and bought, consumers more or less actively use their creativity to try to give their own meanings to the products and services that they buy. As du Gay et al. (1997: 103) put it, meanings are constructed 'in an ongoing cycle of commodification – where producers make new products or different versions of old products as a result of consumers' activities – and appropriation – where consumers make those products meaningful, sometimes making them achieve a new "register" of meaning that affects production in some way.' Consumption may thus be seen as a form of production. Consumers produce symbols and meanings that are incorporated into the system of representation in which people act and make sense of their everyday life (Firat and Venkatesh, 1995: 258). They construct culture through the creative work associated with consumption. Therefore, consumers are not necessarily passive victims of capitalism but may well have a more active role in shaping the meanings of products and brands (Mackay, 1997; Miller, 1995).

So the view of the consumer as a 'couch potato' is, in fact, outdated, as Solomon (2003) maintains. But people do not necessarily pick and choose the brands that speak to them, quite autonomously as many contemporary postmodern scholars seem to suggest. The prevalent consumer culture provides only a limited matrix of intelligibility in which people's subjectivities as consumers and as citizens are constituted and within which they can operate. Moreover, the terms of the dialogue and the cycle of commodification in which products and brands are created as cultural artifacts are not necessarily equal. Marketers (including advertisers, designers and retail buyers) are powerful cultural gatekeepers. Together with editors, journalists, reviewers and 'experts' of many sorts they have a significant influence on what is eventually supplied and offered to consumers in the market. As Solomon (2003: 59) writes, 'a paradox of consumerspace is that the abundance of choice is in some ways illusory'. Many of the choices consumers make are largely predetermined, influenced by the judgments of cultural gatekeepers who steadily winnow down the options before people ever see them.

Consequently, consumers should not be studied as autonomous subjects. Nor should they be understood as detached and independent 'postmodern consumers' celebrating the world of goods and markets. Instead, consumers and marketers should be studied together, in a dialogue or interaction, as participants in cycles of commodification and as producers of culture. As such, they also should be studied as moral and political actors, involved in, constrained and enabled by various forms and relations of power.

Box 1.2   Taking a cultural approach to studying the marketplace

The cultural approach to marketing and consumer research pays attention to cultural structures and, in particular, to structures-in-use. Let us exemplify what this means in practice. Studying a space such as a shopping mall from this perspective means, first of all, that you understand the mall as a textual construct and shopping as a cultural form that is interrelated with other cultural forms, representations and practices that make up a 'way of life'. It also means that you pay attention to the ways in which disparate structures meet in and flow through the use of such a complex site as a shopping mall.

In practice, your task is to identify the sorts of discourses that are present in the context of a mall and how they are practiced and displayed in the everyday use and management of such a space; for instance, how economic discourse becomes practiced in the ways in which a mall is managed or in the ways in which pricing strategies are implemented; or, how aesthetic discourse becomes practiced through particular product displays, use of colors and lay out. That is to say, you pay attention to how cultural discourse and discursive practice are interplayed in the empirical context of a mall.

Moreover, such a study acknowledges that this interplay is not any neutral or innocent one but embedded in a field of power. You therefore pay attention to the ways in which particular politics are played out in a mall, focusing, for instance, on zoning permits, the micropolitics of corporeal discipline, or gender-specific targeting and display of products.

Methodically, you have several options to conduct such a study. You may conduct an ethnographic study, for instance, and immerse yourself into the life a particular mall for a period of time, obtaining data through observation and photography, for instance. You may also use empirical materials, such as architectural drawings of the mall, advertising materials, or managerial documents such as memos of meetings of personnel.

Source: Frow and Morris (2003)

Practical relevance of cultural knowledge on the marketplace

The approach to cultural marketing and consumer research that we discuss in this book seems increasingly relevant for all market actors from both business and socio-political perspectives. It provides firms and marketers as well as consumers, consumer organizations and consumer policy-makers with new conceptual tools and methods for gaining a better understanding of the cultural complexity of the marketplace and helps them to reflect on their roles in the market.

FOR FIRMS AND MARKETERS, this sort of cultural studies perspective and the cultural knowledge and competence it provides is becoming increasingly important. To carry out successful, innovative, socially responsible and customer-oriented marketing strategies, marketers would seem to need to improve their ability to recognize and understand the prevalent symbols, myths, images, values and cultural narratives of the culture of their target markets. It enables them, as recent examples show (Holt, 2003), to design products and services that add value and make sense in the everyday life of their customers, and thus helps them to build and manage strong and appealing brands.

Box 1.3   Practical relevance: the role of myths in creative advertising design

To exemplify the ways in which the cultural approach may be beneficial for marketing practice, we take a case on creative advertising design. In a study published in the *Journal of Advertising*, Venkataramani, Holbrook and Stern (2001) studied the creative process underlying advertising design. Their aim was to empirically explore which characteristics of the design process may foster the development of a creative ad that also fulfils its communicative goals. Towards this end, they studied the advertising design process as it occurs in the creative teams of five advertising agencies. The creative team members were asked to tell their thoughts as they worked on a task of designing a print ad for a new product. The empirical data of this study thus consisted of the team members' verbal protocols and the ads they produced (which were also submitted to 'expert' judges to be evaluated).

In analyzing the work of these different teams, the authors found out that copywriters and art directors heavily relied on particular mythic orientations and themes in planning their ads. The authors categorized the mythic themes as comedy, romance, tragedy and irony. The authors thus made a link between the myths and the creative process in advertising. They displayed how mythic elements and patterns provide cultural resources for marketing professionals such as the advertising creative team members. In doing so, they not only elaborated on the ways in which ads embody mythic patterns – as the large bulk of previous studies has done – but also on *how* mythical resources can be used in the practice of marketing management.

Interestingly, their findings suggest that the over-reliance on a particular mythic type may inhibit creativity, whereas idea generation that draws inspiration from more than one of the mythic types appears to produce more effective outcomes. In other words, a mode of creative working that does not narrow its horizons to the execution of one primary mythic theme, but relies instead on a multi-mythical approach, may produce more effective advertising. In practice, this sort of multi-mythical working means that after generating ideas from a particular myth, executing these ideas (for example, as headlines and visuals), and then screening them, the creative team then circles back to draw on another, different myth for additional ideas and subsequent screening. In this way, the team members can systematically tap diverse myths and be disciplined in screening resulting ideas before making selections for further explorations. This finding – though exploratory in nature – suggests that advertising agencies can enhance their effectiveness by actively encouraging creative teams to sample from multiple and divergent cultural resources and stories.

(Continued)

More generally, this sort of approach, which focuses on the ways in which cultural resources such as myths are made use of in creative work, can enlarge our understanding of the creative work process, not only in advertising but also in product design and development. As creativity is widely understood as a balance between freedom and constraints – production of new and innovative ideas occurs in the presence of external restrictions such as budgets, time limits and client satisfaction – this sort of cultural approach enables marketing practitioners to capture and acknowledge the *cultural constraints* that shape and affect the creative work. Designers, art directors and copywriters all inevitably draw from a set of particular cultural discourses that provide a sort of frame for their work. And consumers need to be able to recognize these discourses, and thus to interpret the creative work from a sufficiently similar frame, to be able to decode the preferred meanings encoded in the ads or products.

Source: Venkataramani et al. (2001)

Overall, the success and financial profits of marketers would seem to be increasingly dependent upon the ability of marketers and strategy-makers to interpret, understand, anticipate and control the consumption-related ascription of meaning that is relevant for their markets and products. In a recent study on mobile phones and everyday life, for instance, Neil Holloway, Managing Director, Microsoft UK states that:

> We must be aware that technology for its own sake is never as powerful a tool as technology that makes sense in the everyday life of a user. We must constantly make sure that the tools that we provide are useful, affordable and comprehensible. (Crabtree et al., 2003: 1)

According to Crabtree et al. (2003), people have a highly developed sense of what a cell phone means, symbolizes or says about its owner and being aware of this symbolic potential most people attempt to manage it, particularly if the product carries potential symbolic dangers. Their study shows that, in some cases, even if consumers benefited from using a particular product and could actually afford to buy the product, they could not necessarily do so because of the symbolic meanings attached to the product. A plumber participating in the study, for example, said that he could not even think about buying an expensive camera phone in the 1990s because he assumed that his customers might think that 'he is making too much money' and thus charging too much. As Jack the plumber explains:

> I couldn't get a picture phone – people would think, he must be an expensive plumber. So I'd have to use it in private if I got one at all, but it would be handy for taking a picture of a boiler or something like that. (Crabtree et al., 2003: 27)

Moreover, and importantly, the sort of discursive approach to cultural marketing and consumer research that we discuss here, and the theoretical and methodological tools involved, encourage marketers to reflect on their own role in producing social order and in constituting particular modes of being for people. To be able to carry out socially responsible business, marketers need to develop their ability to analyze the social, political, economic, moral and religious effects of their marketing texts and practices on various consumer audiences in particular. This sort of reflexivity is crucial knowing the all-pervasive and constitutive role of marketing and consumption in contemporary Western society. The marketing segmentation strategies of companies, for instance, may play a key role in producing particular agencies for whole subcultures of people (Peñaloza, 1994).

FOR CONSUMER ORGANIZATIONS AND CONSUMER POLICY-MAKERS the cultural approach provides new conceptual and methodological tools for understanding the dynamics of the struggle of meaning in the market, and to actively engage in it as well in their attempts to guard the rights of the consumer. Both policy-makers and consumer organizations need to understand and develop strategies that are sensitive to the insidious, complex relations of power in which the subjectivity and freedom of the consumer–citizen is produced and shaped in the market. The different forms and mechanisms of power (Foucault, 1978, 1980, 1983) that prevail in the market may well produce profound detrimental effects on individuals, groups, and society as a whole. Such negative relations and forces of power that permeate the marketplace may manifest themselves, in marketing texts for example, as racial or gender-related stereotypes that sustain inequality or as ideological ideals that marginalize difference, thus constraining and repressing innovation and creativity in all areas of human and social life (Hall, 1992a). The cultural studies approach that we discuss here helps to detect such forms and mechanisms of power/knowledge.

Overall, cultural methods and knowledge help marketers and policy-makers as well as marketing and consumer researchers to reflect on their role as cultural gatekeepers and intermediators, in the systems of representation where the wants, meanings, ideas, norms and values associated with marketplace behavior are discursively produced. As a critical cultural studies approach (Denzin, 2001a), it particularly encourages consumer and marketing researchers to study how corporate and governmental actors and institutions – and the academic scholars and experts they rely on – are involved in fixing the conceptual and interpretive repertoires and discursive practices that are available in the markets.

Case Study 1.1   Tribal marketing

(Source: Bernard Cova and Véronique Cova (2002) 'Tribal Marketing: the Tribalisation of Society and Its Impact on the Conduct of Marketing', *European Journal of Marketing*, 36 (5/6): 595–620)

What does it mean for the conduct of marketing if the company takes a cultural approach? How could marketers benefit from thinking of the notion of subject? This example aims to answer to these questions. It draws on studies conducted by Bernard and Véronique Cova (2002) and shows how Salomon successfully followed principles of so-called tribal marketing in launching their in-line rollers. To a large extent, Salomon's success seems to be based on re-conceptualizing the (individualistic, detached and passive) subject, as well as on rethinking the consumer–product and the marketer–consumer relationships.

Inspired by Maffesoli, Cova and Cova note that the quest for community, instead of individualism, is characteristic of contemporary societies. Contemporary communities – or tribes – may be characterized as shifting gatherings of emotionally bonded people, and they exist in no other form but the symbolically and ritually manifested commitment of their members. Rituals become enacted and displayed in particular physical or virtual spaces or occasions that provide a momentary home for the tribe. For instance, in France there were regular local in-line roller gatherings, called Friday Night Fever, where skaters set off for a night skate through the city. In these gatherings sacred cult objects, ritual clothing, words, idols, icons and sacred images are used to reaffirm and strengthen the underlying values of the tribe.

The primary marketing task is to support the tribe in its very being. Marketers should aim to provide products and services that enable a sense of tribal belonging and membership to be established and fostered. This being the aim, the focus of interest is not on consumers' individual values or opinions, but on practices through which tribes are brought into being. Therefore, the marketer is well advised to favor market knowledge based on detecting signs and symbols, conducting observations on places where the tribe gathers, and undertaking desk research on everything that can be said or written about the tribe in newspapers and books, on chat lines, diffusion lists, or Net forums. This is because the underlying logic, shared experiences, interpretation, representations, discourse and action of tribes goes unnoticed through statistical surveys.

Importantly, marketers should consider the product or service from the angle of its *linking value* instead of its use value: the linking value refers to the product's contribution to establishing and/or reinforcing bonds *between* individuals. Whereas the individualistic approach to relationship marketing aims at creating and developing a relation between the brand or the firm and a customer, the tribal approach prefers to recreate and support the relation between customers. Moreover, as the very aim is more at supporting than controlling the tribe, marketers should not treat members of the tribe as 'end users' nor as a 'target group' but rather as partners and co-developers of products and services. This recognition that tribes are a source of competencies forces marketers to lower the boundaries of the company. The tribe is not outside the company, it is part of the company network, just as the company is part of the tribe.

(Continued)

Below you will find a concrete phase-to-phase strategy that Salomon followed in investigating the ways of supporting the in-line roller tribe:

Phase 1   Ethnomarketing: Salomon moves close to the in-line skaters (1995–6)

- Analysis of rituals and practice codes
- Encounters with the milieu
- Presence at in-line events
- Participant observation of in-line skaters

Phase 2   Co-design: Salomon launches its in-line activities (1997–8)

- Design of products in collaboration with skaters
- Work on distinctive features of the products with skaters
- Product tests by a team of skaters supported by Salomon

Phase 3   Tribal support: Salomon takes root in the in-line skater tribe (1999)

- Salomon is an embedded actor who shares the values of the tribe
- Salomon supports in-line events not by placing an ad (streamer) but by promoting the practice (contests)
- Salomon creates new events and helps in the building of in-line structures
- Salomon supports the shared passion of in-line skaters

EXERCISE 1.1   Branding in cultural research

This exercise aims to draw attention to the ways in which branding, a key theme in marketing, is understood in a cultural approach. The task is to read the following influential texts, all of which are concerned with branding in the cultural framework, and to contrast them with the views of the more conventional brand management literature. In reading the texts, try to answer to the following questions:

1 How is 'brand meaning' conceptualized in each of the text?
2 How is 'culture' understood in them?
3 How is the consumer understood in them?
4 What is the relation between 'marketing practice' and 'brand meanings'?
5 Is it supposed that marketing managers exert control over brand meanings? On what grounds?
6 How is politics taken into account when branding is assessed?

Aaker, David and Joachimsthaler, Erich (2000) *Brand Leadership*. New York: Knopf.

Fournier, Susan (1998) 'Consumers and Their Brands: Developing Relationship Theory in Consumer Research', *Journal of Consumer Research*, 24 (March), 343–74.

Holt, Douglas (2002) 'Why Do Brands Cause Trouble? A Dialectic Theory of Consumer Culture and Branding', *Journal of Consumer Research*, 29 (June): 70–90.

McAlexander, James H., Schouten, John W. and Koenig, Harold F. (2002) 'Building Brand Community', *Journal of Marketing*, 66 (Jan.) 38–54.

Thompson, Craig, J. and Arsel, Zeynep (2004) 'The Starbucks Brandscape and Consumers' (Anticorporate) Experiences of Glocalization', *Journal of Consumer Research*, 31 (Dec.): 631–42.

FURTHER READING

The following textbooks provide an easy introduction to the basic concepts and typical research questions of cultural studies.

The book edited by Stuart Hall offers a comprehensive account of the ways in which visual images, language and discourse work as systems of representation:

- Hall, Stuart (ed.) (1997) *Representation: Cultural Representations and Signifying Processes*. London: Sage.

Graeme Turner gives a thorough account of the conceptual foundations and theoretical legacies of British Cultural Studies, which informs much of the contemporary cultural research on marketplace activity.

- Turner, Graeme (1990) *British Cultural Studies: An Introduction*. New York and London: Routledge.

There are few textbooks that discuss marketing and consumer behavior from the cultural perspective. The following, however, illustrate how consumption, production and everyday life may be studied from a cultural perspective.

- du Gay, Paul, Hall, Stuart, James, Linda, Mackay, Hugh and Negus, Keith (1997) *Doing Cultural Studies: The Story of the Sony Walkman*. London: Sage.
- Mackay, Hugh (ed.) (1997) *Consumption and Everyday Life*. London: Sage.

(Continued)

Arnould and Thompson provide a general overview of the development of cultural research in the field of consumer inquiry:

- Arnould, Eric J. and Thompson, Craig J. (2005) 'Consumer Culture Theory (CCT): Twenty Years of Research', *Journal of Consumer Research*, 31 (March): 868–82.

2

Evaluating Cultural Research

CHAPTER SUMMARY

This chapter discusses the perspective on validity and evaluation adopted in the book. The objective is to discuss and elaborate on:

- general questions of validity, reliability and generalization in cultural research;
- principles of good epistemic practice in cultural marketing and consumer research; and
- the nature of practical and theoretical contributions in cultural marketing and consumer research.

Introduction

Textbooks on qualitative methods often discuss the criteria for evaluating the quality of the research process towards the end of the book. This might imply the idea that the study is first carried out and reported by the researcher and then is evaluated by some external audience. Placing the discussion on evaluation here, in our second chapter, we wish to emphasize that the criteria for evaluating the quality of a study are rooted in the specifics of the theoretical and methodological perspective chosen for the study and should thus guide methodological choices in the different phases of the research process.

It is our contention, however, that there are no absolute or objective criteria for good cultural research (Holt, 1991; Schwandt, 1996; Smith and Deemer, 2003). All knowledge claims and their evaluation take place within a particular conceptual framework through which the world is described and explained. These interpretive frameworks are culturally constructed through social interaction in historically and locally specific systems of representation and are thus infused with values, norms and role expectations. Therefore our knowledge of the world and the criteria that we use to evaluate knowledge are always contextual, plural, contested and subject to change.

We have no way of transcending or breaking out of our historical and cultural circumstances in order to produce objective accounts of reality or to reproduce the meaning or intention of social actors. As John Smith and Deborah Deemer (2003) put it, we cannot deny our human finitude and adopt a God's-eye point of view. This is something that we just have to accept and learn to live with. It seems worth citing Thomas Schwandt at some length here to illuminate the idea:

> [w]e must learn to live with uncertainty, with the absence of final vindications, without the hope of solutions in the form of epistemological guarantees. Contingency, fallibilism, dialogue, and deliberation mark our way of being in the world. But these ontological conditions are not the equivalent to eternal ambiguity, the lack of commitment, the inability to act in the face of uncertainty. (1996: 59)

One way of living with this uncertainty is to see cultural research as an act of construction that is practical and moral and not properly speaking epistemological (Smith and Deemer, 2003). Then also judgments about the goodness or badness of research are taken as practical and moral judgments and not as epistemological ones. Another way of coping with this finitude is to search for epistemic authority from the consensus and transformative criticism of the relevant scientific communities (e.g., Longino, 2002). In both cases, perhaps, the criteria for good research are not discovered but negotiated. They are derived from community consensus among researchers regarding what is trustworthy and useful, as well as what has meaning for action and further steps, at a certain time and under certain conditions. As such they are constantly reworked and open to transformation.

In any event, the lack of certain final, ultimate criteria does not mean that 'anything goes'. Despite the fact that we have no definite solution to the problem of validity in cultural research, as researchers and citizens we do constantly make judgments: and we must make judgments. As Smith and Deemer (2003: 440) have argued, to say that these judgments cannot be grounded extra-linguistically does not mean that we are free from the obligation to engage in as open and unconstrained a dialogue as possible in order to justify and revise our assessments (also Pulkkinen, 2000). David Silverman (1993: 186–93), for example, has argued that social science can overcome relativism by making three contributions to society. It can participate in debates about public policy, provide people with new opportunities to make their own choices, and offer new perspectives to practitioners and various social actors. This would seem to apply in the context of cultural marketing and consumer research as well.

So since we continuously do make judgments, as scholars and educators, about the quality of research work, it seems only fair to try to be as explicit as possible about the principles according to which we pass this judgment. In making judgments about the quality of research, people often have a set of ideas about what characterizes good research. It seldom boils down to a list of characteristics that can be used as a simple yardstick to sort out and scale different pieces of work from 'poor' to 'outstanding'. It is rather open-ended, in part unarticulated and subject to constant reinterpretation (Smith and Deemer, 2003). Production of cultural knowledge is a social process in which we construct reality as we go along. In this process we also construct the criteria for judging the process and its outcomes.

In this chapter, we make an attempt to specify a set of ideas and principles that we see as fit for evaluating cultural research from the perspective that we have taken in this book. We emphasize, however, that we propose these ideas in the hope that they stimulate critical thinking and creativity. We are *not* presenting them as some sort of strict, normative criteria that will guarantee the quality of your work. We rather encourage you to challenge and develop further the ideas that we discuss here as well as to re-work the criteria we suggest according to the particular research problems and contexts that you work with.

First, we discuss the views and assumptions of validity, reliability and generalization upon which cultural research is based. Then, we outline and briefly discuss a set of characteristics that add, in our view, to the overall quality of cultural research. In the chapters that follow, these characteristics will be discussed in more detail. Finally, we address the relevance and contribution of cultural research.

Questions of validity, reliability and generalization

Academic research is conventionally evaluated in terms of three basic criteria: reliability, validity and generalizability. Discussion of these criteria is often premised upon the traditional values associated with the a cluster of views that Philip Kitcher (2002) has labeled 'The Realist Package',[1] which social scientists have traditionally used to guide their judgments. In cultural research many of the cognitive values and norms associated with these epistemological views have been rejected. Cultural marketing and consumer research tends to go against the conception of knowledge as a value-free search for causal accounts of phenomena, which can be empirically tested and confirmed against observation using all available or representative evidence.

Nevertheless, questions of validity cannot be easily dismissed. As Yvonna Lincoln and Egon Guba (2003: 274–5) point out, the – sometimes irritating – question remains whether or not the 'co-created constructions' that we produce in a study are sufficiently trustworthy and authentic (isomorphic to some reality, related to the way others construct their social worlds) that it is safe to act on their implications? Can they be trusted to provide some purchase on some important human phenomenon? Next we shall try to tackle some of these issues through discussing basic questions about validity, reliability and generalization in cultural research.

Validity

The concept of validity is a highly debated topic in social research since it has no single, generally agreed-upon definition (Winter, 2000).Validity generally refers to the truth or accuracy of the representations and generalizations made by the researcher; how true the claims made in the study are or how accurate the interpretations are. Hammersley (1987: 69), for example, maintains that an 'account is valid or true if it represents accurately those features of the phenomena that it is intended to describe, explain or theorise'. Sometimes discussions on validity also revolve around objectivity of research. In cultural research, this way of thinking about validity is problematic because it is believed that knowledge is never value-free and that no method can deliver an ultimate truth about the state of matters in social life.

Since cultural research is usually based on the understanding that claims of knowledge and truth about social reality are always culturally constructed in complex networks of power, and thus never value-free, it seems inappropriate to talk about the 'objectivity' or 'objective truth' of research 'findings'. The objectivity and accuracy of those claims is always subject to contestation and negotiation. Many of the widely used techniques for improving the validity of research, such as using systematic methods for analyzing data as well as assessing and accounting for the impact of the context and the researcher on the setting, seem self-evidently relevant and necessary for producing intellectually rigorous, creative and critical accounts of social reality. But there are no grounds for claiming that using these methods and procedures makes the research process more objective or provides a more accurate representation of the research phenomenon. We simply have no access to the truth, the whole truth and nothing but the truth, about how things are. Therefore, if conceived as techniques of producing findings and conclusions that accurately reflect the 'real' situation in the research setting, some of the procedures commonly suggested for establishing the validity of qualitative research, such as triangulation, are inconsistent with the basic assumptions that we have outlined for cultural marketing and consumer research.

Triangulation usually refers to combining multiple theories, methods, observers and empirical materials to produce a more accurate, comprehensive and objective representation of the object of study. In investigator triangulation, for instance, multiple investigators are assigned to study a phenomenon independently and using the same methods. If their findings coincide and if they arrive at the same conclusions, then the validity of those findings and conclusions has been established. If the findings and conclusions differ substantially, then further study is needed to 'uncover the "true" and "certain" finding' (Guion, 2002: 2). Similarly, in a case study validity of findings and conclusions is often sought by using multiple methods, for example, interviewing, observation, document analysis and survey methods. If the findings obtained with all these methods correspond and draw the same or similar conclusions, then the validity of those findings and conclusions has been established. (The weight of evidence supports them.)

Triangulation, in this form, is usually based on the assumption that by overcoming partial or biased views and by looking at an object from more than one standpoint it is possible to produce a more 'true' and certain representation of the object. In the natural sciences, particularly with concrete physical objects, this may well make sense. But in cultural research, which focuses on social reality, the object of knowledge *is* different from different perspectives. And the different points of view cannot be merged into a single, 'true' and 'certain' representation of the object. Triangulation, from this perspective, is thus better conceived as a 'display of multiple, refracted realities simultaneously' (Denzin and Lincoln, 2003: 8; Richardson, 2000).

In cultural research, it is stressed that realities are culturally constructed and also accounts of those realities are cultural constructions. Therefore, the aim is not to discover indisputable facts about a single social reality. As Silverman (1993: 157–8) has pointed out, it seems naïve to assume that aggregating data from different sources will unproblematically add up to provide a more complete picture; we cannot simply aggregate data in order to arrive at an overall 'truth'. Moreover, the task, in assessing the validity of research, is not to adjudicate between different competing versions of accounts and descriptions but to understand the 'situated work that they do' (p. 158). As Silverman has argued, the 'major problem with triangulation as a test of validity is that, by counterposing different contexts, it ignores the context bound and skillful character of social interaction and assumes that members are "cultural dopes" who need a sociologist to dispel their illusions' (p. 158).

Cultural research often does rely on the use of multiple methods and materials (for example, interviews, focus groups, media texts and documentary material) to understand the interplay between cultural discourses and everyday discursive practices in a particular setting. The aim, however, is not so much to get a more objective representation of the cultural practice in the setting or to secure an in-depth understanding of it. Rather, the combination of multiple methods, empirical materials, perspectives and observers in a single study is best understood as a strategy that 'adds rigor, breadth, complexity, richness and depth to the inquiry' (Denzin and Lincoln, 2003: 8). Multiple materials are often also needed to contextualize the analysis. Moreover, multiple materials highlight the pervasive nature of cultural beliefs, values and norms; the meanings related to body height, for instance, become practiced and produced throughout the social life, and can therefore be 'read' from a variety of empirical sources, from announcements of birth, to daily conversations and advertising images (Valtonen, 2004b).

In general, validity cannot be achieved through correct use of method alone. Even a rigorous use of particular methods cannot guarantee increased credibility. Using particular methods and procedures may undoubtedly add to the quality of the interpretation in the eyes of the reader of the research report but the credibility of the interpretation cannot be inferred separate from its reading (Holt, 1991). By using specific techniques and following certain protocols researchers may develop more nuanced and more interesting interpretations and accounts of empirical phenomena that appeal to the reader. Some methods are obviously also more practical or better suited for studying particular research phenomena and problems than others. But there are no grounds for claiming that these methodological procedures make the interpretations and accounts more trustworthy. What is trustworthy to some, may be suspect for others. This is not merely an abstract epistemological position but also something that can be observed in the everyday practice of research communities.

To illustrate, in Finland there are two competing research organizations that produce economic evaluations and forecasts and also carry out research to support political decision-making in key issues of economic and social policy. The one institute is sponsored mainly by industry (www.etla.fi) and the other by labor unions (www.labour.fi). It would be no surprise if those who identify with the interests of industry tended to find the reports produced by the labor union-sponsored research institute less trustworthy than the reports produced by the industry-sponsored research institute – and vice versa. In our personal experience, this is exactly what people appear to do. So, even in the field of economics, which is known for its claims to objective knowledge, perspectives do seem to matter. Knowledge is not disinterested, apolitical or neutral but in some sense ideological, political and permeated with values.

Consequently, agreements about validity are subject to community negotiations about what is accepted as truth, and the result of dialogue and argumentation in the research community. Such a communicative and pragmatic concept of validity is never fixed but created and recreated by a community narrative that is subject to the historical conditions that gave rise to the community (Lincoln and Guba, 2003: 273).

This does not mean, however, that empirical 'evidence' does not count in any way. Despite the fact that validity cannot be established on 'the weight of evidence', the claims that are made in the study have to agree or to be somehow in line with the data on which those claims are based. Cultural research focuses on texts and the use of language, typically investigating the ways in which everyday life is organized within, and through, language and signifying practices. These texts, which constitute the data that are analyzed, place limits on the specific ways in which they can be interpreted and understood. Therefore, as we shall argue in Chapter 9, there may be many 'wrong' interpretations of a text; but there is always more than one good interpretation of it.

In this book, we tend to take the view that the validity of research is something that the audience of the research reports and papers decides on – whether or not you want it or accept it. Research is ultimately evaluated by the community of scholars who judge the interpretations that are produced. However, inspired by Silverman (1993), we tend to value cultural research that participates in debates about public policy and contributes to the ongoing cultural dialogues by providing people with new opportunities to make sense of their everyday life. Particularly, research that problematizes taken-for-granted ideas and questions received wisdoms in an attempt to offer new perspectives to consumers, marketers and policy-makers seems 'valid'. In other words, the criteria for judging the adequacy of cultural marketing and consumer research tend to be pragmatic; it can be evaluated by the degree to which it makes possible new and meaningful interpretations of the social and political phenomena it investigates (Howarth, 2000: 130). Nevertheless, we challenge you to work out your own set of criteria that is applicable to the particular perspective that you take in your study (for starters see Lincoln and Guba, 2003).

Overall, we take the view that the appropriateness and adequacy of the theorizing in cultural marketing and consumer research may not be assessed simply in terms of its analytical ability nor in terms of the guidance it offers for marketing practitioners and political decision-makers. With many constructionist scholars, we maintain that theorizing must also be assessed in terms of its general moral and political implications and that as academics and social 'scientists', consumer researchers have an important political role and responsibility in society (Lincoln and Guba, 2003; Schwandt, 1996). If we believe that research is not about finding and discovering but constructing reality, we must acknowledge that ethical issues become paramount. Researchers must take moral responsibility for what they construct.

Scholarly work carries moral authority and inevitably involves participation in relations of power whether or not the 'scholars' themselves are aware of it. There is, therefore, a need to reflect critically on the ways in which this power is or should be used or defused – even if we acknowledge that there is no position outside the field of power. Therefore, it seems necessary to consider what sort of a story our research tells of human beings, society and nature; how it justifies our everyday thinking and acting, and how it possibly silences alternatives.

Reliability

Reliability usually refers to the degree to which the findings of a study are independent of accidental circumstances of their production (Kirk and Miller, 1986: 20). It deals with replicability, the question whether or not some future researchers could repeat the research project and come up with the same results, interpretations and claims. In quantitative research, for example, reliability usually refers to the extent to which an experiment, test, or measurement yields the same result or consistent measurements on repeated trials. This is needed for drawing conclusions, formulating theories and making claims about the generalizability of the study. It is a necessary but not sufficient condition for validity.

According to this logic, qualitative researchers are sometimes advised to make the research process transparent by describing the different methodological practices and processes in a sufficiently detailed manner in the research report (Yin, 1989: 45). This principle also applies to cultural research but the idea, of course, is not that some other researchers would actually replicate the study in an attempt to verify that the methodological procedures yield consistent findings and conclusions in repeated studies. Cultural knowledge is contextual, and it is not usually possible to produce 'consistent measurements' of social reality. The methodological procedures are rather explicitly specified primarily to allow evaluators to draw their conclusions about the quality of the study.

Besides the methodological transparency (data production process, analytical procedures and principles, how interpretations were developed, and conclusions drawn), cultural researchers should also pay particular attention to theoretical transparency. That is, you should make explicit the theoretical stance from which the interpretation takes place. This is because the theoretical frame produces particular interpretations and excludes others as we shall discuss in the analytical chapters.

Moreover, reliability refers to the overall practice of conducting research in a systematic and rigorous manner. It is important, for instance, that the interviews and focus groups are carefully recorded and transcribed. Similarly in ethnographic research, it is important that you make systematic and sufficiently elaborate field-notes (see, e.g., Emerson et al., 1995; Silverman, 1993: 146–7). Also, the typically large data set needs to be carefully coded and organized. Such measures not only allow public access to the data but make the data analysis easier. If the transcripts are incomplete, for example because some parts of the texts are inaudible or unclear, you may not be able to do the analysis or you may have problems getting started with the process. Just take a piece of text that you have analyzed in the past, cross out a couple of important sentences, and then try to make sense of it again. If a key utterance is missing, it may take a long time to figure out what is going on in the piece of text. In the same vein, it is important to be careful when you are dealing with a language that is not your native language. Errors in trans-lation may cause errors in interpretation.

Generalization

Generalization and transferability are controversial issues in cultural marketing and consumer research and in qualitative inquiry more generally. It is a widely shared view that to be valid or useful the findings of a study must be transferable to some other contexts and situations. There seems to be no general agreement, however, on what this means in qualitative research.

In quantitative research, which still appears to set the terms for discussion on the issue, *generalization* refers to the extension of research findings and conclusions from a study conducted on a sample population to the population at large. It is a question of external validity. This, of course, is not something that qualitative researchers should set out to do in the first place (Alasuutari, 1995; Denzin and Lincoln, 2003; Stake, 1995). The small samples that they typically focus on are unlikely to be statistically representative of any larger populations. Therefore, the quantitative notions of generalizability, the logic of sampling and statistical infer-ence do not apply and are of no use in assessing the wider relevance of cultural marketing and consumer research.

In many cases, however, this is not really a problem, as Pertti Alasuutari, (1995) has argued. Cultural research is concerned with understanding and interpreting the historically specific rules and conventions that structure the production of meanings in particular historical contexts. These rules and conventions, and the cultural practices that they entail, are, often, fairly well known to the members of the culture in which they apply. Therefore, in many cases generalization is not a problem. The challenge rather is to understand and interpret these taken-for-granted but poorly understood cultural practices.

To illustrate, the belief that men are more tech-savvy or technologically inclined than women would seem to be a fairly generally shared belief in many Western countries (e.g., Green and Adams, 2001). There would seem to be no need to show that such a belief is fairly generally shared. Therefore, in cultural research on the topic, the focus of interest is not whether this idea is widespread but rather on the cultural practices through which the representation of men as tech-savvy is produced, and perhaps contested and transformed, in everyday life. The focus is also on the historically and locally specific discourses that sustain such representations and constitute the conditions of possibility for the representation of gender and technological competence. Cultural researchers could study, for example, the cultural practices (texts, talk and signifying practices) through which these ideas are reproduced day after day in ordinary families, schools and the marketplace. They could observe, for example, how the father is called in from the garage to change the light bulb when a light has gone out, or the ways in which teenage girls construct and perform their female gender identity in talk by exaggerating their lack of technological skills in class. Or they could study the conversations between sales people and customers, observing how female customers are being ignored by retail sales people, patronized or offended by pushy sales techniques, and treated better when accompanied by a father, husband or any other male (*San Jose Mercury News*, 11 January 2004). In the evaluative criteria of such studies, quantitative notions of generalizability are misplaced.

The question of *transferability*, that is, whether or not the results of the study can be transferred and applied to other contexts and situations by the readers of the research report or article, however, is relevant also in qualitative research. Transferability does not necessarily involve broad theoretical claims but invites readers and evaluators to make connections between elements of a study and their own understandings and personal experience. Transferability, in this sense, refers to the degree to which readers can transfer the results of the study to other contexts and situations with which they are familiar. Robert Stake (1995, 2003; Stake and Trumbull, 1982), refers to these processes as *naturalistic generalization,* arguing that if the empirical case is described with a sufficiently descriptive narrative readers may be able to vicariously experience these happenings and draw conclusions.

To illustrate, a person, let's call her Ann, might read a research report on a study that focuses on the ways in which women are discursively produced and reproduced as technically and mechanically incompetent through cultural practices, for example, through gendered division of labor in the household (men use tools and machines; women clean and cook). Reading a description of how this takes place in the empirical setting of the study, Ann realizes that she constantly engages in similar practices. She remembers how she called in her husband, Jim to carve the Thanksgiving turkey when the dinner was ready to be served because it was 'too complicated a task' for her to do. And yet, she had just produced a fourteen-person dinner party through a skillful process of planning, coordinating, scheduling, executing and timing of different cooking procedures and preparations, using half-a-dozen different electrical appliances. If she could pull off such a project, why would she not be able to slice up the turkey? And when she recognizes a similarity between the practices described in the study and her own life, she starts to see even more connections. She observes how her teenage daughter recurrently seductively talks about her lack of technological competence when talking to her boyfriend on the cell phone. This leads her, thus, to infer that some aspects of the conclusions made in the research apply in her own family and probably also more generally.

To improve the transferability of research findings and conclusions, qualitative researchers are therefore often advised to supply a highly detailed 'thick description' of their research situation and methods (Geertz, 1973). It is believed that such a description allows readers to 'see the phenomena in their own experience and research' (Dyer and Wilkins, 1989: 617), and thus make informed judgments about whether or not and to what degree they can transfer the findings to their own situations. In cultural marketing and consumer research, this is undoubtedly a good methodological practice that may add to the convincingness and insightfulness of the analysis.

But what can we say about more theoretical forms of transferability? Knowledge produced in cultural research is contingent, situated and partial; it is context-specific and the claims that are made refer only to specific historical, social, cultural and material circumstances (time, place and people) in which the study was made. Can the results of cultural analysis also be transferred vertically? Can we make *theoretical generalizations* that apply over different contexts?

Talk about theoretical generalizations and transferability sometimes implies the idea that the aim of research is to produce universal causal laws and theories that can be refuted or confirmed by independent testing and which serve as the basis for predicting comparable or future events and processes. In the field of marketing, Hunt (1983: 693), for example, has argued that the objective is to seek law-like generalizations that 'specify a universal conditional ... which is capable of yielding predictive statements (hypotheses) which are composed of terms that have empirical referents and, thus, permit empirical testing'.

Cultural research, however, is not concerned with predicting or with causal explanations of social phenomena, particularly if they take the form of subsuming empirical events under universal laws or depend on the positing of intrinsic causal properties of objects. It is believed that there are no universal causal laws in the social sciences comparable with those in the natural sciences, and that it is not the task of social scientists to delineate the inherent properties or causal mechanisms of objects (Howarth, 2000). Therefore, the aim is not to generate or test theories by elaborating on the 'dynamics present within single settings' (Eisenhardt, 1989: 534) if this refers to specific features of a causal mechanism, for example, the psychological and social processes through which norms, values or 'culture' exert their effects or cause social behavior. The results of cultural research are not to be generalized to apply in the context of particular causal mechanisms. In this specific sense, cultural marketing and consumer research is not concerned with producing theoretical generalizations.

To conclude, we wish to emphasize that even if we did not want to say anything about the causal mechanisms of the 'real world', we need to specify the ways in which the insights gained in the study are relevant or transferable to situations other than the one being studied. Cultural marketing and consumer research is concerned with analyzing language and signifying practices to learn about the cultural practices through which people are governed and make sense of their world. This analysis may be viewed as a generalizing operation as such (Alasuutari, 1995). As language gives us a particular version of reality, objects or sites of analysis can be looked at as texts. And the structures of those texts can be analyzed to gain an understanding of the wider cultural structures, institutions and practices that produce them. Texts are thus studied for the cultural forms they realize and make available. The aim of cultural marketing and consumer research is, therefore, to gain a better understanding of the historically and locally specific cultural practices and systems of representation that structure the production of meanings in the market. Generally, institutionalized and culturally standard discourses tend to take the form of fairly enduring albeit continuously negotiated cultural regimes. Therefore, knowledge about these practices and representational systems is largely transferable and can be applied to the historical and cultural context in which they were studied.

General principles of good epistemic practice

It is our contention that doing cultural marketing and consumer research does not boil down to a linear or mechanistic process of performing certain well-rehearsed tasks, employing rigorous methods. Rather, as Silverman (1993: 144) argues, the real issue is 'how our research can be both intellectually challenging and rigorous and critical'. So, we prefer to characterize the process of doing cultural marketing and consumer research as a continuous process of inquiry that involves critical thinking. The role of evaluative criteria, in this process, is not to outline a set of techniques and procedures for producing more trustworthy representations of the empirical reality of the marketplace. They rather serve as a basis for critical thinking, continuous self-evaluation and self-reflection throughout the research project.

In everyday talk, the term 'critical' is usually understood as '*inclined to judge severely and find fault'*. It is something negative. We, however, understand 'critical' as something more positive, creative and productive. In general, critical thinking can be understood as an active and systematic cognitive strategy to examine, evaluate and understand events and to solve problems (Levy, 1997). In research practice it could well mean that the researcher makes every attempt to systematically gather, weigh and synthesize information, as well as to form reasonable inferences, judgments and conclusions. But even more so, we see being critical as an analytical and diagnostic perspective. Critical thinking involves an attitude that is both open-minded and skeptical. It entails identifying and questioning underlying assumptions and beliefs as well as discerning hidden or implicit values. This might mean, for example, that researchers make an attempt to produce a critical account of the motivating questions, institutional frameworks and disciplinary rules by which their research imperatives are formed (Denzin and Lincoln, 2003). From a single scholar as well as from a research community, being critical in this sense requires tolerance for uncertainty and ambiguity, so that individuals and groups can feel comfortable to explore alternative perspectives and explanations in an attempt to interpret and understand complex cultural processes and practices.

In the following sections we discuss some of the principles of good epistemic practice which we have found useful and practical, and which are, we hope, also ethical. We shall elaborate on these ideas and principles in the chapters that follow. Here our purpose is only to outline a set of important issues. We begin with a list of evaluative criteria that could well constitute the items of a reviewer report form as used by many international journals. To sort out the 'high impact' articles from 'low impact' articles, reviewers are advised to evaluate manuscripts based on criteria such as the following:

- importance of the topics and issues to the field of inquiry;
- contribution to existing research and theoretical debates;
- conceptual rigor: explicit specification of concepts and theoretical perspectives, clarity of objectives, appropriate treatment of relevant literature, logical reasoning, etc.;
- methodological rigor: appropriate methods, appropriate and sufficient data, rigorous and innovative analysis;
- Clarity of writing and argumentation.

These criteria would seem self-evidently relevant for cultural marketing and consumer research. In the following sections we try to discuss some ways of producing cultural knowledge that satisfies these criteria.

Formulating appropriate research questions

One of the most important indicators of quality in all academic research is the use of theoretical constructs and methodologies that are appropriate for the subject matter and the objectives specified for the study. The theoretical and methodological perspective we specify in this book, as with most cultural marketing and consumer research in general, is not suitable for many of the typical formulations of research problems and questions that can be found in the marketing and consumer behavior literature.

Qualitative research, in general, is not particularly suitable for research questions that imply general causal relationships or prediction of outcomes – in one way or another. Neither is it good for experimentally examining or measuring in terms of quantity, amount, intensity or frequency. Qualitative methods are best suited for studies in which the emphasis is on analysis and description of qualities and meanings of entities and processes (Denzin and Lincoln, 2003). In cultural approaches to marketplace phenomena, the analytical focus is particularly on meaning-making, on the ways in which meanings are created, made use of, contested and changed in the markets and how these meanings (constitute the conditions of possibility for subjectivity and agency) guide and constrain action both in the marketplace and in society more generally.

So, the appropriate research questions in cultural marketing and consumer research tend to be of the form *how*. The aim is to elaborate on and gain a better understanding of *how* social reality is constructed and social order achieved in everyday discursive practices within an existing cultural and institutional structure. How do particular people in particular contexts make use of the available cultural categories, rationalities and representations to make sense of their life and to achieve social order? How do culturally standard or institutionalized discourses come into being and are structured? What sort of subject positions do they offer and impose on people who enter them? What forms of being, thinking and acting as well as rights and obligations do these subject positions entail?

Thus if your objective is to investigate the impact, value or importance of various factors and variables, for example, you are better off using quantitative methods and theoretical approaches based on a 'realist' approach. In business studies, it may, in fact, be sometimes necessary to take such a quantitative view on the world and look for predictable processes and accurate measurements of relatively enduring features. Marketing managers may, for example, want to get accurate information about the market share of their brands and a retail buyer may wish to predict the demand for particular products as precisely as possible.

Understandably, many marketing students and scholars are used to formulating research questions in terms of quantity or a 'factors-and-outcomes-logic' (Potter, 2003: 786) of some kind that implies cause-and-effect relations, without giving much thought to it.

We argue, however, that it might sometimes be fruitful to problematize these received ways of defining research objectives and to consider other ways of looking at the issue at hand. So, instead of investigating the impact of a 'subculture' on brand image, one could consider studying the different ways in which members of this subculture make use of the meanings of the brand as a cultural artifact to construct their collective identity as a subculture as well as to make sense of their selves, others and social relations in their everyday life.

Box 2.1 Cultural marketing and consumer research – analytic focus

To illustrate the nature of the research questions and interests that characterize the cultural approach to marketing and consumer research, we take a study carried out by Craig Thompson and Maura Troester (2002) as an example. They studied the cultural construction of consumer values in the context of natural health micro-culture. Their aim was to uncover the imbrigated layers of cultural meaning that structure consumers' actions and shape their interpretations of personal experience in a given social context. By theorizing values as narrative structures they were able to highlight the cultural content through which the micro-cultural value system became meaningful to consumers and to develop an understanding of the meaning-based linkages between natural health values, the salient consumption goals that these values respectively engendered, and the specific consumption practices through which these value–goal pairs were enacted. Among other things, they also concluded that the forces of postmodern fragmentation do not exist in opposition to the historical, cultural and sociological structuring of consumer meanings and practices. But, these structuring processes now assume more complex forms (p. 566).

Defining a clear theoretical and methodological perspective

In some approaches to qualitative research, research methodology is taken to be inductive and initially theory-free. Theory is achieved at the end of the research process (e.g., Eisenhardt, 1989). It is our view, however, that to avoid lapsing into ad hoc use of common-sense interpretations, it is necessary to define the data within a well-articulated analytic scheme (Silverman, 1993, 1998). While some may argue that qualitative research is inductive, because it involves careful analysis of data it is important to recognize that this analysis is influenced and even partly made possible by researchers' assumptions about social reality and methodology (G. Miller, 1997). The researcher is inevitably bound within a net of epistemological and ontological premises that become self-validating.

Qualitative researchers should, therefore, begin with a theoretical and methodological perspective and choose methods and data that give an account of the structure and meaning in the data from within that perspective. This does not mean, however, that the phenomena under focus should be theorized in the sense of presenting theoretical propositions or hypotheses to be tested through data analysis. By 'theory' we mean a set of concepts that offer a way of looking at the research phenomenon (Silverman, 1993). Theory, in this sense, guides understanding and makes it possible. It is grounded on abstract principles and beliefs about ontology (subjectivity, reality), epistemology (knowledge) and methodology (appropriate methods of inquiry) that shape the ways in which the researcher sees the world and acts in it.

We do not mean, however, that the theoretical perspective initially chosen for the study is fixed once and for all. Rather, it may have to be modified and rearticulated to suit the particular empirical phenomena and problems that are addressed. Therefore, the theoretical framework must be sufficiently open and flexible enough to be stretched and restructured in the process of applications. The idea is to avoid essentialist and reductionist theories of society, which tend to predetermine the outcomes of research (Howarth, 2000).

The theoretical and methodological perspective specified for a study thus guides the research process. It is essential in defining the research problem and in making methodological choices. It also serves as the basis of evaluation for the study. Therefore, it is important to make an attempt to specify the analytic perspective and the basic assumptions on which the study is based as explicitly as possible. Particularly, questions of validity and generalization need to be addressed to avoid the situation where readers and evaluators systematically misinterpret your work.

Building on, challenging and contributing to existing literature

Silverman (1998) argues that analytic depth is one of the most important criteria for evaluating the quality of qualitative research. He emphasizes that it is important to demonstrate that our research has mobilized the conceptual apparatus of our social science disciplines, and thereby, helped to build useful theories. Therefore, researchers should not only make explicit the theoretical concepts that they use but also the contribution of the research to existing research and theoretical debates as well as to journal-specific hot topics and issues in the field.

It goes without saying, perhaps, that the main theoretical section of a paper or a research report should locate the project in relation to some established tradition of academic work, either continuing or challenging it (Taylor, 2000: 41). To be able to do this, it is necessary to know the literature on this tradition fairly well and be familiar with the assumptions of the expected audience to some extent. This is needed not only for being able to anticipate criticisms and to argue against them, but also for producing interesting and insightful knowledge claims. As Davis (1971) has argued, interesting is something that the audience does not find obvious, irrelevant or absurd in the light of their preconceptions and pre-understandings. We shall discuss the key role of the audience in academic research in more detail in Part 4, which deals with writing cultural research.

It is obviously also necessary to be sufficiently explicit about what exactly is the knowledge gained about marketplace phenomena or about the conduct of cultural research. There is no reason to expect that the reviewers and evaluators of your work will detect this contribution if you fail to specify it yourself. For marketing and consumer research-related journals, a description of the managerial contribution and marketing implications of the study is usually also needed. We shall discuss the relevance and theoretical contribution of cultural marketing research more specifically in the last section of this chapter.

Using appropriate analytical procedures for rigorous and insightful analysis

The specification of evaluative criteria for what is rigorous and insightful analysis is firmly rooted in the philosophical commitments and theoretical perspectives of the study. The methodological perspective that we discuss here is based on the assumption that it is not enough to define standards and norms only for the use of analytical methods – for instance, for doing good narrative analysis or discourse analysis. Instead, you need to consider the goodness in broader terms. In particular, you have to consider it in relation to the philosophical commitments that inform your approach to interpretation – what you mean by interpretation. This notion should also be followed throughout the study, throughout the process of interpretation, not only during the stage of conducting analysis (Denzin and Lincoln, 2003: 274–5).

Moreover, a central issue in evaluating the quality of the cultural analysis involves the correspondence between a theoretical paradigm and the observations made by the researcher, for example, the theoretical concepts and the observations that are supposed to represent them (Peräkylä, 1997). The methodological perspective that we specify in this book, for example, does not allow the possibility of making claims about the inner psychological states of individuals. It is not designed to provide information about how people feel or really think.

Moreover, it seems that different methods and techniques of data-gathering seem to be better suited for different purposes. The choice of these methods and techniques has to be argued for and justified. In the field of cultural studies, for example, quantitative methods have been customarily dismissed as objectionable tools of the positivist paradigm. Quantitative methods have been used to model and test general causal explanations about social phenomena, which have no place in cultural research. Some scholars have argued, however, that, if applied with circumspection and imagination, quantitative methods, particularly the survey method, might well be useful in cultural research on marketplace phenomena. Particularly Justin Lewis (1997) has argued that the survey questionnaire could potentially be used as a research tool for mapping out the context in which processes of representation take place, and where messages are given meaning.

This is undoubtedly an innovative and interesting idea. However, we emphasize that if quantitative methods, for example, the survey, are used to complement cultural research, there is a need to explicitly define and specify the methodological conditions and ways in which different quantitative and qualitative methods can be utilized as complementary, paradigmatically commensurable methods. The same naturally also applies for all available qualitative methods, such as projective techniques, observation, interviews, focus groups, which can be used in many ways and for many analytical purposes.

The criteria for rigorous and insightful analysis also depend on the research community in which it is assessed. In this sense, the question closely relates to the role of the existing literature and audience in defining evaluative criteria. What is considered insightful in one body of literature or research community may be 'déjà vu' in another. In the same vein, the criteria for rigor may vary from one research community to another; the criteria for conversation analysis, for instance, differ significantly from those in the autoethnographic tradition.

Overall, analytic integrity would seem to be a self-evidently central goal in cultural marketing and consumer research. This would seem to require, to begin with, that the researcher overcomes the temptation to jump to easy conclusions just because there appears to be some evidence that leads in an interesting direction. We shall discuss these issues in the course of the book in more detail. In Chapter 10 we discuss specifically the criteria for analyzing and interpreting cultural data and in Chapter 11 we focus on writing and reflexivity, which are also important for the rigorousness and creativity of the research process.

Practical relevance

In marketing research, the value and quality of any study are often evaluated in terms of its perceived usefulness in the 'real world'. If we do not want to say anything about the mind–independent reality, how can the insights gained in the study be relevant for real people with real problems? And how can the findings of cultural research best be fed back into society?

First, we wish to note that there are several different schools of thought and serious debates on the ontology of the real and what it implies for cultural studies and their practical and political relevance (see, e.g., Wetherell, 2001). Different authors and institutional actors are being interpreted and categorized in different ways into opposing camps, such as weak and strong constructivists or realists and relativists. Although the topics of these discussions are undoubtedly important, we consider the simple categorizations that the debates sometimes boil down to largely 'political' – discursive – practices through which scholars are constructing their identity and trying to achieve social order in the world of academia. We do not want to engage in this practice of 'calling people names' explicitly by swearing loyalty to any of these camps – which are contested social constructions anyway (see, e.g., Hammersley, 2003 vs. Potter, 2003). But we encourage you to work out for yourself the nature of reality and whether or not and under which conditions it makes sense to think that there are more or less 'correct' interpretations of it. Philosophically these debates involve very difficult and controversial issues, which cannot be solved in this book.

Nevertheless, as we have explained, the methodological perspective that we discuss in this book is based on the acknowledgment that as finite human beings we have no way of 'really' knowing, producing objective and true accounts of reality. This does not mean that we *deny* that reality. We rather prefer to focus our attention on the ways in which it is represented in text, talk and signifying practices, and try to learn as much as possible from that.

However, we see the practical relevance of cultural research in its ability to participate in the ongoing cultural dialogues by providing people with new opportunities to make sense of their everyday life (Gergen and Gergen, 2003; Silverman, 1993; Taylor, 2000).

It can provide firms and marketers as well as consumer organizations and consumer policy-makers with new conceptual tools and methods for gaining a better understanding of the cultural complexity of the marketplace. It also helps them to reflect on their roles in the market. Cultural research problematizes taken-for-granted ideas and questions received wisdoms in an attempt to offer new perspectives to consumers, marketers and policy-makers. It thus can provide a space for alternative constructions of real-life phenomena or marginal versions of them. Doing this, it may challenge established authorities, explanations and attributions of responsibility.

Cultural marketing and consumer research does not simply attempt to retrieve and reconstruct the meanings of social actors to make intelligible meanings that are initially unclear, incomplete or suppressed (Howarth, 2000: 128–9). Nor does it try to uncover the 'true' underlying meanings of texts and actions, which are deliberately concealed by ideological practices or discourses. The aim is not to demystify surface meanings and practices to discover some deep truth, for example, class struggle or the psychology of the unconscious, which explains cultural practices.

Instead, cultural marketing research can provide novel interpretations of events and practices by elucidating their meaning by analyzing the way in which political forces and social and market actors construct meanings within incomplete and undecidable social structures (Howarth, 2000: 129). It also locates these everyday discursive practices in larger historical and social contexts, so that they may acquire a different significance and provide the basis for a possible critique and transformation of existing practices and social meanings.

Theoretical contribution

Academic journals and PhD committees expect original, novel explanations that have a clear bearing not only on practical and managerial problems or burning social issues but also, and more importantly, on current theoretical discussions. Cultural research is usually practiced within a particular field of theoretical discipline – or disciplines – and it is also expected to contribute to a particular body of disciplinary knowledge (Atkinson, et al., 2001a). Therefore, you should make explicit the contribution of the study to the existing research and the theoretical debates that it involves. But what is a 'theory' and what constitutes a theoretical contribution in cultural knowledge? And what is a theoretically sophisticated piece of research?

What is a theory?

There is little consensus on what exactly theory is and what constitutes a strong versus a weak theory in social sciences (see, e.g., DiMaggio, 1995). Generally, theory often refers to an account that answers questions of why. It deals with connections among phenomena and tells a story about why and how acts, events, structure and thought occur.

Traditionally, in marketing and consumer research, theory has been understood as a set of propositions about a phenomenon, preferably a causal explanation, which comprises a set of concepts and causal laws that describe the phenomenon, and which is based on empirical facts (tested and verified hypotheses). The adequacy of such a theory is evaluated as a matter of correspondence of the objects, processes, and relations described in the propositions of the theory with the objects, procedures and relations in the domain of the natural world that the theory purports to explain (Longino, 1996). Theory, in this view, thus needs to be a well-substantiated causal explanation of some aspect of the natural world.

In cultural research, however, many of the assumptions on which the traditional view of theory builds are rejected, as we have explained, and 'theory' rather refers to a set of explanatory concepts that offer a way of looking at the world (Silverman, 1993: 1–2). It also specifies a logic or dynamic that justifies the selection of those concepts as relevant for understanding the phenomena in focus. Theory thus gives a point of view; it guides understanding and makes it possible. As such, theory is essential in defining the research problem and in making methodological choices. But it is also developed and modified by good research. The adequacy of such a theory is evaluated on the basis of its ability to make room for artful and new insights on the phenomena that the theory is supposed to describe and account for.

Theory, in cultural research, is therefore a semantic construction, providing us with a conceptual framework that helps us to interpret the world around us. It is based on a set of ontological beliefs and it involves cognitive (and non-cognitive) norms and values that guide research practice. From this perspective, theory can be understood as a specification of a structure, which is not true or false but just a structure that is realized in some actual system. (Longino, 1996: 274.) The adequacy of such theories is determined by their ability to map some subset of the relations and structures posited in the theory onto some portion of the world that is to be described and understood. According to this sort of semantic or model theoretic view, the adequacy of the theory is therefore evaluated on the basis of its ability to pick out the relations and structures that we are interested in. As Longino explains:

> A model guides our interactions with and interventions in the world. We want models that guide the interactions and interventions we seek. Given that different subcommunities

within the larger scientific community are interested in different relations or that they may be interested in objects under different descriptions, different models … may well be equally adequate and provide knowledge, in the sense of an ability to redirect our interactions and interventions, even in the absence of general consensus as to what is important. (1996: 275)

Consequently, cultural knowledge is based on a body of diverse theories and their articulations onto the world that changes over time in response to the changing cognitive needs of those who develop and use theories. The task therefore is not to find one best or correct theory. Rather, the aim is to articulate and elaborate on a number of theories, generated from the different subject positions involved. As Longino (1996: 276) argues, if we recognize the partiality of theories, we can recognize pluralism in the community as one of the conditions for the continued development of knowledge. From this perspective, 'theory-building' entails construction and elaboration of new or revised concepts and frameworks that provide meaningful insights into the phenomena that we are interested in. It involves challenging and extending existing knowledge by revealing the partiality of existing theories and by changing the focus to aspects of phenomena and processes that existing models conceal. In this sense, theory-building is ongoing. There is no terminus of inquiry that just *is* the set of truths about the world, as Longino has noted.

What constitutes a strong theoretical contribution in cultural research?

One way to approach this question is to ask what constitutes a good theory. As Helen Longino (1995: 385) has argued, traditionally theories have been evaluated in terms of constitutive values such as the following: accuracy, simplicity, internal and external consistency, breadth of scope (explanatory power) and fruitfulness. Many of these criteria and standards have to do with traditional notions of validity, sanctioning what counts for truth or what enhances the likelihood of the truth of a theory. As we argued above, when discussing questions of validity, such criteria for theory-building are inconsistent with the basic assumptions and analytic focus of cultural marketing and consumer research. Longino (1995: 386–90), however, has introduced an alternative set of theoretical values, which would seem useful for discussing theoretical contribution in the context of cultural research. These values function as theoretical virtues, as qualities of a theory that are regarded as desirable and which hence guide judgments between alternatives. These virtues are empirical adequacy, novelty, ontological heterogeneity, complexity of interaction, applicability to human needs, and diffusion or decentralization of power. Next we shall discuss how these virtues could be taken to guide theoretical work in cultural marketing and consumer research.

The relevance of *empirical adequacy* and *novelty* seems quite straightforward for theoretical work. Good cultural research is not only theoretically sophisticated but also empirically well grounded. The claims of a theory thus have to agree with the data that it aims to describe. (Why would we collect data, if we did not try to make use of them?) Moreover, the objective of all scientific work is to add to our knowledge and understanding of the world. Ideally, therefore, research produces novel theories that differ significantly from the existing theories either by postulating different entities and processes, adopting different principles of explanation, incorporating alternative metaphors, or by attempting to describe and explain phenomena that have not previously been the subject of investigation (Longino, 1995: 286).

The virtue of *ontological heterogeneity* is based on the value of polyvocality (Gergen and Gergen, 2003) and the idea that cultural research should report on and be attentive to the lifeworlds and voices of individuals and social groups that reflect the heterogeneity of social life (Atkinson et al., 2001b: 8). Any theory posits implicitly or explicitly an ontology. It characterizes what is to count as a real entity in its domain. Therefore, a good theory grants parity to different kinds of entities and thus avoids treating apparently different entities as versions of a standard or paradigmatic member of the domain (Longino, 1995: 387).

To give an example, theories that are characterized by ontological heterogeneity try to avoid taking the white, Western middle-class male, for instance, as the standard type of social actor – contrary to what is often the case. Focusing only on such a standard type may be problematic because when ontological priority is given to this standard type, difference is easily treated as a departure from, or failure to fully meet the standard. This is not only an ethical problem but may also prohibit marketers from identifying new business opportunities in the 'margins' of the potential target market. Recently, such problems have been recognized in the consumer electronics industry, for example, where marketing has customarily been geared to serve the needs and interests of their male customers, as we discussed earlier.

Hence, as Kenneth Gergen and Mary Gergen (2003) point out, qualitative researchers are encouraged to recognize both within themselves as scholars and within those who join their research as participants the multiplicity of competing and often contradictory values, political impulses, conceptions of the good, notions of desire, and senses of self. The challenge of polyvocality becomes even more radical if we acknowledge that all parties to the research may 'contain multitudes' (2003: 595). A crucial question is, therefore, whether the theories we build enable participating parties to give expression to their multiplicity as well as to the complexity and range of contradictions that are typical of social life.

The virtues of *complexity, applicability to current human needs and diffusion of power* revolve around the same issues as ontological heterogeneity. Complexity of relationships values theories that treat relationships between entities and processes as mutual, rather than unidirectional, and as involving multiple rather than single factors (Longino, 1995: 388). In cultural marketing and consumer research, for example, the relationship between marketers and consumers is theorized as an ongoing dialogue of commodification, as discussed in Chapter 1, not as a unidirectional relationship where marketers target and direct marketing activities toward consumers in an attempt to have an impact on their behaviors. The idea is to search for new ways of giving consumers a more active role and a more symmetrical position in market exchanges. This is motivated by the basic value and objective of producing knowledge that is applicable to human needs and which enhances the diffusion of power in social life, which is perhaps the ultimate epistemic goal of cultural marketing and consumer research.

Note

1   This 'package', might typically include some or all of the following views, which, according to Kitcher (2002), form the stock of traditional philosophy of science, and which are typical for mainstream marketing research. (1) The aim of science is to accept true statements (Veritism). (2) Truth is correspondence to mind-independent reality (Correspondentism). (3) The acceptance of statements in science is guided by rules of method (Methodism). (4) Individual scientists aim to contribute to the attainment of a single, complete, true account of nature (Monism).

FURTHER READING

The following texts provide a thorough discussion on the epistemological debates that inform the cultural approach to marketing and consumer research discussed in this book:

- Schwandt, Thomas A. (2003) 'Three Epistemological Stances for Qualitative Inquiry: Interpretivism, Hermeneutics, and Social Constructionism', in N.K. Denzin and N.S. Lincoln (eds), *The Landscape of Qualitative Research*. London: Sage. pp. 292–331.
- Schwandt, Thomas A. (1996) 'Farewell to Criteology', *Qualitative Inquiry*, 2: 8–72.
- Smith, John K. and Deemer, Deborah (2003) 'The Problem of Criteria in the Age of Relativism', in N.K. Denzin and N.S. Lincoln (eds), *Collecting and Interpreting Qualitative Materials*. London: Sage. pp. 427–57.

Part 2

Cultural Data and Methods

In cultural marketing and consumer research, empirical analysis is based on textual and visual materials, which are all analyzed as cultural texts. These texts can take many forms, ranging from 'naturally occurring' media texts, documentary materials and visibilities to fieldnotes and texts generated through interviews, focus groups and projective techniques. In Part 2 we discuss a range of such empirical materials and methods for generating cultural data that we see fit for analytics of cultural practice.

We take the view that some methods and materials may well be better suited for particular research projects than others, and thus encourage you to reflect on your choice of methods and materials. What is a 'good' data set and what are appropriate research methods for a study largely depend on the theoretical perspective and research design that you have defined for your study. To some extent, it also depends on what has been studied and reported by others before you in the existing literature. If some method or form of data has been used extensively in the past, there is a good possibility that some other methods and materials will provide fresh insights into the phenomena you are interested in.

Like many contemporary qualitative researchers, we take the view that within the chosen interpretive framework, different methods and empirical materials can be used and combined fairly creatively. While sometimes it is good to carefully analyze a narrow set of data with a specific technique, at other times it may be more fruitful to use multiple empirical materials and methodological tools – or even whatever tools and materials are at hand – to study the marketplace. The objective, in any case, is to choose methods and materials that enable you to learn as much as possible from the phenomenon that you study. So, if new methods and techniques have to be invented – or pieced together – then it is the task of the researcher to do that. However, you are wise if you get informed about and take into account the academic conventions that are relevant for your work – different journals and different PhD committees may have different policies and requirements concerning 'appropriate' data and methods.

Part 2 is organized as follows: in Chapter 3, we discuss ethnographic data and methods; Chapter 4 concentrates on cultural talk and texts; and in Chapter 5 we briefly discuss the ways that visual materials and methods can be used to analyze marketplace culture. Throughout the chapters, we also try to offer examples of previous market-related studies, which illustrate how these methods and materials have been applied in cultural marketing and consumer research.

3

Ethnographies

CHAPTER SUMMARY

This chapter is concerned with the possibilities, challenges and problems of doing ethnographic research on marketplace behavior. The objective is to introduce and discuss:

- the basic principles of ethnography;
- a number of current ethnographic varieties, such as virtual ethnography, critical ethnography and auto-ethnography; and
- the ways in which ethnography and its varieties may be employed to understand marketplace phenomena.

Introduction

In the history of social sciences, ethnography has traditionally been – and still is perhaps – the key methodology of anthropology and cultural research. Ethnography refers, briefly put, to a research process in which the researcher closely engages in the daily life of some social setting and collects data using ethnographic methods of observation and participation – an experience labeled as the fieldwork – and then writes accounts of this process.

In recent years, ethnography and ethnographic data have also invited vivid interest in the field of marketing and consumer research. *Journal of Consumer Research*, for example, has published several ethnographies that investigate, for instance, the ways in which people form communities around particular brands and consumption artifacts (e.g., Schouten and McAlexander, 1995), the role of consumption activities in feasts such as Thanksgiving Day (Wallendorf and Arnould, 1991), or the role of mass-mediated advertising in the social life of adolescents (Ritson and Elliott, 1999).

Moreover, a number of ethnographies have been conducted to gain insight into the ways in which marketing activities are performed. These sorts of studies focus on marketing practitioners, as members of organizations who carry out various activities of marketing management such as service delivery (Arnould and Price, 1993), product development and strategy execution (Dougherty, 1988).

Recently, new ethnographic varieties such as critical ethnography (Peñaloza, 1994, 2000, 2001), visual ethnography (Peñaloza, 1998), virtual ethnography (Kozinets, 2002b) and autoethnography (Valtonen, 2004b) have also been introduced for the study of marketplace behavior and interaction. These new varieties follow ethnographic principles but take a particular focus in terms of either the aim of the study or the way in which ethnographic fieldwork is conducted.

Altogether, all these studies show that ethnography, as well as ethnographic methods and data, can provide important perspectives both for marketing strategy formulation, for theory-building and for questioning assumptions that govern prevailing marketing inquiry.

In this chapter, we concentrate on elaborating the role of ethnography, ethnographic methods and ethnographic data in cultural marketing and consumer research. Our purpose is mainly to discuss the possibilities, challenges and problems of doing ethnographic research on marketplace behavior and interaction from the cultural perspective we have specified in this book. We do not go into the nitty-gritty of ethnographic fieldwork. Nor do we immerse ourselves into the details of the philosophical controversies that recent discussions on ethnography involve. We rather prefer to cite sources, throughout the text, where the ideas that we discuss are developed further and elaborated on in more detail.

In particular, the aim is to bring to the fore current ethnographic varieties such as *virtual ethnography, critical ethnography, and autoethnography*.[1] We argue that these new types of ethnography offer, first of all, appropriate approaches and useful tools for capturing some of the conditions that characterize contemporary society, such as the increasingly virtual nature of marketplace behavior. Moreover, these current forms of ethnography offer methodological solutions to theoretical questions that characterize cultural marketing and consumer research. Critical ethnography and autoethnography, for instance, may offer excellent ways of capturing the all-pervasive nature of cultural production – the ways in which culture permeates all of society (Hall, 1997a) – and the multiple ways in which culture, market and politics come together.

Moreover, it is our contention that ethnographic research practices can be fruitfully employed in various sorts of studies, which may or may not strictly adhere to the orthodox accounts of ethnography as an epistemic practice. With certain restrictions, ethnography may well be combined with a whole range of other research practices, be they textual, historical, narrative, or statistical. And ethnographic methods and data may well be employed in many sorts of qualitative studies. For example, the ethnographic method of observation and the practice of making notes and keeping a journal during the research process are fruitful practices in many sorts of studies.

Ethnography in cultural marketing and consumer research

A brief history of ethnography

Originally, ethnography was a methodology developed and employed by anthropologists who sought to develop an understanding of 'strange' cultures in distant places.[2] The 'strange' was defined from the point of view of the Western way of life; forms of life and people that differed from Western standards were defined as 'others'. Still today 'the Other' constitutes a key concept of anthropology and ethnography. Yet, the concept no longer refers uniquely to some geographically defined distant place and its strange inhabitants. In the course of its history, anthropology has witnessed a shift from studying distant cultures to close and familiar ones; that is, to studying, for instance, the ways in which some groups of people are constructed as 'others' in contemporary Western societies. The Chicago School of Sociology, in particular, has played a significant role in the process of turning attention to familiar and nearby cultures through their studies of urban life and urban communities (for a review see, e.g., van Loon, 2001).

This shift has contributed to the field of marketing and consumer research, as it has brought to the fore the multiple ways in which marketing and consumption play a role in constituting and mediating cultural values and norms. For instance, Daniel Miller's (1998) ethnographic study on routine shopping behavior in North London – he observed typical acts of routine shopping over a period of one year – describes the ways in which family relations are negotiated through shopping. The ethnographic study of Melanie Wallendorf and Eric Arnould (1991), in turn, elaborate on the multiple ways in which consumer artifacts and consumption activities are infused in rituals through which festivities such as Thanksgiving Day are constructed and negotiated.

Besides this geographical turn, ethnography has witnessed a tremendous theoretical turn, or, to be more precise, theoretical evolvement and plurification. While many of the early ethnographic studies were largely based on a structural-functionalist frame, the work of Clifford Geertz (1973), in particular, has been influential in diffusing interpretive perspectives to ethnographic inquiry. Currently ethnography is employed within a wide range of theoretical schools of thought and empirical areas – such as media studies, women's studies, educational research, and marketing and consumer research – and therefore, it presents a profusion of different theoretical and disciplinary perspectives.

As a result of these developments, the reasons for doing ethnographic research have multiplied and the methods of ethnography have become highly refined and diverse (Vidich and Lyman, 2003). Therefore, it is perhaps best characterized by diversity (Atkinson et al., 2001b). Despite this diversity, ethnography involves some distinctive characteristics. A fundamental characteristic is its dual nature: ethnography includes (1) the *fieldwork* and (2) its textual or visual representation, the *fieldwork report*. Briefly put, hence, ethnography is 'a research process in which the ethnographer closely observes, records, and engages in the daily life of another culture – an experience labeled as the fieldwork method – and then writes accounts of this culture, emphasizing descriptive detail' (Marcus and Fischer, 1999: 18).

In the remainder of this section we introduce some of the contemporary debates relating to these two phases of an ethnographic inquiry. We start by discussing the nature of the fieldwork and two key themes related to it: how to define and understand the field and the people under study. Then, we present the ethnographic methods used in the field and the nature of the data gathered and produced. After this we turn to discuss the question of writing an ethnographic report based on the fieldwork. We close the section by taking up questions related to ethnographic knowledge production.

Fieldwork: research site and people

Ethnography is, first and foremost, the study of social phenomena *in situ*. In its basic form, ethnographic fieldwork consists of a researcher spending an extended period of time in a particular research setting, having direct and sustained social contact with the agents under study. Ethnography is therefore firmly rooted in the first-hand exploration of a particular social and cultural setting (Atkinson et al., 2001b: 5). It is based on an assumption that by entering into close and relatively prolonged face-to-face interaction with people in their everyday lives, ethnographers can develop an understanding of the often tacit ways in which people make sense of their lives in the setting in question. Hammersley and Atkinson (1995: 1) have summarized the key features of ethnographic fieldwork in the following way:

> In its most characteristic form it involves the ethnographer participating, overtly or covertly in people's daily lives for an extended period of time, watching what happens, listening to what is said, asking questions – in fact, collecting whatever data are available to throw light on the issues that are the focus of the research. (Hammersley and Atkinson, 1995: 1)

But, how to define 'the field'? What constitutes a setting? Traditionally, anthropologists have focused on a certain spatially defined setting, such as a village or a specific urban area. In the contemporary mass-mediated and technology-intensive world, which is characterized by global cultural flows, this way of delineating the research setting has, however, become problematic. Cultural meanings, ideals and practices become produced and mediated beyond spatial boundaries (Appadurai, 1996). The ethnographic study of Robert Kozinets (2002a) well illustrates this point. In his study on a one-week-long antimarket event called Burning Man, much of the fieldwork is actually conducted outside the physical research setting in which the event takes place. Before the event, he makes informal observations of the Internet community of Burning Man participants and after the event he continues to carry out e-mail interviews. In Kozinets' study, the research setting, thus, may not be confined to the venue or the area in the desert where the event takes place, but an essential part of the setting is constituted by the virtual environment where the participants interact. We shall provide a case example of his study at the end of this section.

Though, it may often be quite relevant to concentrate on a particular geographically defined area or physically bounded setting. The notion of servicescape
(Bitner, 1992), in particular, highlights the strategic importance of the physical
surroundings in the service business. Servicescape refers to the physical setting or
environment of a place and it includes dimensions such as ambience, spatial layout and functionality, and signs and symbolic artifacts. These dimensions affect the
ways in which both customers and employees behave and interact in the space
and experience it. As Mary Jo Bitner remarks, ethnographic methods are appropriate for examining the servicescape. For instance, in research on the effect of
facility layout options on customer/employee interaction patterns, direct observation may be a fruitful method (1992: 68).

Let us consider what it means to conduct an ethnographic study in a servicescape from the perspective we have outlined in this book. If you examine a
particular holiday resort, for instance, the starting point is that this resort is not
taken as given. Rather, the research attention is drawn to the ways in which that
particular setting is produced as a 'holiday resort'. This means, for instance, that
you need to analyze the ways in which the resort setting is physically and spatially
organized and constructed as a 'holiday resort': how the houses are built, how the
paths and passages are organized, how the fields and gardens are made, how shops
and restaurants are organized, and how people take part in this process of making
a holiday resort by their shopping behavior or sun-bathing, for instance. These
practices are enabled and framed by some discourses – and the practices simultaneously reproduce and shape these discourses – and it is these discourses you
should try to identify. They shape the ways in which various kinds of human
action can be initiated, conducted and also interpreted meaningfully.

In the same vein, the prevailing discourses related to the setting frame and shape
the ways in which the ethnographer may meaningfully conduct the fieldwork.
Think of conducting ethnography in malls that are public places and characterized by short stays relative to conducting an inquiry in homes that are private
places and involve long-term stays. As the nature of these and all other types of
settings are culturally constructed differently, the ethnographer has to adopt and
modify the way fieldwork is organized, conducted and negotiated case-by-case.
For instance, as the nature of several contemporary professions tends to be rather
mobile, and organized around nets of several kinds, the researcher has to invent
particular 'mobile ethnographies', to use Barbara Czarniawska's term (2004), for
investigating them ethnographically.

Besides the problematics related to the conceptualization of the setting, the
fieldwork involves the problematics related to the ways in which the *people under
study* are conceptualized. Conventionally, in anthropologically inspired studies in
particular, there has been a tendency to consider people under study as 'natives'
who form achieved or ascribed 'communities' or 'subcultures'. Roughly put, these
communities and subcultures refer to forms of social organizations that include
interpersonal relationships, a particular social structure, a unique ethos and a set of
shared beliefs and values, rituals and modes of symbolic expression.

This way to comprehend the people under study has also been followed in
marketing and consumer studies. There are a number of studies that have focused

on 'consumption oriented subcultures' that have emerged around some consumer artifacts such as Harley–Davidson motorcycles (Schouten and McAlexander, 1995). These authors define 'a subculture of consumption as a distinctive subgroup of society that self-selects on the basis of a shared commitment to a particular product class, brand, or consumption activity' (Schouten and McAlexander, 1995: 43). Moreover, the term 'brand community' has been introduced by Albert Muniz and Thomas O'Guinn (2001). With the term they refer to 'a specialized, non-geographically bound community, based on a set of social relations among admirers of a brand' (p. 412). Like other communities, these authors argue, brand communities are marked by a shared consciousness, rituals and traditions, and a sense of moral responsibility.

However, as we have discussed earlier in this book, the concept of subculture can be somewhat problematic, particularly if it relies on a view of culture as some sort of a systemic ideational unity (Helliwell and Hindes, 1999). Often subculture also refers to some subordinate or deviant group of people. People under study are considered deviant with respect to a 'wider culture' that is being resisted or renegotiated. As Robert Kozinets points out, the prefix 'sub' ascribes a secondary rank to the entity it modifies (for a brief overview of the critics of the subculture literature, see Kozinets, 2001: 68–9).

Moreover, the notions of subculture and community sometimes entail – implicitly or explicitly – a presumption of commonality and a shared system of meanings, as if the consumption of a particular object, a particular brand of motorcycles, for instance, automatically expressed a commonly shared identity. To avoid this sort of romantic oversimplification it is important to rely on conceptualizations of culture and subculture that permit the exploration of the cultural heterogeneity of particular communities, as Kozinets (2001) remarks. His ethnography on *Star Trek*-related consumption phenomena portrays a group of devoted consumers socially constructing their reality as a community of *Star Trek* enthusiasts. This sort of community may well be constructed by a set of overlapping and even conflicting practices, identities and meanings, as he points out. His study also illustrates that it is important to take account that in the construction of communities, people use a particular interconnected system of commercially produced images, texts and objects. In focusing on community building, the researcher should therefore investigate the intertextual linkages of objects, texts and ideologies in cultural systems of meaning, and take account of the contextual embeddedness of meanings as they are embodied in and negotiated by cultural members in particular social situations (Kozinets, 2001: 68–9).

Moreover, contemporary consumption-related communities are increasingly characterized by impermanence. In marketing and consumer research, new forms and conceptualizations of community have thus been discussed. Arnould and Price (1993) have elaborated on *periodic communities*, such as those formed during vacation trips. They tend to be based on weak social ties but in some cases also on strong but short-lived social ties. Kozinets (2002a: 20), in turn, has studied *hyper-communities*, which are well-organized, short-lived but caring and sharing communities 'whose explicit attraction to participants is [their] promise of an intense but temporary community experience'. Hypercommunities, such as the Burning

Man community, often dissolve shortly after they have been formed and they may be strong precisely because they are temporary (p. 35). Both of these conceptualizations draw attention to speed and temporariness as major determinants of cultural and social life.

In the approach to cultural marketing and consumer research that we elaborate on in this book, questions of community are primarily studied by analyzing and describing the ways in which particular identities and subjectivities are produced, reproduced and contested for particular individuals or groups of people in particular research settings. The analytic focus is thus on the techniques through which people under study, the 'natives' or 'local subjects', are produced. In studying a consumption-oriented community such as a Vespa-club, for instance, the ethnographer might observe and account for the techniques and practices through which members of the community represent themselves as, and thus make themselves 'Vespa-people': how they talk about themselves as Vespa-people, how they represent themselves in their personal Web pages and in the Vespa community website, how the Vespa brand is displayed in the clothes of the members of the community, and so forth. More precisely, what is addressed is the relationship between cultural production of these kinds of subjects and the setting in which such subjects can be produced, named and empowered to act meaningfully. The point is not to presume a community or subculture as such but to analyze the ways in which the community is formed through discursive (and material) practices, and to understand the interrelationships between these discursive practices, media imagery, subcultures and wider cultural practices. The prevailing social categories such as race, age and gender obviously also play an important role in the construction and negotiation of these sorts of communities.

Ethnographic methods and data

Once the setting is decided and access negotiated, the ethnographer enters the field and combines various methods of inquiry to produce historically, locally and politically situated accounts of it. In practice, she or he investigates it through a set of basic ethnographic methods: participation, observation – and writing.

Participation and observation

In most common ethnographic forms, the ethnographer participates, to a greater or lesser extent, in the field he or she is studying. The very basic idea of this practice is that through participation, ethnographers become insiders over time. This in turn enables the ethnographer to 'come to see the world through the eyes of the participants'. By gaining this 'insider's' perspective – which is an essential part of the traditional ethnographic ethos – the researcher is able to produce an account of social setting that is faithful to the perspectives of the participants. However, in conducting ethnography the point is *not* merely to produce an empathetic description of insider's views but to produce a theoretical description. That is, the ethnographer should adopt the viewpoint of a professional stranger who brings an analytical approach to the cultural phenomenon in question. In any case, one of the core tasks of an ethnographer is to manage the tension between these stances of insider and outsider that the researcher takes in doing ethnographic research.

Observation as a research method means that the ethnographer systematically observes everyday events, interactions, conversations and the use of objects in social settings over time. Observation focuses on naturally occurring constellations of social behaviors. That is, the researcher may observe the complex ways in which Thanksgiving feasts are produced and consumed in homes (Wallendorf and Arnould, 1991) or the ways in which guides orchestrate customer satisfaction on commercial white-water river rafting trips (Arnould and Price, 1993). Generally speaking, the strength of observational methods is that they allow the ethnographer to record the mundane features of everyday life that tend to remain unremarkable, even to participants themselves. These features may be so common and routine-like that the participants would not necessarily come to talk about them in an interview situation, or they may have a limited reporting capability about them. For instance, the suppression of evidence of using branded products at Thanksgiving feasts and their inclusion in ordinary US meals are consumption behaviors that consumers do not typically report when talking about their food patterns and habits but they still have marketing strategy implications, as Arnould and Wallendorf (1994: 487) point out.

Observation may involve both participant and non-participant observation, or a combination of both. These forms are differentiated from each other by the membership role that the researcher adopts (Arnould and Wallendorf, 1994: 486–9). In participant observation, the researcher is present in the setting and actively participates in its activities while doing observations. For instance, the ethnographer takes part in the Thanksgiving feasts and makes detailed observations of them. Participant observation tends to be central in ethnography, since it, as discussed above, enables the ethnographer to become an insider, and in doing so it provides access to the 'backstage' areas of the phenomenon in question.

In non-participant observation, the researcher observes and records naturalistic behavior but does not become a part of the unfolding events. This form of observation may well be useful in situations where it is important that the general taken-for-granted scripts of, for instance, employee – customer interaction are not disrupted by the researcher. In this form of observation, the researcher may be present in the field to collect data without interacting with participants. Or, alternatively, he or she may study naturally occurring data such as videotapes of service encounters without even being present in the field.

Learning to observe analytically is a basic ethnographic skill that takes time to develop. It is not just a matter of looking and recording but of knowing what to look for and how to reflect on what is seen. Recording of observations (making written notes, mechanical observation using cameras and recorders) is another basic skill since recordings constitute a major data set for ethnographic research. Whatever form you use, one simple rule of thumb is to record the field data as soon as possible: in the setting or immediately after it, or at the end of the day.

In addition to observation, ethnographic inquiry often involves *interviews,* which may vary from more casual conversations to prolonged in-depth interviews. We shall discuss the topic of interviewing in more detail in Chapter 4.

Quite often, ethnographies that in particular follow premises inscribed in the tradition of naturalistic inquiry (e.g., Lincoln and Guba, 1985; Belk et al., 1988), make rather empiricist and positivistic assumptions concerning the fieldwork. In such research, it is implicitly assumed that by 'being there' and seeing 'what really takes place' the ethnographer can come closer to some essential truth about social life. They tend to adopt the rather idealistic view that the 'real' can be revealed by a trained observer's eyes. In the approach that we have been discussing here, it is not maintained that observations can reveal 'the truth' about some event, but rather that observations of some event are inevitably already interpreted, and that what they can produce is not 'the truth' (in realistic terms) but 'truthful accounts' (in regard to the chosen interpretive framework).

Another common premise that informs the use of ethnographic methods is that they enable researchers to produce *detailed* data on social and marketplace behavior. We accept this premise, and in the approach that we have been discussing here, this feature is of particular interest. This is because the detailed nature of the data enables the researcher to address the ways in which cultural (micro) practices interplay with (larger) cultural discourses and structures. That is, the ethnographer is able to analyze the discourses that structure social behavior in that setting, and to investigate the complex ways in which these discourses become embodied, embedded and negotiated in particular local settings.

With Eric Arnould and Melanie Wallendorf (1994: 485), we also wish to stress that in making a detailed investigation of the setting in and through which social life is reproduced one often needs *multiple sources of data.* This means that besides the dominant set of methods of observation and interviews, one may also take photographs or gather material cultural artifacts such as brochures, flyers, business cards, newsletters or newspapers to generate detailed and varying perspectives of the setting in question.

To give a concrete example of the nature of ethnographic data, we quote in Box 3.1 Peñaloza's description of the data collected in her study on Mexican immigrants.

Box 3.1   Ethnographic fieldwork data

'The output of data collection efforts consisted of maps of the field sites, 300 photographs, 50 artifacts (brochures, business cards, flyers and local newspapers), and 839 pages of text. This included a set of fieldnotes (311 handwritten pages compiled from 223 hours of field observation), transcriptions of the tape-recorded interviews (141 pages typed), and a journal of personal reflections (387 handwritten pages).'

Source: Peñaloza (1994: 38)

The ethnographic study on the Burning Man festival conducted by Robert Kozinets (2002a), in turn, illustrates the ways in which the Internet may also play a role in the data-gathering function of a 'conventional' ethnography (we shall discuss 'virtual ethnography' in more detail in the next section) (see Box 3.2).

Box 3.2   Using the Internet as part of a conventional ethnography

'My investigation of Burning Man and its community began in October 1996. At this time, I began informal observation of the very active Internet community of Burning Man participants. I downloaded and analyzed Burning Man–related photographs, articles, documents, reminiscences, computer-mediated communications and other cultural data available through mass-media channels and on the Internet. After approximately three years of building a knowledge base, I intensified my research with six days of participant observation at the weeklong Burning Man 1999 event. Following this, I maintained e-mail contact with several participants I had met and interviewed. Participating as a member of the community, I created and maintained a Burning Man Research website, actively surfed online sites, and subscribed to and participated on three major Burning Man mailing lists. This year of intensified online activity was followed by a further six days of participation-observation at Burning Man 2000'.

Source: Kozinets (2002a: 23)

Ethnographic writing

Let us turn to discussion of the other part of an ethnographic inquiry, *writing*. Basically, an ethnographic report expresses an understanding of a cultural setting gained through fieldwork. It is developed from a set of written fieldnotes, interview transcripts and other documents. In the more traditional and realist approaches to ethnography, the role of these fieldnotes and the final ethnographic report is to present a 'documentary' and 'authentic' description of the fieldwork setting. In recent decades, however, the assumption of such realist writing has been under severe attack.

The critical examination of textual practices – often referred to as the 'crisis of representation' – relates to a wider series of intellectual crises that ethnography, and social research in general, has gone through (Clifford and Marcus, 1986; Marcus and Fischer, 1999). Poststructuralists and postmodernist critiques have challenged the assumptions of 'positivist' arguments and realist approaches to knowledge, truth and objectivity, and in doing so, they have contributed to a major re-examination and re-fashioning of ethnographic epistemology and methodology. As a result, previously taken-for-granted assumptions of a researcher somehow directly capturing and representing 'authentic' experiences of Others were problematized. Rather, the focus was directed to the ways in which ethnographic knowledge was culturally and socially constructed.

As contemporary ethnographers acknowledge that they make culture rather than discover it, particular attention is paid to the ways in which ethnographic textual practices make up culture (Richardson, 2000). As a result, there has been an enhanced interest in ethnographic writing. Ethnographic writing is no longer understood as a form of transparent representation of a pre-existing culture but as a textual construction of reality. Recently, ethnographers have developed a number of innovative and non-realist forms of writing, and we shall discuss them in more detail in Part 4. Common ethnographical writing forms to be mentioned here include 'confessional tales' from the field or 'impressionist tales' (van Maanen, 1988; for a discussion see also Thompson et al., 1998: 111–13).

This increased concern about the constitutive role of textual practices relates both to fieldnotes and final reports. While fieldnotes typically express a documentary intent, the creation of fieldnotes is a product of textualization that makes up a particular world, as Emerson et al. (1995) discuss in their book. To illustrate this point, we offer a little exercise that takes up the questions of *voice, power and reflexivity.* These very questions are currently considered central not only to ethnographic writing, but to every aspect of the research process (Coffey, 1999; Peñaloza, 1994; Thompson et al., 1998). In the reminder of this section, we shall concentrate on discussing these themes, which all relate to the production of ethnographic knowledge.

EXERCISE 3.1   Writing fieldnotes

Consider, for instance, observing a social situation such as lunch breaks in your academy. How do you write up people when making fieldnotes? Perhaps you would label them as 'professors', 'students', 'PhD students', and 'other faculty members'? Try to reflect upon the ways in which fieldnotes become constructed. How those interpretations and not others came about? What kind of power relation is inscribed in these labels? Whose voice is written in the fieldnotes? Whose is excluded?

Ethnographic knowledge production

To conclude, let us consider the complex role of the researcher who is the primary 'means' through which ethnographic knowledge becomes produced. The question of the researcher and the researcher's self has always been the subject of debate and scrutiny in ethnographic research (Coffey, 1999). Ethnographers enter the field as professional researchers but also as gendered, racial and bodily beings who must constantly negotiate different field roles and positions during the fieldwork. In trying to analyze and understand the field in question, the ethnographer is undeniably part of the complexities of the field.

In ethnographic textbooks, general emphasis has been on the ways in which the researcher negotiates and manages relationships between the self and others in the field ('good' relations are presumed to produce 'good' knowledge) and how the ethnographer is likely to 'affect' the field and the knowledge produced. In contemporary debates, the notion of reflexivity has become more central. It is a highly controversial issue, but it would be out of the scope of our book to immerse ourselves in these debates.

Generally speaking, *reflexivity* refers to social scientists' efforts to critically examine their constitutive role in the research process and the relationships between the knower and the known. Reflexivity goes, therefore, beyond the researcher's concern with questions of 'bias' or 'distorting the setting' through participation. Rather, the researcher is seen as a situated knowledge producer who, in this production, is involved in complex power relations (Coffey, 1999). A reflexive approach, hence, recognizes the centrality of the subjectivity of the researcher to the production and representation of ethnographic knowledge. Reflexivity should not, therefore, be misunderstood as a mechanism that neutralizes ethnographers' subjectivity, but rather, as a one that highlights it. As Marcus and Fischer summarize:

> [Ethnographers] are thus motivated to emphasize the reflexive dimension that has always underlain ethnographic research. This reflexivity demands not only an adequate critical understanding of oneself through all phases of research, but ultimately such an understanding of one's own society as well. (1999: 109–10)

Due to the vivid ongoing debate on reflexivity, in recent research reports there can be found several sorts of 'self-reflexive' accounts, from personal confessions to mere lists of personal attributes, such as 'white middle-class woman of certain age'. We align ourselves with theorists who argue that reflexivity needs to be extended beyond personalized reflections and biographical confessions, and that it should entail, above all, a critical elaboration of the paradigmatic conventions and assumptions that the researcher follows (Rosaldo, 1989; Thompson et al., 1998: 114). This sort of reflexive approach directs the researcher to carry out systematic analysis of the implicit system that shapes, guides and constrains knowledge production. It means that the researcher should, first and foremost, reflect upon the taken-for-granted core assumptions and ideological positions that underlie the research conventions, theoretical concerns and accepted rules of knowledge.

In practice, hence, ethnographers should attempt to articulate the assumptions which they take with them into the field. They should have an ongoing conversation about what they know and how they know it. This sort of continuing examination of the starting assumptions forms one way of learning about the field setting. Ethnographers should also consider the ways in which their paradigmatic positions are imposed on all stages of the research process – from the questions they ask to those they ignore, whom they study and whom they ignore, from problem formation to analysis. Analytic categories, concepts and standard modes of representations that are used in the construction of knowledge all express an underlying ideological content that can be revealed – in part, and only in part – by reflexive analyses (Thompson et al., 1998: 109).

This sort of reflexive approach is needed since the researchers' paradigmatic – as well as socio-cultural – background, prepares him/her to construct knowledge claims about specific issues, and not others. In other words, it reveals how researchers' paradigmatic and ideological orientations frame the phenomenon in a particular way, excluding other ways. The study of Thompson, Stern and Arnould (1998) well illustrates this point. They critically examine and counter-read published ethnographic marketing research texts. This re-reading from different paradigms show how alternative interpretations may arise; interpretations that give voices to issues that the original text had placed in a marginal position or excluded altogether.

All in all, this critical and reflexive practice that has troubled ethnography, has paved the way for the new varieties of ethnography. Next we shall discuss virtual ethnography, critical ethnography and autoethnography as possible ways of collecting ethnographic data for cultural marketing and consumer research.

Virtual ethnography

Virtual ethnography is an ethnographic variety that has emerged and developed, in particular, in line with the proliferation of the Internet. It refers, simply put, to an ethnography that is undertaken in computer-mediated environments. Researchers in various fields have realized that cyberspace provides a relevant ethnographic field site, and they have developed the ways in which ethnographic research methods can assist the understanding of online environments (Hine, 2000; Jones, 1999). As these cyberspaces are often, implicitly or explicitly, market-oriented in their focus, marketers and marketing academics also have shown an increasing interest in understanding and researching contemporary cyberspace (Brown et al., 2003; MacLaran and Catterall, 2002).

In previous literature, virtual ethnography has also been labeled as 'netnography' (Kozinets, 2002b), 'cyber ethnography' or 'on-line ethnography', but we use the term 'virtual ethnography'. To date, virtual ethnography mostly relates to the use of the Internet, and also we concentrate on this particular space. We believe, however, that the emergence of new mobile digital technologies may provide interesting possibilities for conducting virtual ethnographies in the future.

We start the section by discussing the particularities of this ethnographic variety, and then we turn to discuss the ways in which it has been applied in marketing and consumer inquiry.

What is virtual ethnography?

Virtual ethnography involves, briefly put, the transplantation of ethnography to cyberspace, which is studied as a context of social and cultural relations in its own right. Newsgroups, for instance, may be viewed as a form of social action, and therefore treated as appropriate sites and objects of analysis for ethnographic inquiry. The task of virtual ethnographers, then, is to study the social, cultural and political formations that can be found in this particular cyberspace.

Virtual ethnographers not only acknowledge that the Internet represents a place where culture and social relations are formed and reformed, but also emphasize that the Internet itself is a specific cultural artifact (Hine, 2000: 9). It is a technology that has been produced by particular people with particular contextually situated goals and priorities. As a research site, the Internet is thus shaped by the ways in which it is marketed, taught and used. These specific features of the cyberspace should therefore be considered and reflected upon when doing virtual ethnography. Moreover, as the very notion of virtual depends on a vague or questionable distinction between real and virtual, in focusing heavily on the specific features of 'virtuality', researchers may inadvertently reproduce a distinction in which they do not believe.

Moving ethnography to an online setting involves a re-examination of some of the basic epistemic practices that typically characterize ethnographic work. First of all, there is a shift in focus from face-to-face interaction to virtual forms of interaction (Kozinets, 2002b). For example, virtual ethnography may partly be based on online interviewing, which is a special kind of interactive situation that requires special kind of interpretive skills from the researcher (MacLaran and Catterall, 2002). Whilst non-verbal cues such as eye contact and body language are crucial ways to create rapport in face-to-face interviews, online interviews must rely on different kinds of paralinguistic cues. Commonly used examples of such cues are emoticons, that is, smiling or frowning faces such as ;) or :(. Moreover, the use of capitals and exclamation marks represent ways to communicate emotions and points of emphasis in an online interview. In virtual ethnography, these sorts of textual cues are to be submitted to the analysis, as part of the interviews to be interpreted.

Secondly, the nature of the field and the way it is defined has to be reformulated in virtual ethnography. Virtual ethnographers cannot rely upon physical boundaries in defining their site; instead, they commonly rely on connection and shared practices (Hine, 2000). This means, for instance, that they may consider newsgroups as research sites to which people log on in order to form social relations although participants do not meet physically.

Thirdly, while conventional ethnographers typically 'go to the field', 'are in the field' and 'return from the field' – which constitutes an essential part of the professional identity of an ethnographer – virtual ethnographers seldom travel anywhere from their place of work. Nevertheless, they still have to negotiate access to the research site. They have to gain entry to Internet newsgroups, for instance. They also need to make decisions about the length of their stay in the field – does the research question necessitate a prolonged engagement in online setting or not. Moreover, they need to consider whether involved presence and in-depth immersion into that particular setting is needed. This relates to the choice of online ethnographic methods: whether to use participant or non-participant methods? Like in conventional ethnography, so in virtual ethnography researchers may either participate in the interaction that takes place in the research setting or they can just observe it by 'lurking', for example, which refers to monitoring a website through non-participant observation (see, e.g., MacLaran and Catterall, 2002: 323–4). Altogether these latter examples illustrate that there are also a number of symmetries between the virtual and the more 'conventional' forms of ethnography.

Virtual ethnography in marketing and consumer inquiry

Marketing and consumer researchers as well as marketers have recognized the increasing importance of virtual environments in creating, sustaining and mediating culture, particularly in contemporary Western societies. The new computer-mediated environments create virtual worlds where people can entertain themselves, pursue their hobbies, buy and sell products, express their ideas and values, as well as interact and form relationships with each other, participating in various types of virtual communities. Therefore, the new virtual environments and particularly the virtual communities they involve provide a rich source of information on a wide range of marketing-related topics (Kozinets, 2002a, 2002b; MacLaran and Catterall, 2002; Solomon, 2003).

Virtual communities come in many forms and perform a wide variety of functions for consumers (see Solomon, 2003: 138–9). More and more people are logging on to various 'communities of relationships', such as matchmaking websites and online dating services, in hope of finding intimate friends and forming personal relationships of various sorts. 'Communities of transaction', such as eBay, have also become popular sites for buying and selling goods and services. There are also 'communities of interests' of various types which allow people to learn and share their knowledge about topics that interest them as well as to locate others who share those interests. These online communities – sometimes also referred to as 'electronic or virtual tribes' – are forms of community where people may maintain their anonymity and do not necessarily meet physically, but nevertheless share some common interest. People 'meet' and interact in these communities through electronic chat rooms, mailing lists, news groups and bulletin boards as well as through Internet games based on Multi-User-Dungeons (MUDs), for example.

For marketing and consumer researchers, *virtual brand communities* are a particularly interesting form of online community. They refer to specialized, non-geographically bound groups of people, based on a structured set of social relations among admirers of a brand (Solomon, 2003: 136). Many of these communities are created or at least nurtured by companies as part of their customer relationship management or brand management strategies. But there are also virtual brand communities that have been formed by the customers of the brand, independently of the company. For instance, there are newsgroups devoted to Harley–Davidson motorcycles (Schouten and McAlexander, 1995), Saab cars and MacIntosh computers (Muniz and O'Guinn, 2001). There are also a number of anti-brand communities and communities that are devoted to actively boycotting particular firms or politicians.

In virtual brand communities consumers often engage in discussions where they try to inform and influence fellow consumers about products and brands. Doing this, they also talk about themselves and express their personal views and values, thus providing marketers with interesting information about the potential and actual customers of the brand as well as about the image of their brand in the market. For marketers and consumer researchers these virtual environments and communities may therefore constitute an important source of data (see, e.g., Brown et al., 2003).

Analyzing these brand communities, the personal Web pages and weblogs of the members of the brand community, if available, also constitute an important source of data. As the study of Schau and Gilly shows (2003), in personal websites consumers construct identities by associating themselves with commercial signs and symbols to represent and express their self-concepts.

Critical ethnography

Critical ethnography is a style of analysis and a discourse embedded within conventional ethnography (Foley and Valenzuela, 2005; Thomas, 1993). We first discuss its basic features and then turn to elaborate on the ways in which such a methodology can contribute to marketing and consumer research. For that purpose, we use the critical ethnography conducted by Lisa Peñaloza (1994) among Mexican immigrants as an example.

What is critical ethnography?

Critical ethnography is based on basic ethnographic methods and principles: it addresses social life in a particular context and employs conventional ethnographic methods. What differentiates critical ethnography from the more traditional forms of ethnography is the explicitly political nature of the approach. As Jim Thomas summarizes:

> Critical ethnography is a way of applying a subversive worldview to the conventional logic of cultural inquiry. It does not stand in opposition to conventional ethnography. Rather, it offers a more direct style of thinking about the relationships among knowledge, society, and political action. The central premise is that one can be both scientific and critical, and that ethnographic description offers a powerful means of critiquing culture and the role of research in it. (Thomas, 1993: vii)

Critical ethnography thus not only critically analyzes and challenges the conventional, received views and accounts of social reality but also directs attention to the ways in which particular forms of research produce and sustain these views.

The core of critical scholarship in critical ethnography is, first of all, that the commonsense assumptions and beliefs upon which social existence is built are questioned. Critical ethnographers – like cultural researchers in general – recognize that we live in a reality that presents itself as taken-for-granted, and it is precisely this taken-for-granted nature of social reality that calls for further analysis. It is emphasized that even the most benign beliefs, cultural symbols, representations and linguistic categories that are shared in a culture may inhibit, repress and constrain the thinking and acting of the members of that culture. Critical ethnography, therefore, sets out to critically analyze the forms of social control that these cultural and discursive practices entail. Importantly, critical ethnographers also work toward realizing alternative ways of seeing, thinking and acting. Therefore, while conventional ethnography asks 'what is?', critical ethnography asks 'what could be?' (Thomas, 1993). This means that some sort of emancipatory spirit is inscribed into critical ethnography.

Secondly, critical ethnographers draw particular attention to the role of research in producing both restricting and emancipating alternative possibilities. It carefully describes, analyzes and opens to scrutiny agendas, power relations and assumptions that govern research (Thomas, 1993). This is needed because the questions that we ask, and the specific ways that we conceptualize and operationalize phenomena, are inevitably infused with values that tend to remain implicit unless critically assessed. Critical ethnography is also concerned with the relationship of power and subjectivity of not only the researcher but also the researched. In this sense, critical cthnography entails the sort of critical reflexive practice that we discussed earlier (Coffey, 1999; Thompson et al., 1998).

Thirdly, critical ethnography aims to situate the knowledge that it produces in a broader social, economic and political context. This means that critical ethnographers do not merely describe the cultural beliefs and systems of meanings that prevail in the field, but also seek to link these descriptions to broader structures of power and control.

Under these basic principles of critical ethnography, applications may range from modest rethinking of conventional concepts to more direct engagement that includes political activism (Thomas, 1993: 17). Douglas Foley and Angela Valenzuela (2005) offer a good state-of-the-art account of critical ethnography, elaborating on the ways in which it is currently employed. According to their analysis, in current research practice, critical ethnography tends to take the form of academic cultural critiques, applied policy studies and studies, that serve particular political movements. For those interested in this methodology, we highly recommend their article.

Critical ethnography in marketing and consumer inquiry

Discussing the ways in which critical ethnography may be applied and utilized in the field of marketing and consumer research, we use the study of Lisa Peñaloza, 'Atravesando Fronteras/Border Crossings: a Critical Ethnographic Exploration of the Consumer Acculturation of Mexican Immigrants' (Peñaloza,1994) as a case in point. The study investigates the dynamic processes through which Mexican immigrants adapt to the US environment. The study looks at how these Latino consumers express both Mexican and US culture in their consumption practices, and importantly also how marketers deal with this consumer group. The study contributes to our understanding of the processes of consumer acculturation by elaborating on the complex ways in which marketing and consumption practices play into these processes. (The term 'consumer acculturation' describes the processes through which people from one culture adapt to live in another.)

What makes this study a piece of critical ethnography? Peñaloza herself explains (1994: 36) that the concerns of a critical ethnographer include (1) the relations between the researcher and the researched, (2) the agency of those being investigated (that is, how people are treated during the course of the study, how they are represented in the written account, and whether the study incorporates their interests) and (3) the importance of situating the work within the global economy. We shall concentrate, in particular, on the two latter themes: agency of those being investigated, and situating the work within the global economy.

Generally, as Peñaloza notes, Mexican immigrants tended to be a somewhat 'invisible' group of people and it was marketers who actually 'saw' and acknowledged this previously invisible group of people due to the new market potential they represented. This group of people, as she notes, also tended to be treated – implicitly or explicitly – as one homogeneous group, as if they were all the same, all merely *Others*. Through her study, Peñaloza critically analyzes and problematizes this comprehension, providing a more subtle description of the differences prevailing within the group. This critique which provides a more elaborate understanding of the largest minority group in the United States, is vital across the spectrum of education, health care, social services provision, community organizing, politics, employment and marketing. This sort of knowledge provides tools for public policy-makers to elaborate, for instance, on what the market can and cannot do in community development. For firms, it provides a more thorough understanding of the nature of this group among which the differences are often at least as great as between Latinos/as and non-Latinos/as.

In the spirit of critical ethnography, Peñaloza also analyzes the ways in which research plays a role in constituting particular agencies for Mexican immigrants. She maintains that research is always based on a set of tacit rules about how the world is and how it should be, and thus involves a built-in ideology that gives a rather narrow perspective to what is studied. The question therefore arises, what sort of research conventions and assumptions sustain the homogeneous picture of immigrants? She proposes that the prevailing assimilation model – and attendant discursive practices – may be used in ways that have smoothed over options other than assimilation and rendered unintelligible the increasing heterogeneity of the US market (p. 52).

Importantly, her study suggests that marketers are critically important agents of consumer acculturation (Peñaloza, 1994: 50–1). By targeting Latinos with market offerings associated with Mexican culture, marketers have facilitated the institutionalization of Mexican culture in the United States. By providing user-friendly access to mainstream US products and services for Mexican immigrants, marketers have also facilitated their assimilation of those items.

Accordingly, the study of Peñaloza elaborated on the ways in which marketing practices may play a key role in producing and shaping agencies for people. In doing so, marketing practices have potential social and political impacts in society. For critical marketing ethnographers, therefore, seemingly 'normal' marketing practices such as segmentation strategies are not neutral in any way. Rather, they are treated as technologies through which agencies are effectively reproduced and/or neutralized (Peñaloza, 1994: 51) and, therefore, as something that needs to be carefully and critically analyzed. As she notes, 'issues brought to the fore in a critical marketing ethnography include the cultural role of market practices, discourses, agents, and institutions in constituting such agencies' (Peñaloza, 2000: 86).

Finally, in line with the principles of critical ethnography, Peñaloza situates her findings into a broader economic context. She devotes particular attention to the historical, cultural and economic processes and practices through which the subject positions of Mexican immigrants have evolved and taken form over time. Moreover, discussing the conditions of global economy, global movements of capital and labor as well as the global dynamics of cultural interpenetration, she also challenges consumer researchers to rethink the categories that they use when investigating consumer behavior that transcends national borders (Peñaloza, 1994: 51).

Autoethnography

Autoethnography refers to an autobiographical genre of research in which researchers study cultural phenomena by analyzing the ways in which they themselves are engaged in cultural practice. In autoethnography, the researcher uses the cultural practices he or she performs and/or observes in the course of his or her everyday life – working, doing shopping and spending time with friends and family – to learn about particular cultural phenomena.

In this section, we present the basic idea of an autoethnographic inquiry. Using one case example of an autoethnography, conducted by Valtonen (2004b), we elaborate on the ways in which this methodology may produce relevant insights into consumer and marketing inquiry, enabling us to advance our theoretical understanding of the complex and all-pervasive ways in which cultural meanings are produced, mediated and sustained in the market. The strength of this methodology is that it enables us to empirically display the multiple ways in which particular cultural discourses are played out and practiced in the course of everyday life, throughout the whole life.

What is autoethnography?

In recent years, social sciences have witnessed a rise of autoethnography (Coffey, 1999; Ellis and Bochner, 2000; Richardson, 2000). The rise can be seen, in part, as a response to the critiques of ethnographic assumptions and conventions that we have outlined at the beginning of this chapter, even though the personal approach is certainly not new direction for ethnographers, neither for social scientists in general. C.W. Mills, for instance, in his classic book *Sociological Imagination*, highlights the importance of the personal in the practice of doing academic research. He remarks: '[Y]ou must learn to use your life experience in your intellectual work: continually to examine and interpret it. In this sense craftsmanship is the center of yourself and you are personally involved in every intellectual product upon which you may work' (Mills, 2000: 196).

The autoethnographic inquiry positions the self at the center of the research process.[3] The autoethnographer is simultaneously the subject and object of the research, observing and interpreting culture through reflecting on his or her personal life experiences. This methodology uses the personal position as a valuable means of investigating culture and in doing so it challenges several conventional academic practices. First it challenges the division between the researcher and the researched. Secondly, by maintaining that personal accounts can be sources of insightful analysis, the autoethnographic tradition openly works against the ideology of detachment that has dominated academic research, including consumer and marketing research (Bristor and Fischer, 1993; Hirschman, 1993). Thirdly, by problematizing the ways in which research may be written and represented, the tradition also reacts against the insularity of academic writing. Autoethnographic research is thus based on making the most of the *situated self* as well as on *writing from that situated position*. It is on these two characteristics that we concentrate in the reminder of this section.

To start, however, we wish to differentiate the autoethnographic perspective from the psychologically and/or phenomenologically inspired introspective tradition that has invited some interest in consumer research. This particular tradition considers researchers' personal introspection as an access to inner thoughts and feelings that are otherwise inaccessible (Gould, 1995). In an autoethnographic research, especially when applied in a framework that is inspired by poststructuralism, the point is not to use the self to provide access to inner feelings otherwise inaccessible. Instead, the idea is to use the self to make visible cultural meanings and practices that are otherwise invisible owing to their taken-for-granted or marginalized nature. As these practices create, shape and constrain modes of being and thinking, they call for critical investigation. We position, therefore, the autoethnographic tradition closer to the critical ethnography than to the introspective tradition (see also Foley and Valenzuela, 2005).

Situated self

The personal approach inhibits particular kinds of insight, but in the autoethnographic tradition, this is not seen as a limitation but as a productive point of departure (van Loon, 2001: 282). The notion of situated self and situated knowledge is obviously acknowledged also by several non-autoethnographic authors. Quoting Renato Rosaldo (1989: 8), the basic idea of situated knowledge may be summarized by arguing that 'all interpretations are provisional; they are made by positioned subjects who are prepared to know certain things and not others'. In the autoethnographic tradition this idea is fully taken advantage of.

This means, in particular, that the personal position of the autoethnographer is made use of to draw attention to positions that commonly go unnoticed in academic discourses. Autoethnography typically produces stories that deviate from the canonical ones. It gives voice to the hidden, forbidden, or silenced stories; stories that matter to people but remain invisible in academic discourses (Ellis and Bochner, 2000). This openly moral, ethical and political standpoint also differentiates an autoethnography from more conventional forms of biographies.

The main objective of this strategy is to alter the taken-for-granted paradigmatic assumptions. As we have already discussed, research conventions privilege certain voices and marginalize and/or exclude others. By paying particular attention to the choice of position from which to voice thoughts and by explicitly including alternative voices, the autoethnographic method makes these implicit forms of academic social control visible. Thereby it also opens new avenues for social scientific theorizing. We illustrate this point by paraphrasing some personal reflections of one of the present authors. Anu Valtonen (2004b) conducted an autoethnographic study that was concerned with the ways in which such a cultural category as 'shortness' becomes produced and sustained both throughout routine social life and throughout various market-related practices.

> My story of shortness emerged from the process of attending the feminist reading group at my business academy. In reading and debating on various bases for subjectivity, such as sex, gender, age, ethnicity, race, class, outlook, education and so forth, I had a vague feeling that something was missing. Why does no one talk about the dimension that has ruled my entire life, height? In trying to understand this silence, I started to remember my life, to identify instances in and through which I had been made to feel short. I also started to keep a diary of my daily life, to observe and make notes of social situations in which height was mentioned; in classes, in the corridor, seminars, talks over coffee, family meetings, when meeting with friends etc. I also came to notice the ways in which height is referred to and produced in the books I read, films I see, and newspapers I scan. I also came to notice the multiple ways in which marketing practices and service encounters kept repeating and reproducing particular height – related meanings. But despite this all-pervasive reproduction of height, the issue of height had been silenced both in the literature on body – it is the issue of weight, not height, that dominates – and in critically informed social studies – there, it is the issues of race and gender that have invited most investigation. (Paraphrased from Valtonen, 2004b)

Why has shortness remained invisible in previous debates? Let us elaborate on that question by reference to a discussion that took place at an academic conference. The author (A.V.) had presented the personal study on shortness, and then a man from the audience, a white male professor of normal height, stood up and said: 'Anu, you are *not* short!' On another occasion another white male professor of normal height repeated the same statement, but he continued, 'Or, actually, I have never thought of it.' That is the point. The latter statement describes the notion of the invisible power in practice (Rosaldo, 1989). The statement concretizes the point that from a particular position we are prepared to see only particular matters and a wide range of matters lie beyond; they are matters that 'we do not think of'. Therefore, what kinds of positions become inscribed as 'normal' in academic discourses have an impact on the kind of knowledge of the phenomenon in question that is produced, and what kind of knowledge remains hidden.

Autoethnographic method may hence give voice to those cultural positions that are systematically marginalized or excluded but that are relevant to the phenomenon in question. In the 'shortness' example, for instance, the issue of height is seldom included in discussions on wage discrimination, although there are studies that show that tall people earn more than short ones. In this regard, the method may work towards a political aim but it may also serve as a fruitful stimulant for opening new theoretical and empirical perspectives for market-related phenomenon.

For instance, the autoethnographic method draws our attention to the multiple ways in which the prevailing discourse of shortness becomes repeated and practiced in different contexts, by different people and by different institutions. This discourse of shortness suggests that a 'short woman' is a deviant. She deviates from the 'normal' category of adulthood and is equated with the child, with attendant qualities of inferiority. This very meaning becomes produced – not only through 'bad advertising creating false images for people' – but also through the material world that is made for people of medium height; through the measurement practices of health clinics and schools doctors' and nurses' comments and growth curves show that short people are deviant; through the friendly advice of friends and workmates to avoid certain types of clothes and to use high heels in order to be more like normal; through emphatic tones of voices; through service encounters that sell children's tickets to people of short stature; through the outlets specialized in serving small-sized women; as well as through advertisements and media. They are all promoting and reinforcing the message: I am small. The message is obviously gendered: a man would wear concealed heels instead of the high-heeled shoes that in the case of a woman do not merely represent a symbol of femininity, but also a symbol of normal height.

All in all, this methodology may advance our theoretical understanding of the complex ways in which the circuit of culture operates in the market. It enables us, in particular, to make explicit the all-pervasive and repetitive nature of cultural reproduction and thereby empirically illustrate the repertoires of repetitive practices (Butler, 1990).

Writing from a personal position

The autoethnographic tradition also places particular emphasis on how to *write and represent* the world being studied. It maintains that personal texts can be sources of insightful analysis. It also maintains an overall critical appreciation of the power relations of textual production and representation of the social world.

In practice, autoethnographic texts may appear in a variety of forms – short stories, poetry, fiction, novels, photographic essays, or performance (see, e.g., Ellis and Bochner, 2000 for a good review). The study on shortness mentioned earlier relates to the narrative tradition (Riessman, 1993), but as an autoethnographic narrative it is a particular one. It is, first and foremost, a thoroughly reflexive narrative that invites the reader to know the world from the position of the writer. It invites the reader to notice the multiple ways in which shortness becomes produced throughout social life, and gives room for the reader's own self-reflection.

Although the story is personal, it is not about the personal feelings of being short. It is not a confession story, but a story with political purpose. Although the author uses her own body as primary data, the focus is not on that body as such, but on the ways in which cultural practices define and label certain bodies as short, and on the particular meanings inscribed in such a label, and on the social and cultural consequences of these particular meanings. These practices are not the property of the author or any other individual. They are shared, as cultural knowledge always is. In that particular story, these public cultural events are drawn attention to, analyzed and displayed.

Notes

1 We do not discuss 'visual ethnography' here, because the book contains an entire chapter that is concerned with the notion of visual.

2 Prominent developers of this methodology include authors such as Bronislaw Malinowski, Margaret Mead and E.E. Evans-Pritchard to mention a few (for a historical review, see for instance Tedlock, 2003: 166–71).

3 Also in conventional ethnography, prolonged fieldwork inevitably involves the researcher in various kinds of autobiographical practice: ethnographers use fieldnotes and research journals to record the feelings, emotions and personal identity work.

FURTHER READING

The following texts provide a thorough account of recent methodological discussions and debates on the different varieties of ethnography.

The *Handbook of Ethnography* is a valuable resource for both graduate students and experienced researchers. It discusses the nature of ethnography, its historical grounding and substantive applications, as well as the different types of research practice that constitute it. The future directions of ethnography are also explored:

- Atkinson, Paul, Coffey, Amanda, Delamont, Sara, Lofland, John and Lofland, Lyn (eds) (2001) *Handbook of Ethnography*. London: Sage.

There are several good texts focusing on the different varieties and new creative applications of ethnography we have discussed above.

Critical ethnography:

- Foley, Douglas and Valenzuela, Angela (2005) 'Critical Ethnography: the Politics of Collaboration', in N.K. Denzin and Y.S. Lincoln (eds), *Handbook of Qualitative Research*. London: Sage. pp. 217–34.

Virtual ethnography:

- Hine, Christine (2000) *Virtual Ethnography*. London: Sage.
- Kozinets, Robert V. (2002b) 'The Field Behind the Screen: Using Netnography for Marketing Research in Online Communities', *Journal of Marketing Research*, 39 (1): 61–72.

Autoethnography:

- Ellis, Carolyn and Bochner, Arthur P. (2000) 'Autoethnography, Personal Narrative, Reflexivity: Researcher as Subject', in N.K. Denzin and Y.S. Lincoln (eds), *Handbook of Qualitative Research*. London: Sage. pp. 733–68.

4

Cultural Texts and Talk

CHAPTER SUMMARY

This chapter focuses on cultural texts and talk, as empirical materials for doing cultural marketing and consumer research. The objective is to discuss the ways in which different spoken and written materials can be obtained, generated and used to gain cultural knowledge of the marketplace. More specifically, the chapter elaborates on:

- media texts and administrative documents as cultural texts;
- interviews and focus groups as cultural talk; and
- the use of projective techniques and elicitation materials to generate cultural texts and talk.

Introduction

In cultural marketing and consumer research, empirical analysis is based on textual and visual materials, which are all analyzed as cultural texts. These texts can take many forms, ranging from naturally occurring media texts, documentary materials and visibilities to fieldnotes and texts generated through interviews, focus groups and projective techniques. In this chapter, we focus on *naturally occurring texts and cultural talk*, elaborating on the ways in which written and spoken empirical materials can be obtained, generated and used to gain cultural knowledge of the marketplace.

By 'cultural texts' and 'cultural talk' we refer to social texts that are produced, shared and used in culturally specific, socially organized ways. As we have explained, these texts are studied for the cultural discourses and discursive practices that they realize and make available. Cultural texts and talk are thus not taken as transparent representations or accurate portrayals of marketplace phenomena – they only give us access to particular accounts of those phenomena. Neither interview data nor focus group discussions, for example, merely reflect people's subjective experience or cognitive representations of objects, events and categories pre-existing in the social and natural world (Atkinson and Silverman, 1997; Silverman, 1998). The cultural talk that is generated through interviews and focus groups is rather taken as a complex cultural, socio-psychological product, constructed in particular, context-specific ways to carry out relationships and to constitute what is real, true and good in a particular community (Gergen, 1997; Potter and Wetherell, 1987).

By the same token, *institutional documents and factual accounts* such as annual reports and policy documents are seen as social texts that are constructed according to particular conventions and to make things happen. As Potter (1996: 108) has argued, factual accounts and descriptions have a double orientation. They have an 'action orientation', in the sense that they are used to accomplish an action, and they have an 'epistemological orientation' in the sense that they are constructed in particular ways in order to build up their status as a factual version. As such, documentary and archival data do not necessarily differ very much from many media texts or marketing communications.

In the sections that follow, we first briefly discuss media texts and documentary materials as naturally occurring cultural texts. Then we take up the somewhat controversial issue of doing interviews and focus groups to generate cultural talk for cultural analysis. It is our contention that interviews and focus groups must be viewed and analyzed as cultural practice and as particular forms of social interaction. But as such they may well be useful means of generating cultural talk. We conclude the chapter by exploring the possibilities of generating cultural text by means of projective techniques and elicitation materials.

Naturally occurring textual materials

Much of marketing and consumer research takes place in literate societies and self-documenting cultures, where different kinds of text are continuously written, read and archived (Atkinson and Coffey, 1997: 45). In such environments, there are plenty of 'naturally occurring data' available for cultural research. Different sorts of media texts, administrative documents and archival materials, produced by members of cultures themselves, can be used as empirical materials, and there is no need necessarily to do interviews or carry out focus groups to collect data.

In various professional, organizational and academic settings, there are lots of *documentary materials* that can be analyzed to learn about the cultural discourses and discursive practices through which social reality is produced and everyday practices are organized in those settings. In contemporary business organizations, for example, managers, knowledge workers and staff members of different sorts are all routinely required to 'do paperwork' for administrative purposes, and the written records and documents that these employees produce may serve as an important source of empirical data for cultural research. They can be analyzed for the local, firm-specific forms of government and organizational cultures that they entail. But as cultural texts, these materials may also tell much about the prevalent cultural discourses in which these organizations operate.

Moreover, in Western market economies, both organizations and individuals produce various sorts of texts and documents for self-presentation and image-management. Firms produce annual reports, press releases and marketing communications for general marketing, brand management and shareholder management purposes, for example. Governmental and non-governmental organizations generate different kinds of educational materials, reports, policy documents, histories and general informative texts. Individual consumer-citizens create personal Web pages, résumés and curriculum vitae of different types to advertise themselves and to appear desirable in the job market. Increasingly, individuals also place personal ads and resort to online dating services to form meaningful social relationships and to find potential spouses. All these texts, when available publicly or by permission, constitute a rich source of empirical data for cultural marketing and consumer research. They can be studied to learn about the discursive practices through which individuals and organizations publicize themselves and compete with others in the same 'market'; how they justify themselves to potential employers, partners, spouses, clients, shareholders and boards of directors for example. Contextualized within wider systems of representation, these texts may provide valuable cultural knowledge of the marketplace.

Media texts and cultural products of different types, such as films, TV shows, popular magazines and novels, have been studied extensively in the field of cultural studies for the forms of cultural discourse they draw from and produce. This material is an equally useful source of naturally occurring data for cultural marketing and consumer research. Popular TV shows and magazines, and recently also different Internet-based discussion forums and online communities, can be analyzed particularly to learn about contemporary consumer culture. Much as advertisers and designers, journalists and media producers may serve as important cultural intermediators, by producing and circulating symbolic forms, goods and services, they may also play a critical role in cultural processes. On the one hand, they need to accommodate the expectations and preferences of their audiences in the content that they produce. On the other hand, they also function as significant shapers of taste. They introduce new ideas, concepts, fashions and lifestyles, thus exerting power and authority from their position within important cultural institutions.

To sum up, in Western literate societies, there are numerous types of naturally occurring cultural texts, ranging from administrative documents to personal Web pages, available for empirical analysis. For cultural marketing and consumer research, these materials constitute important sources of data, which may often not only be easier to obtain but also constitute more appropriate data than interview and focus group materials, which have traditionally been used in qualitative marketing research, as we shall discuss in the next section of this chapter.

Personal interviews

In the field of marketing and consumer research, qualitative research is often associated – if not equated – with personal interviews. Qualitative researchers are pictured as investigators who try to reveal the hidden mechanisms and complex processes of the market and social life by probing first-person accounts from individual consumers and other market actors. In much of the existing literature, researchers have put special faith in the interview as the primary means of data collection, apparently because it has been viewed as a powerful tool for extracting information, both facts and feelings, from informants. Many scholars seem to believe that with correct interview techniques the researcher has 'the opportunity to step into the mind of another person, to see and experience the world as they do themselves' (McCracken, 1988: 9). In cultural marketing and consumer research, however, interview materials have no privileged (epistemic) status as empirical evidence of what goes on in the real world. An interview is not a mirror of some external world, nor is it a window to the inner life of a person (Denzin, 2001b: 25). The interview is rather taken as a particular form of social interaction, guided and constrained not only by the cultural discourses that are relevant for the topic and context of the interview, but also by particular cultural conventions about how interviews are to be performed both by the interviewee and the interviewer.

Paul Atkinson and David Silverman (1997), for example, have argued that predominant ways of doing interviews tend to take the form of confessionals that construct the interiority of the subject through a set of well-rehearsed discursive practices. As Atkinson and Silverman put it, the technology of the interview generates a type of encounter in which the agenda of questioning and the formulaic patterns of exchange reveal the predictable in the guise of a private confession (p. 314). Hence, in relying heavily on personal interviews, qualitative researchers often place the biographical and the narrated self at the heart of social inquiry, thus recapitulating, in an uncritical fashion, particular features of what Atkinson and Silverman refer to as the 'Interview society' – a society of the spectacle where personal interviews and the confessional mode of discourse have been turned into a form of entertainment, in the form of 'heart-to-heart'-type TV talk shows and radio programs for example.

From this perspective, the interview is not so much a method of gathering information, but rather a vehicle for producing cultural talk, which can be analyzed to gain cultural knowledge about the marketplace. This view of interviewing rejects the assumption of the subject behind the respondent as a 'passive vessel of answers', a repository of facts, feelings and information (Gubrium and Holstein, 2003b: 31). Interview participants are rather understood as actively involved in using the available cultural resources and discursive practices to construct meaningful accounts of social reality. When telling their life stories, for example, people do not necessarily tell stories that are completely their own but borrow from the narrative and discursive resources that seem appropriate and are available to them. The interview is thus viewed and analyzed as a performance in which people enact cultural meanings (Denzin, 2001b: 27).

The focus in analyzing interview materials thus shifts from 'tapping into people's minds' to collect information about their views and facts about marketplace phenomena, to cultural meanings and practices through which members of a culture construct social reality. More specifically, as we have explained in Chapter 1 (see also Part 5), the analytic focus lies on the ways in which marketplace phenomena are represented or produced discursively in text, talk, images and signifying practices.

Consequently, contrary to what is often believed, interview data are not necessarily in any way better or more authentic than some other forms of cultural data. As Gubrium and Holstein (2003b: 29) put it, in in-depth interviews, we 'do' authentic experiences as much as we do opinion offering. Nevertheless, if viewed and analyzed as jointly produced by the interviewees and the interviewers, cultural talk generated through personal interviews may well be useful for cultural marketing and consumer research. Interviews may allow researchers to collect data on the ways in which institutionalized discourses are resisted and contested in everyday discursive practices, for example (Holt, 2002; Thompson and Haytko, 1997).

Recently, new ways of conducting interviews have been developed that are based on having the interviewer and respondents collaborate in constructing the narratives. As Gubrium and Holstein (2003b: 32) note, the interview is being reconceptualized as an occasion for purposefully animated participants to construct versions of reality interactionally rather than merely to extract information from respondents. One way of animating the interviewees is to have them discuss cultural phenomena in focus groups and to use projective techniques to prompt cultural talk. These methods will be discussed in the following sections of this chapter.

Focus groups

For several decades the focus group method has been the mainstay of commercial qualitative market research, and recently its usage has also been increasing within academic research. Focus groups are discussions where a number of volunteering participants[1] are invited to come to discuss a particular subject matter in a focused, yet open and free-flowing manner for a limited time, normally for about two hours. Focus groups can involve different group compositions (groups of strangers, pre-existing social groups, lay people or professionals, etc.) as well as diverse group tasks (brainstorming, discussion on opinions, etc.) that obviously shape the scope and nature of group interaction.

There is a moderator in the group who guides and facilitates the discussion, but the key responsibility for the discussion is placed on the participants. The moderator actually seeks to encourage participants to talk to one another, ask questions from each other and comment on each others' views. This explicit emphasis on *group interaction* to generate data differentiates focus groups from group interviews where the group is formed for collecting individual-level data in a group setting. In group interviews, the moderator typically asks questions from each participant in turn instead of encouraging them to interact with each other (Barbour and Kitzinger, 1999).

The focus group method might be employed within a variety of theoretical and methodological frames. In this section we discuss and elaborate on the ways in which focus groups may be employed in culturally oriented research on marketing and consumption. Towards this aim, we discuss the particularities of focus group interaction, and the cultural data generated through it. We illustrate our discussion by drawing on a study conducted by Anu Valtonen, who applied focus groups to gain insight into the problematized notion of time and free time.

Focus groups as a site for cultural talk

The defining feature of focus groups is the social interaction among participants and among participants and the moderator. These group interactions and the talk produced through them are necessarily framed and shaped by larger social and cultural structures. For the group talk to be meaningful and to acquire a degree of social understanding it must draw on the available stock of cultural discourses and discursive practices. Therefore, although focus groups are divorced from the 'natural' cultural setting, and 'artificially' formed for the researcher's purposes, there is no reason to consider the group conversation as 'un-natural'. Besides, naturally occurring discussion is subject to the same kind of interactional and contextual constraints as the 'contrived' speech of focus groups (Hollander, 2004; Madriz, 2000).

This view of focus groups fully acknowledges that people say different things in different contexts, but this does not mean that one set of statements is distorted and the other is not. Different statements are merely produced in different contexts. Accordingly, the 'social influence' of the group is taken into account, but it is not considered a problem. On the contrary, it is considered a fruitful catalyst for displaying the ways in which multiple and overlapping discourses foster speech and particular silences. Focus group interaction illuminates the taken-for-granted ways of talking about the subject matter in focus as well as the routine silencing of certain parts of it. For instance, in talking about violence in a group setting men would not necessarily admit that they are afraid of violence in front of other men, but this *is* part of the phenomenon, not a deficiency of the method (Hollander, 2004). The nature of conformity, groupthink and social desirability pressures are not thought to obscure the data but rather these *are* the data because they are important elements of social interaction. The social dynamics of group behavior is not therefore seen as something that needs to be overcome by judicious preparation and moderation, but as an important part of the phenomenon under study.

Hence, the common concerns that participants do not speak 'their true thoughts' in front of others or that conformity pressures lead them to adjust their sayings to match those of others are not an issue in a cultural frame. These sorts of concerns are based on the view that posits the individual as the unquestionable unit of analysis – an individual who has 'real' opinions and beliefs that she or he is able to express in private but not with the presence of others. In cultural marketing and consumer research, however, these sorts of 'real' opinions are not the focus of interest, as we have explained.

In cultural research, focus groups are not conceptualized as a mere research instrument but rather as a research site, where processes of social interaction and culture are put to use and played out. Group members – both participants and moderators – are treated as cultural members who draw from and produce particular cultural discourses when discussing the topic in focus. In this discussion they create an audience for each other, and therefore the focus group situation provides a sort of theater where participants tell stories about themselves for themselves and in doing so they reflect upon the taken-for-granted conduct of life and become aware of it. They thus 'write culture together', to use Madriz's (2000) expression. In this sense, groups provide room for reflecting and commenting on culture – and on what our life is all about. In doing so groups may also foster collective identity and provide a point of contact to initiate grass-roots change (Madriz, 2000).

Next we illustrate how focus groups may be used in cultural research, using as an example a study on free time carried out by one of the authors (Valtonen, 2004a). In this study, the accounts that the participants of the focus group produced were not viewed as giving any direct access to how people actually spend their free time or how they 'really' perform their daily consumption activities. Instead, focus groups were used to get access to the shared representational and symbolic machinery of free time. The researcher was thus not interested in whether the participants lied or 'spoke the truth' when they talked about their daily life and free time. In either case, the conversation still draws from and produces particular cultural discourses.

Insightful interactions

The defining feature of focus groups, social interaction, offers particular sources of insights for a cultural analyst (Kitzinger and Farquhar, 1999). In this section we briefly outline the analytical potential of the different forms of group interaction such as arguments, mutual reinforcement, jokes, story-telling, silences, laughs and strong disagreements.

First, the participant-centered nature of focus group interaction heightens the opportunities for participants to decide the scope, direction and content of the discussion (Madriz, 2000). As the major responsibility for discussion is put on the shoulders of participants, they may pursue their own priorities and use their own terms and vocabulary in treating the topic in focus. Therefore, the group makes it possible to gain insight into how particular market segments, such as surgeons or dog owners, for instance, create their life worlds – the world they take for granted – in discussing with each other. The vocabulary that the presumed members of the market segments use, the contents of their talk, the arguments, silences and jokes, all display the systems of representation that they draw from and take for granted.

To further exemplify the rich nature of participant-centered talk let us consider a discussion on free time (Valtonen, 2004a). In this study, the group discussion centered upon general cultural categories that are customarily used for discussing free time. Accordingly, the participants were asked to tell about their everyday life, how their normal day goes, how they spend their weekends, holidays, etc. The discussion covered shared cultural categories, symbols, meanings and vocabularies related to free time, such as Friday, saunas, summer cottages, mobile phones, coffee, commuting, summer holidays, one's own time, Canary Islands or Christmas. In order to become a group, participants in a way negotiate what 'we' are as a group, what do 'we' have in common, and therefore, the discussion tends to center on collective and common topics rather than individual ones, on topics that are widely available and shared. Moreover, although participants were asked to talk about their own life at the time, the conversation widened to cover different temporal, spatial and social spheres. It covered past, present and future; experiences at home and abroad, in cities and the countryside, one's own experiences, as well as those of friends, parents, children, etc. In this sense, the group generates the kind of talk that may be characterized as rich and comprehensive and that makes the shared and taken for-granted issues visible and researchable.

Importantly, the participant-centered nature of interaction also invites talk that brings cultural representations and issues that are contested or under negotiation to the fore. When some established cultural order is challenged, it typically becomes expressed and negotiated in the social sphere – in the media, in public debates – and also focus groups provide room for that kind of negotiation. In practice, therefore, the mere amount of talk on particular topics may indicate that this topic is under cultural negotiation, not accepted as granted. Discussing free time, for instance, the participants recurrently engaged in hesitant and reflective talk about and even debates on 'what is free time, after all'. Once this or any other sort of socio-economic category becomes challenged in society it typically invites morally loaded forms of talk. For instance, talk about health problems caused by merging categories of work and free time may be read as signs of a threatened temporal order.

Moreover, focus groups open up space for participants to speak out on issues they find more worthy of discussion than the topic in question. In practice, therefore, although the moderator offers the topics to be discussed by asking questions, the participants generate their own questions: they begin to discuss issues of interest to them without waiting for questions from the moderator. This is important for a cultural analysis, because it enables culturally relevant topics to emerge, topics that otherwise might remain untouched. For instance, in a study on free time, the discussion guide did not include the issue of sleep, because the researcher uncritically followed the prevailing assumption of free time as time filled with leisure activities; despite this, however, the participants did talk a lot about sleeping (Valtonen, 2004a). The focus group interaction thus offers a possibility for a researcher to enlarge his or her pre-understanding and horizon of interpretation (these concepts will be discussed later, in Part 3).

Furthermore, the 'sensitive moments' of interaction, moments in which things go intensely but meaningfully 'wrong' may turn out to be fruitful for cultural analysis because they bring the cultural assumptions into sharp relief (Kitzinger and Farquhar, 1999). These moments that stand out may be indicated by explicit comments from research participants, hesitation and awkwardness, reactions of surprise or shock, individual defensiveness or tentative collective elaboration. While routine group talk displays the acceptable range of discourse, the sensitive moments map out the boundaries: they mark the limits of safe and acceptable everyday conversation in this particular context. By paying attention to sensitive moments, or to the ways in which respondents try to defend themselves in these moments, or how new or deviant information is incorporated or sidelined, researchers can identify underlying assumptions and question the nature of everyday talk. In Box 4.1, we illustrate the idea of sensitive moments through an example from the study on free time that we have discussed in this section.

Box 4.1   A sensitive moment

This example is taken from a focus group formed for the purpose of discussing free time. It aims to illustrate the thoroughly cultural nature of group interaction and the ways in which 'sensitive moments' in the group may be fruitful in offering insight into the phenomenon under study. The extract is from the very beginning of a focus group session, where a group of 'fathers of small children' were chosen as participants. The female moderator starts the group by an opening speech, and the 'sensitive moment' refers here to the moment when this speech is interrupted by a male participant.

Moderator:	*So, let's start. First of all, I welcome you all again. My name is Anu, and for the next hour and a half or so, I'm going to talk with you about your free time. It's the male viewpoint that is of interest here, how do you, as men, make yourselves free, what is your free time like during the week and on weekends … I'll tape-record this discussion, but this device* [I point at my MD] *is just a tool for making notes, so you can forget it, I won't give it to anybody …*
Male participant:	*No copies for the wife?* [with a humorous tone – all the others laugh]
Moderator:	[laughing as well] *Well, if you insist, we can arrange it. Do you prefer MD or C-cassette? So, we could start with everyone telling what kind of family you have, and what a typical day is like? Could you, for example, start, please?*

In terms of group dynamics, this kind of brief intervention might be considered a good start for the group. It happens at the very beginning of the group, when the participants often feel a bit insecure. The intervention generates a common laugh, which is generally a good sign of a relaxed atmosphere. When people laugh together, they 'find' each other and start to become a group.

   If we take a look at what the moderator said before that intervention, we notice that participants were addressed as 'men' and were thus invited to talk from the male position. From that particular position, the idea of free time seems to carry a meaning of something hidden and forbidden, something that should *not* be told to wives. The statement 'No copies for the wife?' is just mentioned once, laughed at and then silenced by mutual agreement. All of the people in the group, including the moderator, tacitly

(Continued)

know that there is a risk of crossing a cultural boundary if this topic is pursued further. It simply could not be discussed any further, in any detailed way, in this context. The group would enter into the (too) dirty side of free time.

The little 'sensitive moment', hence, provides understanding of the phenomenon under study. It displays particular cultural meanings related to 'male free time' and gives a lead to consider the dirty and tabooed side of free time and associated meanings more generally. The moment also illustrates that moderating occurs according to a set of cultural rules incorporated into the interaction. It further illustrates how moderators perform their task and are interpreted in the group not only through written or spoken language, but also through visible and watching bodies. People are present in a group as gendered and embodied beings.

Managing interactions

In the literature on focus groups, there are numerous books on the basic practices and principles of conducting 'successful' focus groups, which give operational guidance for managing interaction in the group (e.g., Morgan, 1993). Although it is somewhat problematic to define any sort of group discussion as 'successful', in cultural research it generally makes sense to pursue to a free-floating, lively and comprehensive discussion of the topic in question. Such discussions have the potential of providing a set of data that is rich in cultural meanings and representations.

Typically, the discussion on moderation draws from psychological literature, revolving around professional skills and personal characteristics that are needed for being a moderator. In methodological textbooks things like empathy, warmth and listening skills are often mentioned as desirable characteristics of a good moderator. We acknowledge this, but we also recommend would-be moderators to familiarize themselves with the discursive and rhetorical practices that may be used in bringing groups to life and in managing the various troubles and opportunities that arise. The book by Claudia Puchta and Jonathan Potter (2004), for instance, gives an excellent account of the focus group interaction by considering in detail what happens when the moderator and volunteer participants come together in a focus group. They draw attention to the skilled practices and subtle processes through which moderators set people at their ease, elicit opinions, manage disagreements, generate a range of views, encourage participants to be animated and involved, guide the discussion in the required direction and keep participants focused. This sort of analysis helps awareness of the subtle ways in which particular discourses become offered by the researcher during a group and draw attention to the detailed procedures through which the moderator may *produce* particular knowledge, not merely gather it.

The same authors also provide a fruitful example of the ways in which individual opinions become produced in a market research focus group (Puchta and Potter, 2002). They do not treat opinions as ready-made cognitive objects but as entities that are worked up during the group interaction. Analyzing the interaction in focus groups in a detailed manner, the authors are able to display the practices through which moderators produce particular formulations. They show, for instance, how moderators display attention to freestanding opinion formulations and display inattention to rhetorically embedded formulations, or how the moderators provide explicit formulations of the kind of contributions that are welcome. Overall, they problematize the idea of focus group participants as uncomplicated information storage facilities, who need only the proper instructions from the facilitator or a comfortable group composition to open their hearts and minds to the researcher. Participants are better understood as cultural members who mutually negotiate cultural meanings when engaging in a group discussion. And the moderator inevitably takes part in this negotiation.

The negotiation is not static but evolving in line with the phase structure of the group – beginning, middle and end. The beginning of a group, in particular, is an important phase. Its function is to introduce the topic to be discussed and, above all, to invite and motivate the participants to enter in the discussion. The moderator attempts to do this by welcoming, describing the topic and the rules of the groups, and by placing the participants in the cultural position from which they are supposed to talk (for example, 'as fathers', 'as owners of a BMW', 'as long-distance runners'). The moderator exercises power at this phase, but, little by little, the balance of power is tilted toward the group when the discussion proper is under way. At the end, the moderator reclaims the power in order to close the group, by thanking, giving incentives, or asking if there is anything participants would like to add.

The group criteria play an important role in shaping the nature of the group interaction and discussion. Methodological textbooks tend to emphasize that group members should have some kind of shared basis; shared values, interest, or histories that make it possible for participants to enter and engage in the same language game. Commonly, the basis for similarity is created by an appropriate group composition, that is, groups are composed so that participants are likely to have something in common at the outset. This homogeneity is typically created either in regard to the substantial research topic, and/or to the demographics (Morgan, 1993). Moreover, as several cultural studies scholars have discussed, the practice of sharing food carries a strong symbolic message of unity and coherence. It creates bonds among the participants. Therefore, some food – sandwiches, fruit, cookies, beverages such as wine or beer – are commonly served in a group. The beverages also convey a message that it is to be a free-form discussion and they demarcate a time-out situation that characterizes focus groups; it represents a time set apart from the ongoing business of everyday life.

The researcher must also try to figure out what the various relationships are amongst the participants, and how the setting and facilitator might affect these relationships. Do the participants, for instance, have any pre-existing social connection? What is the relative status of the various participants? The researcher also should consider what kinds of talk might be encouraged or discouraged in this sort of group context, and how particular elicitation materials such as advertisements or products may be employed in order to encourage or discourage particular speech. Moreover, the researcher should pay attention to the moderator's habitus – no matter whether it is the researcher him or herself or somebody else – and consider the ways in which he or she is located in relation to the participants. How do his or her own identity, dress, accent and behavior influence how the moderator is seen? Does the presence of particular symbols (such as a wedding ring, which displays marital status) invite or inhibit particular speeches? Is the moderator using particular discursive practices that locate him/her as 'one of us', 'outsider' or 'authority'? All these sorts of group dynamics may be taken into account when planning the groups, but, they can never be thoroughly planned nor managed. Therefore, they should be given particular attention in analyzing and reporting the group discussions.

Projective techniques and elicitation materials

Projective techniques, vignettes and elicitation materials of all sorts can be useful methods of generating cultural talk. They are particularly useful if used in conjunction with interviews and focus groups. The idea with using these methods is to elicit narratives, descriptions, comments and other verbal accounts from focus group participants or interviewees by showing them specifically designed elicitation materials that, it is hoped, will stimulate discussion and direct participants' attention to the topic of interest. Short stories, pictures, photographs, quotations or phrases, which depict scenarios and situations or moral dilemmas, for example, can be used for such purposes.

Whereas in traditional qualitative marketing research projective techniques and elicitation materials have conventionally been used to tap into the deep personal meanings, feelings and latent needs of people (Branthwaite and Lunn, 1985; Hussey and Duncombe, 1999; Rook, 1988; Zaltman and Coulter, 1995), in cultural marketing and consumer research the purpose is solely to have people talk about specific issues. This talk and the accounts that participants produce as responses to the elicitation material are then analyzed for the cultural discourses and discursive practices that they make available.

Vignettes and projective techniques are particularly useful for research focusing on issues that people find difficult to talk about, for example, because they involve embarrassing, moral or abstract issues, and for eliciting ethical frameworks and moral codes (Barter and Renold, 1999). These methods have been used particularly in consumer research, in contexts where more direct questioning methods fail to capture adequate understanding of consumer behavior processes and product symbolism (Belk et al., 1997: 24).

Projective techniques

Projective techniques are originally developed in psychology for psychoanalytic treatment and personality assessment to study repressed feelings and experiences as well as motivations that are hard to verbalize by respondents when questioned directly. In the psychological literature, the use of projective techniques is premised upon the workings of the unconscious and ego defense mechanisms. Projection refers to a defense mechanism in which people attribute their usually personally unacceptable or undesirable thoughts or impulses to other persons (Bateman and Holmes, 1995: 83). In research practice, participants are presented with more or less ambiguous stimuli onto which they are assumed to project their personality (Hussey and Duncombe, 1999). The more unstructured and ambiguous these stimuli are the more participants are assumed to project their personal feelings and values. These externalized and transformed feelings are then analyzed in some narrative form.

In marketing research applications, projective techniques are not necessarily used merely to reveal the workings of the unconscious self. Projective techniques comprise a wide range of qualitative methods, which draw not only from clinical psychology and personality assessment but also from art therapy theory and practice (Zaltman and Coulter, 1995). Alan Branthwaite and Tony Lunn (1985: 109) outline five typical purposes for using these techniques in marketing research. The use of projective techniques may help to:

- overcome self-censorship;
- encourage self-expression and fantasy;
- change perspective;
- inhibit rationalization and cognitive responses; and
- encourage expression of personal emotion.

In marketing and consumer literature, the use of 'projective techniques' has typically denoted asking focus group participants and interviewees to make collages, write fairy tales, do psychodrawings, as well as to respond to photographs, pictures and cartoons for example (Belk et al., 1997, 2003; Branthwaite and Lunn, 1985; Hussey and Duncombe, 1999; Zaltman and Coulter, 1995). These techniques have been used particularly to stimulate participants' thought processes and imagination as well as to surface meanings that people have difficulties in accessing. Elicitation materials have thus been used as probes and stimulus to interviewing. And the use of projective techniques has been based on the logic that a person's behavior is invariably meaningful and expressive of personality and cultural values (Heisley and Levy, 1991: 259).

Branthwaite and Lunn (1985: 111) provide an illustrating example. They describe a market study on shampoo, in which participants of a focus group were asked to describe what, ideally, their hair would feel like after they have washed it with a perfect shampoo. And to help the participants to overcome their rationality and embarrassment of describing this fantasy self-image in front of the other participants, they were given a magic shower cap to wear while they described their ideal hair. Hence, by turning the focus group discussion into a children's play, researchers tried to help the participants loosen their self-control and talk more freely about the topic and thus gained valuable information on product symbolism concerning shampoos.

Often the use of these projective techniques has also involved various 'third-party' techniques and role-playing, in which interviewees or focus group participants are put 'in somebody else's shoes', so to speak, to have them interpret the behaviors and opinions of others rather than their own. Participants of a focus group are requested, for example, to picture themselves as typical users of a brand

and to describe how they think and act. Or interviewees are presented with a vignette containing a verbal or visual description of a situation and asked to comment on the behaviors and thoughts of the people in the situation or to tell a story about them. The stories and accounts that are produced in this way can then be interpreted in various ways, depending on the particular theory that is used to analyze them (Levy, 1981).

In the traditional psychologically oriented marketing research, the analysis and interpretation of projective data is based on the assumption that in interpreting and commenting on others, participants project their own feelings and motivations into the situation. It is assumed that their 'real' feelings and personal meanings can then be inferred from what they say about others. In other words, the aim is to get beyond people's surface cognitions, rational explanations and defensive reactions to direct questioning, so as to be able to tap into people's innermost thoughts, feelings and motives. This, of course, is not the focus of interest in cultural marketing and consumer research, as we have repeatedly emphasized.

In cultural marketing and consumer research, the purpose of using projective techniques and elicitation materials of various sorts is to generate cultural talk about various marketplace phenomena, as we pointed out. Used as complementary techniques in conjunction with interviews or focus groups, projective techniques and elicitation materials may well facilitate the conversation between participants or the dialogue between interviewees and interviewers. Many projective techniques are designed to help participants to express their ideas and construct meanings. For example, if you give a focus group of serious businessmen a set of 'Junior Designer Modeling Clay Sticks' or 'Kid's Dough' to express the use of mobile technology in everyday life, you may help them to get beyond the techno-jargon that they are used to producing when discussing 'technology' – if that is what you want to do.

In marketing research practice, projective techniques are often employed through the use of various kinds of vignettes in interviews and focus groups. Next we shall briefly discuss the ways in which vignettes could be used in cultural marketing and consumer research.

Vignettes and elicitation materials

Vignettes usually refer to short stories about some topic of interest that participants are invited to respond to. These stories can take different forms but the point is that they somehow refer to some issues and topics that are important for the study. Vignettes can contain stories about imaginary people in specific situations and circumstances, short scenarios about future societal developments written by actual political or business leaders, statements from prominent public figures or any other concrete examples of people and their actions on which participants can offer their opinion (Barter and Renold, 1999; Hazel, 1995). Such elicitation materials may well be useful for generating cultural talk in at least three ways.

First, vignettes could be used to *facilitate communication* and interaction between the interviewer and the interviewee. Vignettes and visual elicitation materials, for example, can provide participants with a concrete context for abstract or personally distant issues and thus help them to elaborate on the topic. In case of morally sensitive matters, vignettes may also help participants to maintain some distance from the issues, as commenting on a story is less personal than talking about personal experience (Barter and Renold, 1999). Vignettes can also be used as an 'ice breaker' at the beginning of an interview, to get the interview started and to elicit particular terms (words, metaphors) that the participants use to talk about the phenomenon (Hazel, 1995: 2).

Second, vignettes and elicitation materials can also be used to *elicit stories* in personal interviews. Narratives are sometimes purposely elicited in interviews to generate more elaborate accounts of marketplace phenomena. It is believed that storytelling is a basic form of communication and interaction in social life and therefore having the participants tell stories about the phenomena will produce richer and more interesting data. It is sometimes very difficult, however, to have the participants tell a story on a topic. In our experience, certain types of analytically oriented professionals, in particular, who are used to expressing their ideas in a concise and abstract, scientific-logical manner, rather organize their thoughts and ideas in terms of categories and items of evaluation, specifying detailed lists of features and benefits, for example. Being exposed to a fragment of a story, an image or a concrete object offers them a subject position that may encourage these people set their 'normal', extensively rehearsed rationalized subject aside. But for all sorts of interview participants, elicitation materials may serve as probes and stimuli that encourage the participants to tell stories. Susan Fournier (1998), for example, studied people's relationships with brands and asked the interviewees to tell the story behind different brands in their kitchen cabinet. As a result, she was able to obtain rich data on consumers' product relationships.

Third, vignettes can be used to prompt specific discourses or contested ideas. The idea is to present the participants with texts encoded with particular cultural meanings and discourses and to have them respond to them verbally. With vignettes, specific frames of reference and discourses are thus purposefully offered and suggested for participants' answers. For example, in a study focusing on the representation of the information society among business students, we used a lengthy quote from Bill Gates, which we believed reflected a particular discourse on global economy and the information society and thus referred to some important points of interest in our study. The quote was a scenario, in which he described the everyday life of ordinary people in the information society of the future. Our aim was to analyze the ways in which the participants of the study reproduced and contested the discourse.

To conclude, projective techniques and elicitation materials may be useful tools for generating cultural talk in interviews and focus groups. In commercial market research, for example, various sorts of elicitation materials are routinely used to study the meanings and uses of new and existing products and services. Elicitation materials are often used in combination with focus groups in an attempt to bring the creative potentials of a group into play. At best, elicitation materials and group interaction can energize the group members to generate a whole array of new ideas. Different focus group members provide different, often unanticipated viewpoints on the discussion, thereby enhancing creativity in the group. Focus groups are therefore often employed for generating new ideas for new product concepts, which are then further developed into commercialized products. Or they are used to gain insights into the meanings and uses of preliminary product concepts or existing products, to get feedback from potential or actual customers. In either case, the aim of the moderator is to evoke multiple discourses, in an attempt to generate unanticipated ideas and meanings. For this purpose, different elicitation materials and projective techniques are fruitful.

To illustrate, in developing new hybrid products and service concepts, market researchers may produce stories that describe the potential customers' everyday life with such new hybrid products, for example, stories that depict the customer purchasing an insurance policy from a convenience store or using a technological device that is simultaneously a computer, camera and a TV set. Analyzing the talk that these stories generate in the focus group, market researchers gain an insight into the cultural conditions of possibility for producing the hybrids. Focusing on the cultural meanings and values that guide and constrain the ways in which these products and services can be merged, researchers learn what is culturally acceptable and what is not. They may find out, for instance, that it is culturally acceptable to consider a convenience store as an outlet for purchasing a travel insurance policy but not for a life insurance policy.

Note

1   There are commonly 6–12 participants in a group, but the 'right' number depends on the cultural background and on the subject matter in hand.

FURTHER READING

There are numerous textbooks on the different techniques of carrying out successful focus groups and personal interviews. Relatively few focus on interview data as a form of cultural text. *Postmodern Interviewing* (which is comprised of a set of articles from the *Handbook of Interview Research* by the same authors), however, provides an interesting account of recent developments in the field of interview research:

- Gubrium, Jaber F. and Holstein, James A. (eds) (2003) *Postmodern Interviewing*. London: Sage.

There are currently several good textbooks on textual analysis in its different forms.

The following texts provide thorough introduction to discourse analysis and illustrate how discourse and discursive practice is analyzed in practice:

- Hall, Stuart (1992) 'The West and the Rest: Discourse and Power', in S. Hall and B. Gieben (eds), *Formations of Modernity*. London: Sage/ The Open University. pp. 275–320.
- Potter, Jonathan (1996) *Representing Reality: Discourse, Rhetoric and Social Construction*. London: Sage.
- Potter, Jonathan and Wetherell, Margaret (1987) *Discourse and Social Psychology: Beyond, Attitudes and Behavior*. London: Sage.

5

Visual Materials and Methods

CHAPTER SUMMARY

This chapter focuses on visual representation and on the ways in which visual materials can be used in cultural research both as data and as elicitation materials. Specifically, it takes up themes such as:

- visual culture and visual representation;
- analysis of visual images, visibilities and visual environments; and
- using visual methods to study the cultural dynamics of the marketplace.

Introduction

Visuals, things and qualities that appeal to the sense of sight, and visual representation are important elements of consumer culture. In contemporary Western societies, people are exposed to hundreds of culturally coded images every day. They have breakfast watching morning TV broadcasts, and then go on through their day facing a virtually endless stream of images: on-street ads, neon-light signs, in-store advertising displays, product packages, usage instructions, TV commercials, music videos, and so on. And with the proliferation of the new information and communication technologies – camera phones and portable DVD players for example – the sites of visual representation are continuously multiplying. The cultural meanings and narratives that these images evoke provide consumers not only with norms, standards, ideals and role models but also cultural knowledge, a visual vocabulary and interpretive resources that help them to make sense of their lives. Visual imagery is thus an important part of the systems of representation in and through which social reality is constructed (Hall, 1997a; Schroeder, 2002).

People also communicate and achieve social order partly by using visual symbols and images in various forms. They construct their social and professional identities through particular styles of dress, some wearing dark business suits others colorful ethnic outfits. They perform their gender identity by managing their appearance with the help of make-up and gender-appropriate accessories – guided by a powerful cultural imagery of femininity and masculinity. They even work out at the gym and engage in complex dietary regimes to sculpt their bodies into forms that better correspond to certain culturally desirable images of 'male' or 'female'. The visible forms, colors and textures of material objects and artifacts have symbolic properties and function as visual signs. Industrial designers encode products with particular design features, visual cues that are hoped to evoke specific associations and to give products a particular character, to create a brand image (Karjalainen, 2004). Business organizations design and construct particular office spaces to facilitate organizational learning and retailers design particular store layouts to increase sales.

In contemporary consumer society, therefore, not only images but all kinds of visible objects and arrangements, visibilities, carry meanings. And through the practices of visual representation, people are governed and they govern themselves. It is no surprise, therefore, that throughout history, visual representation has also been used by the political elites to construct particular sorts of realities and subjectivities for particular segments and classes of people. In early British anthropological photography, for example, natives were portrayed in ways that reified the relationship of superiority and inferiority endemic to colonialism (Harper, 2000: 728). Power and visibility are thus interconnected; what is displayed, what people see and how they see it is linked to and shaped by different forms and relations of power.

All in all, visual representation is a basic component of culture and social life. Many contemporary observers have argued, however, that today we are living in more visual and image-saturated cultures than ever before in the history of humankind, and that this, correspondingly, makes understanding the complex cultural construction and multiple social functions of visibilities and visual imagery more important than ever before (Kellner, 2002).

In this chapter we focus on the ways in which the visual as the reflection of culture and as something that contributes to the production, reproduction and transformation of culture can be studied. In accordance with the perspective taken in this book, we take visuality as something that produces specific views of the social world and which is also used by people to construct particular accounts of that social world. First, we discuss the study of visual representation and visual culture, presenting some tools – categories, questions, techniques – for describing, interpreting and analyzing visual images and visibilities (visible things). In the second part of the chapter, we discuss how visual methods can be used in cultural marketing and consumer research.

Studying visual culture and visual representation

The term 'visual culture' is often used to refer to the nature of present-day culture as primarily visual, or to the particular segment of that culture that is visual. By 'visual culture' we refer to everything we see or may visualize. Visual culture is concerned not only with visual images such as paintings, photographs and movies but also with various sorts of other visibilities, such as visible spatial arrangements and material artifacts that communicate through visual means. The meanings of visual images and visibilities should, therefore, be studied as keys to a fuller understanding of the culture in which they are embedded. Images should be analyzed and interpreted by relating them to the social and cultural arrangements in which they are produced.

In the field of marketing and consumer research, there has been a tendency to equate the study of visuals with the study of images, particularly commercially produced images, such as advertising images (Leiss et al., 1986; McQuarrie and Mick, 1999; Scott, 1994). Much of this research has taken either a *cognitive* approach to visual representation, focusing on the perception of visual elements of advertising, or a rather *descriptive* approach, focusing on coding and listing visual elements by means of content analysis (for an overview see, e.g., Scott, 1994: 256–9, also McQuarrie and Mick, 1999). In many of the *interpretive* studies on advertising images, in turn, the analysis of visual images has been grounded on semiotics and literary theories. Semiotic tools have been employed either to develop *reader-response theories* that address the meanings consumers derive from the advertisements (Mick and Buhl, 1992), or to develop *text-interpretive theories* that address the ways in which visual elements convey meanings and make the ad (Scott, 1994). These studies have often drawn from continental traditions of structuralism and semiotics, and thus worked towards social criticism. The focus has been, for example, on decoding ideologies and cultural codes upon which advertisements are built (Leiss et al., 1986; Williamson, 1978). Moreover, the analytical tools provided by feminist literary theories, such as a resisting reading technique, have been used to uncover the implicit ways in which gender becomes written in visuals (Stern, 1993).

The discursive approach to cultural marketing and consumer research that we elaborate on in this book builds primarily on the critical text-interpretive approach to visual analysis. But as we pointed out above, the field of visual culture and visual representation entails a much broader range of visibilities that can be studied to learn about consumer culture. The possible objects of analysis range from facial expressions and body language to visible material artifacts and to the entire visual and spatial organization of social life (see Peñaloza, 1998; Schroeder and Borgeson, 1998). It focuses on visuals, such as advertising images and retail store layouts, as texts or symbolic systems, which draw on specific cultural discourses and systems of representation (Scott, 1994). These systems of representations provide people with a frame of interpretation for both making and reading the images and visibilities. And it is these shared representational systems that are of primary concern in visual analysis – not the ways in which particular individuals interpret particular images. Visuality, the way in which vision is constructed, is thus analyzed in terms of a discourse that makes certain things visible in particular ways and other things unseen (Rose, 2001: 137).

Talking about the study of visual culture we therefore refer to the study of the visual, vision and visibility as inextricably woven into the systems of representation in and through which people make sense of their life and achieve social order. It has to do with something that relates to the sense of sight, and to the manner in which people see, visually represent and conceive of things, other people, environments and situations. It covers the study of images but also issues of visibility, what can be seen and what is observable in a set of social arrangements (see Kendall and Wickham, 1999; Emmison and Smith, 2002). The focus of interest is thus on what is seen and observable in a particular cultural context as well as how these visibilities are discursively constructed. What are the conditions of possibility for seeing in the context – what sort of power arrangements and systems of representation shape visual representation in the context? Through what sort of visual arrangements and practices are objects and people made visible? And what sort of a visual representation of these objects and people are thereby constructed – to what uses have visual images and visibilities been put?

Next we shall discuss how visual culture and visual representation can be studied using two different types of empirical materials that we consider particularly relevant for cultural marketing and consumer research: *visual images*, such as advertisements and media content, as well as *visibilities and visual environments*, such as retail outlets and physical marketplace settings of different sorts. This distinction is somewhat artificial when images, visible objects and spatial arrangements are all studied as forms of visibility that can be examined to gain an understanding of the wider cultural structures and practices that produce them. But here we make this distinction to draw attention to the fact that visual culture and visual representation involve much more than just making and viewing visual images.

Analyzing visual images

In cultural marketing and consumer research, visual images are generally analyzed as texts that are based on a particular visual vocabulary and a visual grammar, much like language. Images communicate through particular codes, that is, rule-governed systems of signs, that are largely shared among members of a particular culture and are used to circulate meanings in and for that culture (see Rose, 2001: 69–99). Images are thus understood as ordered systems of signs, visual cues, whose meanings are arrived at arbitrarily by a cultural convention. And to analyze the meaning of visual images, the signs and the code through which they are put together, as well as the discourses in which the signs get their meanings, need to be analyzed. As Judith Williamson (1978: 17) has put it, we can only understand what images, such as advertisements, mean by finding out *how* they mean, and by analyzing *how* they work in relation to broader, culturally shared systems of meaning.

For this sort of inquiry, semiotic tools may offer analytical precision. Semiotics provide and elaborate analytical vocabulary and a set of tools for taking the image apart and tracing how it works (see Rose, 2001: 69–99). The basic idea in this sort of visual analysis is that specific elements of an image stand for something else. They function as signs.[1] The high heeled shoes, for example, might represent femininity. And the task of the researcher is to establish the cultural meanings carried by the signs and to explore the logic of their patterning (Ball and Smith, 1992).

To give an example, advertisements can be seen as assemblages of signs that produce the meanings that help marketers to build brands. And to understand what advertisements mean, we need to find out how they mean what they do and how they work. According to Williamson (1978), ads often operate by correlative sign-work. They juxtapose the product (a perfume) and another sign (a French film star). And the meanings that are associated with this sign (the sophistication, glamour and beauty associated with film star) are then transferred to the product (the perfume). These signs are further connected to wider systems of meaning (for example, to the ideology that all women should be sophisticated, glamorous and beautiful for male pleasure). As a result, the image could be interpreted to produce the idea that the perfume helps women to perform and achieve the sort of femininity, beauty and female gender identity that all women should try to aspire to in order to please men. This interpretation, however, cannot be made by focusing only on the visual elements of the advertisement as an isolated symbolic system. The image is always connected and gets its meaning in relation to other cultural texts and images within particular discursive systems (see Part 5 and Box 5.1). The meaning of an image is always intertextual, it is dependent upon other texts that it absorbs and transforms (Culler, 2001: 114) and thus it has to be analyzed in its wider cultural contexts.

Gillian Rose (2001: 81–2) offers a useful set of steps through which a semiotic analysis might be initiated. The idea is first to decide what the signs encoded into the image are, and what they signify in themselves, and then analyze the ways in which they relate to other signs both within the image and in other images, exploring their connections to wider systems of meaning. In the field of cultural marketing and consumer research, Schroeder and Borgeson (1998) have suggested a useful set of tools for doing this. They argue that the conventions of art history, when framed with a social science perspective, offer unique contributions to the cultural analysis of visual images. To illustrate how semiotic tools can be employed, we take their visual analysis of the representation of gender in advertising as an example.

Drawing from the conventions of art history, feminist theory and the seminal work of Ervin Goffman (1979) on advertisements, Jonathan Schroeder and Janet Borgerson (1998) study the representation of gender in advertising. Their analysis is based on the assumptions that the particular visual elements of the image – visual cues – are the key to understanding how it creates meaning. To produce a nuanced understanding of gender–related meanings in the sample of ads they have selected, they focus on a set of visual cues that function as nonverbal indicators of status, gender and dominance, and which describe the body as a cultural signifier. Doing this, they combine two basic sets of tools. Informed by art history, and knowledge of the basic objectifying techniques of representation through which women have been traditionally represented in visual art (for example, focus on body parts, representation as sexual object of male pleasure, or object of violence), they study the ways in which women are represented in the ads. This analysis provides a historical and visual background to contextualize the insights that are derived from the analysis. Based on Ervin Goffman's techniques for analyzing gender relations in advertising, they then analyze the ads for sex differences in terms of posture, gesture, touching and gaze. Close attention to these nonverbal cues, together with the insights of feminist theory, enable them to appreciate the subtle but basic distinctions between the representation of females and males in the data and to explore the articulation of the gender ideology in advertising. They argue that it is important to develop such a critical visual literacy on advertising images because ads play an important role in the production and reproduction of gender identities.

It is important to note here, however, that according to the cultural approach to marketing and consumer research that we take in this book, both reading and creating an image is an active process. On the one hand, the decisions of the image maker have profound effects on the kinds of visual and cultural statements that result from their images. They purposively encode specific messages and cultural meanings to the image, using particular techniques and visual cues, according to a specific code. On the other hand the image is read and thus gets it meaning within specific groups of people, who may interpret the images in multiple idiosyncratic ways. Both of these processes, however, are guided and constrained by the systems of representation that are relevant in the context in which the image is read and produced. So, advertising images get their meaning in a complex process of interaction and meaning-making between the image-maker and the consumer, within the discourse and according to the codes that are relevant in the context.

All in all, research of this kind that focuses on pre-existing images is highly relevant for marketing and consumption inquiry. It not only attends to the role of visuals in the circulation of cultural meanings, but also draws attention to the different – often invisible – forms and relations power infused in them. As Schroeder and Borgeson (1998) remark, the more prominent images become the more power they have in our lives, whether they are intended to control or manipulate or not. And most of us are largely unaware of these power effects. Cartoons, for instance, which are often considered harmless entertainment, may play a significant role in the ways in which people comprehend economy and economic processes (Emmison and Smith, 2002). Moreover, for successful brand management through visual design, it is important also for the marketers and firms to understand the potential meanings that may arise in the product–user interaction or when people read ads, in different contexs among different customer target groups.

Case Study 5.1   Advertising in a sign economy

(Source: Robert Goldman and Stephen Papson (2004) *Nike Culture: The Sign of the Swoosh*. London: Sage)

How to think of advertising in cultural terms? In cultural research, the interest is not on how people process advertising messages, nor on planning the most effective communication mix. Rather, advertising is regarded as a rich cultural form that provides insight into the workings of contemporary culture and economy. From this angle, cultural researchers consider ads as

(Continued)

cultural documents and they may, for instance, investigate the ways in which advertising appropriates and playfully reworks cultural imagery. Advertisers, in turn, are typically interested in the ways in which advertising functions as a key cultural mechanism for assembling and reinforcing the value of brands. Ads are purposely structured to boost the value of a brand by attaching it to images that possess social and cultural value and this has made culture a central component of the economy, as Robert Goldman and Stephen Papson point out in their book *Nike Culture*. The key question for advertisers is: *How* to produce sign value by linking a product value with a cultural value? What is the mechanical process this sort of cultural engineering?

Basically, advertising works by appropriating, or drawing on, cultural meanings from other referent systems: it removes meanings from one context and then re-contextualizes those meanings in another context. For instance, the value of one meaning system – such as the Olympic Games – is appropriated to add value to a particular brand. Any meaning system can serve as a referent for this sort of appropriation: a song, a subculture, a celebrity, a television show, or a piece of art. For Nike, for instance, the obvious referent system is the celebrity athlete.

Currently, the Nike swoosh is a commercial symbol that has come to stand for athletic excellence, but initially the swoosh logo was an empty vessel, a mere visual marker that lacked any intrinsic meaning. The swoosh has acquired meaning and value through repeated association with other culturally meaningful referent systems. By placing the swoosh in the same frame with Michael Jordan Nike has been able to draw upon the value and meaning of Michael Jordan. That is, the meaning of Jordan was transferred to the meaning of Nike. Today, Nike is so rich in meaning that it is itself capable of extending value to other objects and persons.

Thinking advertising in this way does not mean that advertisers should reject conventional communication principles such as the importance of attention and recognition. Rather, it directs attention, in particular, to the cultural desirability of the system or reference that the brand is connected to. Do consumers – as cultural members – want to display the brand and thereby become advertisements themselves?

Analyzing visibilities and visual environments

Not only visual images but visibilities of all sorts, such as spatial arrangements of built environments, display of material objects, clothing and body language, play an important role in cultural processes (see Emmison and Smith, 2002). There is, therefore, a whole range of visual materials that can be analyzed to gain cultural knowledge of the marketplace.

From the marketing perspective, it is particularly important to study the ways in which various selling spaces, such as retail outlets, shopping malls and service delivery sites, are visual and also consumed visually. If we think of hospitals, holiday resorts, retail stores or day-care centers, for example, it is apparent that the physical place and surroundings of the service encounter constitute an important source of information for customers and thus contribute significantly to overall service experience (Bitner, 1992). Marketers therefore try to construct brand identity and to create 'complete buyer experience' through purposefully designed servicescapes (Sherry, 1998). The service encounter may be carefully staged (for example, through signage, lighting, store layout and décor), and turned into a more or less tightly scripted service drama with costumed characters. Nike Corporation, for example, has developed a chain of fastidiously designed, highly interactive product showcases, *NikeTown* megastores, where visuals play important roles in enabling and constructing particular consumption experiences. In these stores, buyer experience is designed to arise from looking at goods, walking around, seeing and being seen (Peñaloza, 1998). The space is purposively arranged, designed and displayed to throw off meanings, such as heroic stories of athletics, and in doing so, they also bear the imprint of society and culture.

How can visibilities and visual environments be studied then? Let us take the shopping mall as an example. First, the mall is understood as a textual construct and shopping as a cultural form interrelated with other cultural forms, representations and practices. Attention is thus focused on cultural structures (instead of trying to understand how people experience the visual environment) and structures-in-use (Frow and Morris, 2000: 326). The objective is to identify the sorts of discourses that are present in the context of a mall and how they are practiced and displayed in the everyday use and management of the mall space.

In practice, the task is to observe and analyze the visual objects, signage and the spatial organization of the mall, to learn how people use the visual information contained in these visibilities to navigate and operate in the mall. Particularly, interpersonal interaction (for example, how people interact with each other and with the staff) and interaction between people and material objects (for example, how they pick up goods and how they handle them) in the mall space could be observed, also paying attention to body language. Documentary materials of various sorts concerning the mall could also be obtained.

These sorts of observations and materials could then be analyzed and interpreted as reflections of some broader cultural discourses, which are assumed to condition and shape practices in the mall environment, as well as to guide the ways in which the mall as an institutional form may be designed, organized and managed. One of the tasks of a visual researcher, could be, for example, to study architects' drawings and plans, and the actual architecture of the mall complex to detect the ways in which particular discourses are articulated in the visual design and spatial organization of the mall.

In conducting such a visual inquiry, the researcher may use various techniques of analysis, creatively applying any appropriate theoretical constructs as analytic tools that may be of help in capturing the visual phenomenon under study. Semiotics is one potential source but many other disciplines, such as art history and anthropology, may also offer appropriate tools for visual analysis (see, e.g., Schroeder and Borgeson, 1998). The work of Mary Douglas ([1966] 2002), for instance, provides an interesting viewpoint to the study of visual culture by drawing attention to what is *invisible*, that is, to those elements and objects that are hidden from the public view or put in the backstage areas. Attention could be paid, for example, to rooms associated with animal bodily functions, toilets and baby changing rooms, or product displays that are more or less hidden in a mall. From this conceptual perspective, one could start to ponder what sort of a system of representation conditions certain market-related features to be visible and others invisible.

To conclude, we stress that visual culture and visual representation can be studied using multiple sorts of visual data. Not only advertising images but also visibilities in their many forms constitute appropriate sources of data for cultural marketing and consumer research. The different forms of visibility through which cultural discourses guide and constrain consumer behavior can be observed in numerous different sites of visual representation: streets, museums, shopping malls, computer screens, charts in marketing textbooks, maps of tourist resorts, directional signs – you name it. We recommend that these various forms of the visual be incorporated into the analytic concerns of cultural marketing and consumer research.

EXERCISE 5.1   Beginning to see

Take a look around the space you are in just now. What sorts of indicators of globalization can you see? Pose that same question to yourself in each place you visit during one day. Make a list of what you have seen, and reflect on it. Could any of your reflections serve as an indicator of a broader theoretical interest?

Try to cope for one day without the sense of sight. Reflect on the ways in which your consumption environment changes. Could any of your reflections serve as an indicator of a broader theoretical interest?

Using visual methods to study culture

The development of visual research methods has been informed by different theoretical approaches, such as visual anthropology, visual sociology, cultural studies and visual studies, including photographic and film theory (for a good outline, see, for instance, Pink, 2001). Here, our aim is to introduce and briefly discuss the multiple ways in which the visual methods may be fruitfully applied in cultural marketing and consumer research. First we discuss the documentary use of visuals in cultural research and then we introduce visual methods that are based on collaborating with social actors in the production of visual representations to learn about marketing-related cultural phenomena (Banks, 1995).

Documentary use of visuals

The documentary use of visual methods has a long history in ethnographic research. From the late nineteenth century onwards, photography and cinematography have been used by anthropologists and ethnographers to record information and to produce empirical evidence for their studies. The use of such visual data has often been premised upon the assumption that a photograph or a video clip that portrays social life at the research setting constitutes a record of systematic observation of reality at that setting, at a particular moment. As such, these photos and videos are considered as documents that provide fairly objective evidence for the interpretations and conclusions that the researcher makes.

In cultural marketing and consumer research, however, it is acknowledged that photographs never represent objective evidence – they merely appear realistic, because we have been taught to see them as such. As Douglas Harper (2000: 721) points out, 'the very act of observing is interpretive, for to observe is to choose a point of view'. Therefore, the decisions that the photographer makes, choosing the angle, composition, lighting and the depth of field, may have profound effects on the kinds of interpretations and claims that result from the images. Every picture therefore invites a question: What is left outside or rendered invisible?

Moreover, cameras are not neutral tools but technologies that are inscribed with particular visions of the patterns, purposes and contexts of their use. There are many taken-for-granted conventions and cultural norms about how cameras are to be used, when and where they may be used, and by whom. Therefore, when photographs are taken the social positions of the photographer and the subject come into play, and the role expectations culturally ascribed to these positions may well shape the ways in which this happens. For example, the image of a person carrying and using a camera or a camcorder in a public place often evokes associations with a tourist or a journalist. In the field, a 'visual ethnographer' may well be positioned in one of these social categories and thus endowed with the characteristics, rights and obligations that are culturally coded to the category. Such a positioning of the researcher may well have significant implications for the ways in which field relations are negotiated between the researcher and the researched, and also for the content and nature of the visual materials that the researcher produces.

Hence, the production of visuals, such as photographs and videos, is shaped by the available repertoires of visual representation. What we see and how we visually represent things is not a 'natural' but a culturally constructed process. In cultural marketing and consumer research, this should not, however, be taken as a limitation, but rather as a target for empirical analysis and critical reflection. When analyzing visual documents, you should carefully study the artistic and technical choices of the image-maker to investigate what kinds of visual statements are constructed through those choices (see, e.g., Schroeder and Borgeson, 1998). What sorts of identities, institutional relationships and histories are defined and constructed in those images?

The documentary use of visuals – understood as thoroughly interpretive and arbitrary practice – may well be a fruitful way of studying marketplace behavior. Photography, for example, can be used to support observation, used as a 'visual note-book' (Banks, 1995) that adds detail and nuance to written fieldnotes. The strength of photographs and videos lies particularly in their ability to provide records of activities, physical features and spatial proximities of the context of phenomena (Peñaloza, 1998; Wallendorf and Arnould, 1991). Moreover, visual materials and visual analysis may provide additional information about the research setting and thus help researchers to extend and refine their interpretations.

Particularly in ethnographic research, visual materials may draw researchers' attention to aspects of the setting that easily remain unnoticed, and thus open new perspectives to the phenomenon. As Eric Arnould and Melanie Wallendorf (1994: 488) point out, still and moving pictures taken in natural settings increase, first of all, the ethnographer's ability to interpret the temporal flow of consumption events. They can also help researchers to identify culturally significant moments since those involved with the event are likely to feel a pull to take photos at these moments. For instance, in a study on a Thanksgiving feast, carried out by the authors, photos of a turkey coming out of the oven and food ready to be served provided evidence that turned out to be useful in interpreting the importance of abundance and togetherness for the feast. Moreover, photographs of so-called backstage areas, for example, in the kitchen, may draw attention to features that otherwise are considered insignificant. Finally, photographs also efficiently display the dramaturgy of human interactions and proxemic expressions that may have much interpretive value in trying to understand 'what's going on in the field'.

Collaborative and reflexive use of visuals

Visual methods that are based on collaborative and reflexive use of visuals have been developed as a response to the crisis in representation in ethnography and social science. These methods aim to give the study participants (subjects) an increased voice and authority in interpreting and representing the phenomena under study. Some of the methods, for example, rely on the participants themselves to produce the visual materials that constitute the data for the study. People are typically asked to take photographs or to use images of all sorts, for example, drawings and clippings from magazines, to investigate their own cultures and to tell their own visual stories about their life or about a particular social phenomenon. This visual material is usually accompanied by texts, written or verbal accounts in which the participants expand upon the images. Next we shall discuss a number of specific collaborative and reflexive techniques for using visual materials to study marketplace behavior.

PHOTO-ELICITATION AND AUTODRIVING   Photo-elicitation refers to the use of photographs to provoke responses from interviewees (Harper, 2000; Heisley and Levy, 1991). Photo-elicitation techniques draw from projective and visual research methods. They are based on the assumption that people project their subjectivity and cultural meanings into the pictures they take and into the stories they tell about these pictures (Heisley and Levy, 1991). In photo-elicitation, researchers thus use photographs as probes and stimuli to interviewing, in much the same way as with the projective techniques discussed in Chapter 4. The photographs used for elicitation can be produced in various ways. They can be taken either by the participants themselves, according to specific instructions, or they can be taken by the researcher or a professional photographer. Also, family photo albums can be used.

Photo-elicitation is based on the idea that pictures can be used to elicit cultural representations of phenomena. As Harper (2000: 727) argues, photographs elicit cultural information that can range from normative negotiation of social action to cultural definition. In photo-elicitation, the pictures that people take are often used mainly to elicit verbal responses from participants. Describing the pictures that they have taken or otherwise produced, people tend to provide more elaborate accounts of social and cultural phenomena. The image serves as a stimulus that provides a rich set of visual cues that prompt and help the interviewee to consider and talk about the different aspects of the phenomenon.

Autodriving is a specific technique of photo-elicitation in which the interview is driven by participants who see and possibly also hear their own behavior by means of photographs or videos. The aim of using these techniques is to produce negotiated accounts of consumption-related behavior. It is assumed that photographs offer exciting challenges to informants by encouraging their need to explain themselves (Heisley and Levy, 1991.)

The study of Deborah Heisley and Sidney Levy (1991) provides an example of the ways in which autodriving as a photo-elicitation technique can be carried out. Heisley and Levy tested and developed the autodriving interview technique by studying family meals, focusing particularly on product use and power relations in the family. Three families were photographed by the researcher as they prepared and ate their evening meals. A set of pictures that represented the flow of events that took place were then developed and printed. In a subsequent interview, some of these pictures, which represented the main events of the evening, were shown to the participants in a chronological order. The participants were asked to voice whatever thoughts arose when they looked at the photographs, and the interview was audio-recorded. In a second iteration of autodriving, the participants were asked to go through the photos again while listening to the recording of the first interview. As a result, Heisley and Levy report gaining important information about the use of products as well as about the role behavior and power relations in the family.

PERSONAL VISUAL NARRATIVES   The photographs that people take and keep as mementos can be analyzed for the visual cultural narratives that they produce. As Harper puts it, the pictures that people take 'tell a story of a culture, a story that is repeated with subtle variations'. For example, the photographs that people choose to display in their living rooms or keep in their family photo albums, for example, photographs of their children's graduation and wedding, often reflect the ideals, traditions and values of their family as well as their culture. The images that participants produce or hold on to can therefore be analyzed as cultural artifacts using the methods and techniques for analyzing visual images and visibilities that we discussed above.

In previous research, visual methods that are based on having the participants document their own life or some social phenomena by constructing visual narratives through photography have taken many slightly different forms (for example, reflexive photography, photo novella and photo voice, see Hurworth, 2003). In studies that focus on this sort of personal visual narrative, participants are typically asked to take snapshots of a particular phenomenon or a topic, and then also to talk about and explain their pictures in an interview. In the field of cultural consumer research, Kjeldgaard (2002), for example, studied youth cultures and young consumers' identity strategies partly by means of 'photographic life description'. He gave disposable cameras to a group of high school students and instructed them to take pictures of a week in their life. The young people were given the freedom to photograph whatever they wanted, be it objects, people, or places, but it was suggested that they take pictures that represented who they were or reflected things of importance in their everyday life. Kjeldgaard argues that the use of a camera as a visual technique allowed participants to express themselves in a way that they might not otherwise have done (p. 388). Unfortunately, he does not elaborate on the techniques of visual analysis that he employs but the methods that we have discussed earlier could well have been used for empirical materials such as this.

Usually, participants have been given a disposable camera for the purpose of creating their visual narratives. They have been sent out to take photos and then called in for an interview later. With the new camera phones, however, it is currently possible to have the participants send in their photographs immediately after they have been taken, and even to have them briefly comment on the pictures they have taken. This would seem to offer new possibilities not only for visual research but also for visual ethnography. Also, commercial market research agencies are currently conducting and offering these sorts of studies, often referred to as 'photo-ethnographies'.

COLLAGES   In addition to photographs, images clipped out from magazines and drawings created by the participants may also be used as visual data. The collage technique refers to a method in which participants are asked to represent a topic or phenomenon visually by composing and gluing together a collage of images, drawings and texts on a piece of cardboard or paper. This collage is then used projectively, as a stimulus and probe for subsequent interviews with the participant on the topic. In a recent study on consumer desire Belk, Ger and Askegaard (2003), for example, had their respondents express their fantasies, dreams and visions of desire visually by means of a collage.

In cultural marketing and consumer research, the visual accounts and narratives that people create when making collages are *not* analyzed as first-person accounts that help researchers to reveal personal and unique meanings. The participants do clip out a set of images to represent their views of the phenomenon but the images that they use are already coded with particular visual and cultural symbols and statements. These meanings guide and constrain the ways in which the participants are able to represent the phenomenon. Therefore, collages are rather analyzed as a product of discursive practice, and explored for the cultural meanings and narratives that they reflect and reproduce. To be shared and understood, collages are taken to enter the rules, codes and conventions of visual language and the cultural discourses in which they are embedded (Hall, 1997a: 25). Collages are thus read as visual cultural stories.

EXERCISE 5.2   Using visual methods

Consider a marketing- and consumption-related cultural phenomenon of particular interest to you. In what sense is this phenomenon visible or visually communicable? How could visual methods provide new insight into the phenomenon?

When to use visual methods and materials

It seems self-evident that visual methods and materials should be used only if they help to better achieve the aims of the research. Visual methods may well be more useful for some projects than others. We would also emphasize that you should not make overly simple and uncritical a priori assumptions about the visual nature of phenomena. Rather, you should ask in what sense social reality is visible, observable and recordable. What aspects of culture are visible? Material objects, such as products, inevitably have a visual presence, but the notion of visual culture should not refer only to the material and observable 'visible' aspects of culture. How, for instance, should we represent cultural structures and systems visually?

Overall, we take the view that visual research methods can produce data that enlarge our understanding of marketing and consumption processes, and therefore, they should be used where appropriate – which is not obvious in advance. We have presented some methods, but rapidly evolving technologies provide new opportunities. Importantly, as Pink (2001: 4) remarks, specific uses of visual methods should be creatively developed within individual projects. As Denzin and Lincoln (2003: 5–6) have argued, qualitative research can often be described as 'bricolage': researchers sometimes need to be professional do-it-yourself people, who use the aesthetic and material tools of their craft, deploying whatever strategies, methods, or empirical materials are at hand. So, if new methods and techniques have to be invented – or pieced together – then it is the task of the researcher to do that. Moreover, one is not necessarily obliged to make the visual a central focus of interest in the work. Visual methods and materials are often used in combination with other methods. As Pink (2001: 4) has pointed out, visuals 'may be combined with textual, historical, narrative, statistical or a whole range of other research practices which may intertwine and overlap or link conceptually as the research proceeds'. But in any case, you should bear in mind that the ultimate goal in using visual methods and materials is to gain a better insight into the cultural dimensions of the marketplace as well as to contribute to marketing and consumer theory.

Note

1   A sign consists of the signifier (e.g., the material object, word and image) and the signified (the meaning ascribed to the material object, word or image). There are many ways of describing signs (e.g., icon, index and symbol) and how they carry meanings (e.g., denotative and connotative meanings) but we shall not go into the details of semiotic analysis here. Our aim is merely to discuss some basic ideas and point you towards some useful literature.

FURTHER READING

The following texts provide an easy introduction to the study of visual culture. They also illustrate how visual methods may be employed in cultural research:

- Emmison, Michael and Smith, Philip (2002) *Researching the Visual: Images, Objects, Contexts and Interactions in Social and Cultural Inquiry.* London: Sage.
- Pink, Sarah (2001) *Doing Visual Ethnography.* London: Sage.
- Rose, Gillian (2001) *Visual Methodologies.* London: Sage.

Part 3

Analysis in Cultural Research

Part 3 focuses on the principles and practices of data analysis in cultural marketing and consumer research. The aim is to discuss the theoretical approach to interpretation that is taken in this book, as well as to outline and elaborate on a number of tools and techniques for analyzing cultural texts, talk and visual materials. The discussion is grounded in the view that the particular interpretive frameworks that researchers choose or come to take, play an important role in the process of data analysis. Although cultural analysis is decidedly data oriented, findings do not simply emerge from the data in any theory-free manner. A more or less explicit theoretically informed interpretive framework always guides the process of analysis, making some interpretations and insights available, while obscuring or possibly blocking out some other interpretations and insights that could be made from the data. It is our contention, therefore, that an insightful cultural analysis is both theoretically sophisticated and empirically well grounded – grounded both in theory and data.

Chapter 6, *Interpretation and Interpretive Frameworks*, discusses the concept of an interpretive framework and the basic principles of interpretation. We advocate a mode of analysis and interpretation that encourages the researcher to exercise his or her intuitive and creative capabilities within a particular interpretive framework. With many others, we see data analysis first and foremost as a creative task that requires imagination, not as a mechanical activity – a set of explicitly codified steps that can be followed in a procedural manner, for example. But, this creative activity must be well attuned to the cognitive goals and values that guide the process of analysis. These normative guidelines are not to be understood as impediments to creativity, but rather as something that enables us to make interpretations from our data, and which also make our interpretations comprehensible and acceptable for the people who read, evaluate and use our work.

Chapter 7, *Analysis in Practice,* illustrates the ideas and principles discussed in Chapter 6 through two case examples, one in the context of social marketing, the other in the context of consumer research. These examples concretize both the process of data analysis – how to proceed from vague ideas to grounded interpretations – and the use of particular analytical techniques to gain cultural knowledge of the marketplace. They illustrate the ways in which both sides of cultural practice, institutionalized cultural discourses and everyday discursive practices, can be analyzed to gain cultural knowledge.

Chapter 8, *Criteria for Good Cultural Analysis*, closes Part 3 and the discussion on data analysis by suggesting a set of criteria for conducting a good cultural analysis. These criteria should not be taken, however, as a set of standards and procedures that guarantee the quality of analysis, but rather as guidelines that help orientate the work.

6

Interpretation and Interpretive Frameworks

CHAPTER SUMMARY

This chapter is concerned with the task of analyzing cultural data. It focuses on the process of analysis and interpretation, elaborating on the basic assumptions about interpretation that inform the cultural perspective that we have taken in this book. Overall, the objective is to demystify the process of interpretation by emphasizing that analysis requires rigorous work both with the data *and* with some relevant theoretical literature. More specifically, the chapter:

- discusses the role of interpretive frameworks and theory in data analysis and;
- illustrates the use of some basic analytical tools and techniques, which in our experience can aid in the process of analysis.

Introduction

In the field of social sciences and qualitative inquiry, *interpretation* and the process of *data analysis* can be understood and carried out in a number of different ways. But in general, to analyze usually means to *examine methodically*, for example, by separating the object of analysis into parts and studying their interrelations in order to learn something about the object. When analyzing a data set, a researcher is usually understood to examine the data to *make sense of the data*, and to arrive at an *interpretation* about the phenomena that the data deal with (Coffey and Atkinson, 1996; Silverman, 2000).

Hence, when we carry out 'data analysis', we not only try to examine the data but also to understand the *phenomena* that constitute the focus of interest in the study. Empirical materials merely give access to the phenomena that are to be investigated. As we have pointed out, cultural texts are studied for the cultural forms they realize and make available (see also the discussion on textuality in Part 5). Cultural texts are sites where cultural meanings and forms are accessible to us, rather than a privileged object of study in its own right. Movies, sitcoms, e-mails, newspapers, interviews, photographs, collages, marketing textbooks, time-use surveys and the many other sorts of cultural texts are concrete forms of data submitted to analysis, but they are not the focus of interest in themselves. The objective is to understand and learn about the cultural phenomena to which these empirical materials give access.

Conceived in this way, data analysis cannot be relegated to a set of technical operations and procedures through which researchers reduce, sort and manipulate qualitative data. It also calls for a particular analytic attitude towards the data and the culture under study – a sort of curious, questioning and also playful analytic attitude. As Jim Thomas (1993: 43) has argued, making sense of data is more than just creating a list of typological terms that are then imposed on the data. For example, skilful data analysis does not boil down to identifying a list of 'discourses', 'recurrent themes', or 'descriptive typologies' and then imposing them on the data. By analyzing data, researchers rather work towards making sense of the *cultural dynamics of the marketplace*, for example, by elaborating on the multiple and creative ways in which consumers use countervailing fashion discourses (Thompson and Haytko, 1997); by displaying the peculiar practices through which certain consumption activities, such as the Burning Man festival, are created as sites of resistance (Kozinets, 2002a); or by making us aware of the ways in which seemingly innocent marketplace practices such as targeting produces have normalizing and marginalizing effects in society (Peñaloza, 1994).

Moreover, in cultural marketing and consumer research, it is rarely sufficient to focus the analysis purely on the data in the process of analysis. It is evident that an in-depth grasp of the particularities of the data set is a prerequisite for a good analysis. But to gain new insights into the phenomena that the study focuses on, the researcher needs to take a broader perspective, analyzing also the historical and socio-cultural context in which data are produced and interpreted. Contextualization is an essential phase of well-grounded cultural analysis.

On the whole, analysis and interpretation are activities that go beyond the mere stage of data analysis. The entire research process involves analysis and interpretation. Approaching the phenomenon, trying to understand the literature, comparing different research traditions, reading transcripts and making fieldnotes are all analytical and interpretive practices. They all represent ways of trying to learn about the phenomenon under study and thereby to make sense of it.

In this chapter, we discuss the basic principles and practices of data analysis, elaborating on the theory of interpretation that informs the approach to cultural marketing and consumer research that we have taken in this book. Our discussion is premised upon the assumption that the particular interpretive frameworks that researchers take – explicitly or unknowingly – play an important role in the process of data analysis. In the sections that follow we discuss a number of questions that need to be addressed when constructing interpretive frameworks for cultural analysis. What is the role of theory and theoretical constructs in interpretation? What is meant by interpretation? What sorts of procedures, techniques and methods of analysis are appropriate for interpreting cultural data?

What is an interpretive framework?

It is widely agreed upon among contemporary qualitative researchers that interpretations never simply 'emerge' in the process of making sense of the data. It is rather the *interpretive framework* and attendant principles, constructs, techniques and methods that *produce* particular interpretations. In this context, the term 'interpretive framework' refers to a set of assumptions, ideas and principles that define a particular, theoretically informed perspective and a set of appropriate practices for the process of interpretation, thus opening the data to particular interpretations. Ideally, therefore, a good interpretive framework liberates the imaginative powers of researchers and enables them to see the everyday marketplace reality in new ways – it is able to 'free thought from what it silently thinks, and so enable it to think differently' (Foucault, 1986: 9). In other words, it enables researchers to problematize, challenge and make revised accounts of the taken-for-granted marketplace reality. Therefore, the specification of the interpretive framework is a crucial task in the process of doing cultural marketing and consumer research.

An interpretive framework comprises not only the particular disciplinary theories that inform the conceptualization of research phenomena – the conceptual framework – but also the more wide-ranging philosophical assumptions and commitments that inform methodological choices and guide research practices in the course of the entire research process – what sort of data are collected, what sort of methods and techniques of analysis are used, and how 'interpretation' and 'analysis' are understood in general. An interpretive framework provides the theoretical constructs, analytical focus and general forms of research questions that guide the researcher to read his or her data in a particular way. It also provides a basic view of what is understood as interpretation, and a set of analytical constructs, methods or techniques for conducting a data analysis.

To illustrate, in Part 1 we specified some important theoretical and methodological features of the interpretive framework that informs the analytical perspective we have taken in this book (it is also discussed in the last chapter of the book). On a general level, for example, it is based on a form of constructivist epistemology according to which all knowledge claims take place within a conceptual framework through which the world is described, analyzed and explained. Accordingly, it follows that the theoretical perspective that is defined for the study plays an important role in the process of data analysis and interpretation. This is in line with David Silverman (2000), who has noted that theory without data is empty and data without theory say nothing.

On the level of theory, however, the analytical perspective we have taken is atheoretical, in the sense that it is based on a fairly abstract theory on culture, subjectivity and markets. It primarily focuses on questions of *how* things happen in the marketplace instead of *why*. Although it provides a basic idea of what is analyzed in the data – not the real state of affairs, nor individual feelings and inner experiences, but meanings, systems of representations, and fields of power, for instance – more specific theoretical constructs may be needed to make insightful interpretations about marketplace phenomena. Throughout the book, we have therefore given some examples of the sorts of theories and concepts – for example, the theory on marketing and consumption as a dialogue and a cycle of commodification – that can be employed to arrive at insightful interpretations that contribute to the body of literature on marketing and consumer research. After all, the objective of data analysis and interpretation is to contribute to existing disciplinary knowledge. As Amanda Coffey and Paul Atkinson have argued, qualitative data should be analyzed in close detail to *develop theoretical ideas* about social processes and cultural forms that have *relevance beyond the data* themselves (Coffey and Atkinson, 1996: 163).

On the level of methodology, the interpretive framework we discuss borrows from the established basic principles of qualitative data analysis in advocating the principle and practice of working with the data in as rigorous, comprehensive and detailed a manner as possible. Researchers must 'think through the data' as the common saying suggests. This means that they should familiarize themselves with the data by iterative reading and re-reading, as well as by using appropriate analytical techniques and methods (Alasuutari, 1995; Coffey and Atkinson, 1996; Lofland and Lofland, 1984; Silverman, 2000).

It is important to note, however, that qualitative data analysis cannot be thought of only in terms of techniques and methods. Instead, interpretation always involves improvisational, imaginative and creative aspects, and therefore bears many similarities with the production of art (Coffey, 1999; Richardson, 2000; Spiggle, 1994). However, such artistic endeavors, when not placed in any theoretically informed interpretive frames, run the risk of romanticizing or mystifying the process of interpretation, as Thompson (1997: 451) remarks. He also reminds us that the 'intuitive and creative mode of understanding is not the exclusive province of a rarified artistic sensibility' (p. 451). It comes with expertise, which usually can only be developed through practice and hard work. But as Silverman (2000) recurrently points out, it is never too early to start gaining analytical expertise.

The role of theory in interpretation

As we have pointed out, theory plays a significant role in qualitative research. Already the process of generating data relies on some ontological and epistemological premises, that is, assumptions about the nature of the reality being studied and about the ways in which it can be studied. This does not mean, however, that we advocate that some sort of a rigid theoretical frame be fixed from the outset. The idea is first to define a particular theoretical perspective, which can then be revised in the course of the data analysis (Alasuutari, 1996). In a sense, this means that data and theory are put in a dialogue, and understandings emerge through an iterative process of matching up data and theory, where ideas and preliminary interpretations are tested, challenged and revised.

In cultural research, the primary role of theory is to provide perspectives to the data – to open up the data, not to test it (Alasuutari, 1996; Coffey and Atkinson, 1996). An explicit theoretical perspective leads us to pay attention to and notice certain features in the data that are not visible at the outset. Theory can be considered a source of inspiration, a vehicle that helps to draw the observer's attention to things that would otherwise pass unnoticed. Its role is particularly to enable the researcher to see and find something *new* in the data, something that may be inconceivable at the outset.

As Thomas Schwandt (2003: 294) points out, social inquiry, in general, is a distinctive praxis, a sort of activity that in the process of performing that activity transforms the very theory and aims that guide it. He argues that:

> as one engages in the 'practical' activities of generating and interpreting data to answer questions about the meaning of what others are doing and saying and then transforming that understanding into public knowledge, one inevitably takes up 'theoretical' concerns about what constitutes knowledge and how it is to be justified, about the nature and aim of social theorizing, and so forth. In sum, acting and thinking, practice and theory, are linked in a continuous process of critical reflection and transformation. (2003: 295)

In practice, this sort of dialogical view on data means that during the process of analysis you have constantly to question and revise not only your emerging interpretations and preliminary findings, but also your theoretical perspectives and the research design. It entails questioning and critically reflecting upon methods, findings and theoretical concepts. For example, as the process of analysis proceeds, you need to ask yourself if you are still comfortable with the theoretical perspective and the techniques of analysis that you have chosen for the study. Is your theoretical approach, say contemporary relationship marketing, suggesting interesting questions for your analysis? Which theoretical constructs work best and look likely to be most productive? Are your methods of data analysis, metaphor analysis for example, giving you a strong grip on your data? Do you expect to be able to generate interesting findings using these theoretical and methodological tools? Actually, if you do not need to change your original research design during the research process, there may be reason to believe that your data analysis is inadequate, as Silverman (2000: 121) has pointed out.

All in all, the nature of this sort of reciprocal relationship between the theoretical perspective and the data is well captured by Coffey and Atkinson, who argue:

> Data are there to think with and to think about ... We should bring to them the full range of intellectual resources, derived from theoretical perspectives, substantive traditions, research literature and other sources ... [this means] that methods of data collection and data analysis do not make sense when treated in an intellectual vacuum and divorced from more general and fundamental disciplinary framework. (1996: 153)

In emphasizing the role of the theoretical framework in an analysis, we hence depart from the basic premises of grounded theory, in which data analysis is taken to proceed inductively from data to theory. Grounded theory refers to a mode of qualitative research in which theoretically based generalizations are induced from qualitative data (Glaser and Strauss, 1967). Essentially, grounded theory methods consist of systematic inductive guidelines for analyzing data. These guidelines involve a set of analytical operations and procedures that produce interpretations; findings emerge from the data through a set of operations such as categorization, abstraction, comparison, dimensionalization, integration, iteration and refutation.

Grounded theory has, unquestionably, played a crucial role in introducing, defending and establishing the use of qualitative methods not only in social sciences but also in marketing and consumer research (see, e.g., Spiggle, 1994). With many others, however, we are highly critical of the idea of having a more or less fixed set of operations to be followed in every study, regardless of the nature of the research phenomenon and the theoretical approach taken to it. Factory-like procedures and techniques may seem easy and systematic, but they run the risk of producing trivial, highly expectable outcomes – thus denying the joy of surprise from the researcher. Therefore, in this book we advocate and work towards a more theoretically informed approach to analysis, which also respects the particularities of the phenomena it studies.

Nevertheless, there is no reason to reject the analytical procedures, principles and techniques developed by grounded theory scholars altogether. The principle of carrying out *rigorous* analysis that is well *grounded in the data* is relevant for all sorts of qualitative analyses. To be able to produce insightful results, the researcher needs to use appropriate techniques and persistently work with the data – reading and re-reading transcripts, listening to tapes, organizing and classifying photographs, for example.

EXERCISE 6.1   Theoretical concepts in data analysis – perspectival knowledge

The aim of this exercise is to illustrate the ways in which theoretical concepts open up a particular view of reality. Consider the following marketplace event. A group of customers visits a high-class restaurant. They order a meal, but one of them is not happy with it and complains to the waiter about the poor quality of the food.

  Now, think of the event with the concept of 'consumer satisfaction'. What does the event look like when seen through the lenses provided by this concept? On what sorts of aspects does this concept guide the researcher to focus attention? Then, think of the event with the concept of 'servicescape'. What do you see now? To what sorts of aspects does it direct your attention? Now go on to try different concepts such as 'group pressure', 'habitus', 'quality management', 'hedonic consumption' or 'consumer culture'. Reflect on the ways in which particular theoretical and philosophical assumptions are infused in these concepts and the ways in which they open up a particular view to reality.

Basic assumptions about interpretation

Different philosophical traditions embrace different perspectives on the aim and practice of understanding and interpreting human life. Much like many constructionist and poststructuralist perspectives, the approach to interpretation that we take in this book draws, albeit selectively and critically, from hermeneutic philosophy, which is primarily concerned with the ontology of understanding. Of particular relevance for our purposes are the concepts of pre-understanding and hermeneutic circle, and the idea of a change as the goal of interpretation. We start, however, by discussing the ways in which the notions of meaning, texts and interpreter are understood in this line of thinking.

Meaning, texts and interpreter

First, cultural research is based on a *non-objectivist view of meaning* (Schwandt, 2003: 302). This means that the text being studied is not treated as an 'object out there' that possesses some true meaning in itself, that is, a meaning that could be isolated, discovered or revealed in any simple manner by using correct analytical methods and procedures. Instead, meanings are always negotiated mutually in the act of interpretation. In this view, to interpret a text is to engage in a dialogue with the text. And the nature of this dialogue inevitably depends on the cultural pre-understanding of the interpreter – the accumulation of the beliefs, codes, metaphors, myths, events, practices, institutions and ideologies that govern and shape his or her interpretation (Arnold and Fischer, 1994). Therefore texts are open to multiple interpretations.

As the pre-understanding is apprehended through language, interpretation and understanding are seen as fundamentally linguistic in nature. This is a premise that is largely shared among the various language or sign-based approaches to interpretation, including structuralism and semiotics (Arnold and Fischer, 1994). Basically, all these views emphasize that language shapes and constrains our being in the world in a very basic manner (see the discussion on language in Part 5). It is emphasized that some entity – be it human action or a piece of text – is meaningful only by virtue of the system of meanings to which it belongs. Depending on the system in use, people express and realize a certain way of being in the world.

In acknowledging that all interpretation is a product, in part, of the interpreter's pre-understanding and the system of discourse where it is constructed, the view that meanings are fixed entities that exist independently of the interpreter is rejected. There is no foundational, mind-independent and permanently fixed reality that could be grasped and revealed by using correct methods, as we have explained. Meaning is not an 'object' that can be found. Meaning is rather constantly *coming into being*. Accordingly, the meaning of a particular object or phenomenon, for instance, is not fixed, but temporal and processive in nature. When it is relocated in different discursive contexts it takes on and is given new meanings. To a greater or lesser extent, most of the contemporary approaches to cultural studies and also to cultural marketing and consumer research share these views.

Understandably, this approach to interpretation also rejects the view that to understand the meaning of social action is to grasp the subjective consciousness or intent of actors. It is maintained that it is not possible to penetrate the subjectivity of the other. And it is also considered inappropriate, in a sense, to consider a person's 'own account' of his or her action 'better' or epistemologically privileged than somebody else's interpretation of that behaviour. In cultural research, the aim is rather to understand how people come to interpret their own and others' action as meaningful, and what are the conditions that make particular interpretations possible.

Consequently, a *cultural text is interpreted as an autonomous body of data, as a text that assumes a life of its own*. This means that the aim of an interpretation is not to understand how the text understands itself, but rather to understand the logic of its production. This sort of methodological view has parallels with (post)structuralist and semiotic approaches, while differing from humanistic–naturalistic inquiry, for instance, where texts are commonly treated as representative of informants, personal views and experiences (Arnold and Fischer, 1994).

To illustrate, let us consider a consumer's story of his/her consumption-related experiences as a text to be interpreted. The task of the researcher, then, is not to try to understand the text in the same way as its author, the consumer, nor to try to capture the author's intended meanings. Rather, the purpose of the researcher is to analyze how the author talks about his/her experiences, what the author takes for granted, what sort of ideas and meanings he or she contests and what he or she does not even come to think about. The aim is to identify cultural discourses that offer and sanction particular ways of talking and acting towards things, events and people, while excluding other ways of representing these objects. Therefore, the text can lead to interpretations that do not necessarily coincide with what the author 'meant', but which generate insights beyond his or her realization.

What is the role of the interpreter, the researcher, in the process of interpretation and understanding? *The interpreter is first and foremost a historically and locally situated co-producer of meanings* (Denzin, 2001a: 325), *and as such an ethical and political actor*. As we discussed above, interpretation involves continuously coming-into-understanding. It is a process that is grounded on the pre-understanding of the interpreter, who occupies a particular socio-cultural position. From this position the interpretations that she or he makes are necessarily partial and based on a set of ethical and political commitments. Researchers thus have responsibility for the interpretations they make. For this reason, sensitivity to the ethics and politics of interpretation is usually also included in the evaluative criteria for a good cultural analysis, as we have pointed out in Chapter 2 and as we shall also discuss in Chapter 8.

Pre-understanding

One of the key assumptions of this sort of hermeneutic thinking is that as human beings we all belong to a socio-historically inherited world and tradition, which provides us with a pre-understanding that governs, enables and shapes our interpretations (Arnold and Fischer, 1994; Gadamer, 1989). Importantly, pre-understandings are not something from which researchers should or could free themselves. Traditions, or the systems of representation in which we live, thoroughly shape what we are and how we understand the world, and they cannot be set aside at will or escaped in any simple manner. As Schwandt (2003: 301) remarks, the attempt to set outside the process of tradition would be like trying to step outside our skins.

Therefore, the task of the interpreter is not to strive to free him- or herself of the tradition, but rather to examine the historically inherited and unreflectively held pre-understandings that shape his or her efforts to understand. In this line of thinking, pre-understanding is not regarded as an obstacle that needs to be overcome, as something that an interpreter must strive to get rid of in order to come to a 'clear' and 'un-biased' understanding. On the contrary, hermeneutic philosophy counsels us to capitalize as fully and as consciously as possible on pre-understanding rather than trying to put it aside when doing research. From this perspective, therefore, pre-understanding is considered a starting point for interpretation.

There are two interrelated sets of pre-understandings to be considered in the process of interpreting cultural texts (Arnold and Fischer, 1994; Thompson, 1997). Interpretation is shaped by the interpreter's particular temporally, socially and culturally conditioned knowledge of the subject matter, and by the disciplinary academic knowledge that she or he has. Studying the marketplace, for instance, marketing and consumer researchers draw, willingly or unwillingly, from their stock of personal background knowledge on the topic in question, as well as from the knowledge of accumulated theories and research findings concerning marketing and consumer behaviour, for example, theoretical knowledge of attitudes, networks, consumption rituals, customer relationships, learning, brand management and so forth. The body of disciplinary knowledge sensitizes researchers to know certain issues and not others by offering particular types of questions, and by providing particular 'obvious topics' to be taken under investigation.

Being aware of the disciplinary pre-understanding is crucial, since particular disciplines interpret phenomena and social reality from their particular perspectives and interests. These perspectives and interests offer particular types of questions and interpretive horizons that 'open up' particular phenomena in particular ways for research. For example, questions characteristic of post-structuralist cultural consumer research might ask: How do consumers combine and reformulate different cultural discourses to create novel consumption meanings? Or, how do consumers use fashion meanings to subvert the dominant meanings and values (Thompson and Haytko, 1997)? These types of questions open up an interpretive horizon that makes visible the dynamics between the natural and the problematic order of things, thus guiding the researcher to focus on the naturalized aspects of marketplace reality, on the natural order of things and to their reciprocal counterpart, problematized interpretations.

Pre-understanding provides, hence, an orienting frame of reference, or horizon, from which texts are interpreted and from which particular questions are posed.

An horizon is, both literally and figuratively, everything that is visible from a particular vantage point (Gadamer, 1989: 302). But, this horizon is *subject to change during the process of interpretation*. When the interpreter moves or changes position as his or her understanding evolves, the horizon moves as well. For instance, as critical perspectives are introduced to the marketing discipline, they become part of the pre-understanding of marketing researchers and are thus likely to influence subsequent interpretations (Arnold and Fischer, 1994).

Pre-understanding evolves and changes through dialogue. In the process of analysis, the researcher is continuously engaged in an interpretive dialogue, which may take the form of a concrete social dialogue or a more metaphorical dialogue between the interpreter and the text. Having a dialogue with the text means, for instance, that a particular point in the text, such as a particular sentence or silence, may catch the researcher's attention, inviting the researcher to consider it further. In doing so, the text in a way affords particular possibilities and the researcher seeks to be open to them rather than projecting a predetermined system of meanings on them (Thompson, 1997). A social dialogue, on the other hand, may take the form of 'interpretive groups' of some sort, which are practical and operational forms of dialogical interpretation (Thompson et al., 1989: 140–1). They make visible the ways in which the same text may be interpreted differently and thereby challenge pre-understandings. We shall discuss interpretive groups in more detail in the context of analytical workshops later in this chapter.

The dialogue through which a pre-understanding becomes revised may also take place in an interview situation when respondents speak back to the researcher. To illustrate this – and the analytical value of focusing on various forms of resistance more generally – we take yet another example from the study on free time that we have discussed in the earlier chapters (Valtonen, 2004a). In conducting interviews and focus groups the researcher asked: 'Tell me, what do you do during your free time?'. This single interview question reflects a fairly generally shared understanding that free time is time awake and time filled with various sorts of leisure activities. The question was thus an interpretation in itself. Some of the responses the participants gave, such as 'Why should I do something?', or 'I do nothing, and that's the point', or 'I just sleep, that's my hobby', may be viewed as ways of 'answering back' and resisting the interpretation offered by the researcher. There were obviously answers that were in line with the researcher's interpretation of free time, such as 'I take dance classes' or 'I spend time with my kids'. However, it was precisely these little forms of resistance that caught the attention of the researcher and served as powerful catalysts for insightful findings. They invited, or even forced, the researcher to challenge her taken-for-granted pre-understandings concerning free time, and to problematize several taken-for-granted notions and ideas, such as what counts as 'doing' and why sleep is not taken into account in leisure studies. Through these dialogic processes, the adequacy of the pre-understanding in encompassing the subject matter was tested. As the limits of the pre-understanding were met, a revised horizon of interpretation opened up, enabling the researcher to detect, in a new way, the ways in which the prevalent meanings of free time were being contested.

All in all then, we advise you to listen carefully to what your data tell you, but what they do tell you will be different in light of the different horizons of interpretation that open up, and the different questions you thus learn to ask in the process of analysis.

The hermeneutic circle

A hermeneutic circle is a widely used general process of interpretation in social and human sciences. Briefly put, it refers to an iterative part-to-whole mode of interpretation.[1] It is based on the idea that to understand the part (the specific advertising slogan, a consumer's utterance of service satisfaction, or a marketing act such as price discount), the inquirer must grasp the whole (the institutional context of marketing and advertising, competitive market context, socio-cultural form of life). After gaining some sort of an idea of the whole, specific elements are examined again and again, and each time with a slightly different conception of the whole. In this way, the interpretation proceeds through a series of back-and-forth, part-to-whole iterations. In this process, hence, earlier readings of a text inform later readings, and reciprocally, later readings allow the researcher to recognize and explore patterns not noted in the initial analysis (see Thompson and Haytko, 1997: 20–1). Gradually, an ever-more integrated and comprehensive account of the specific elements as well as of the whole develops.

This sort of general procedural description of the hermeneutic circle does not specify any particular interpretive perspective, as Thompson and Haytko (1997) point out. Researchers always see and describe the world from some theoretical and philosophical perspective and it is this perspective that offers the particular focus, logic and goal for the iterative process of interpretation. For instance, in research that builds on what is known as 'existential phenomenology' (Thompson et al., 1989) in the marketing literature, interpretations are based on probing into the point-of-view of the individual respondent. The task of the interpreter, then, is to focus on and analyze the specific words and expressions that respondents use themselves, as indicators of their 'inner experiences', as the most relevant 'parts' of the whole that is to be studied, the 'whole' being the transcript of the individual's interview or his/her life history.

From the methodological perspective that we take in this book, the 'parts' and 'wholes', and back-and-forth movement, are thought of and defined somewhat differently. The unit of analysis is neither an individual nor a group of individuals, but culture as a system of representation. On the level of culture, therefore, it is the cultural discourses and discursive practices that are analyzed, as reflexively constituting each other. The focus of analysis can be primarily on the cultural discourses that guide and constrain people's lifes, or alternatively on the details of the discursive practices through which these cultural discourses are produced and resisted. Interpretation of both of these two dimensions of cultural practice requires an understanding of the interplay between cultural discourses and discursive practices.

Therefore, in either case, the analysis is based on some sort of an iterative back-and-forth movement between cultural discourses and the different discursive practices. And the emergent understanding of the interplay between cultural discourses and the ways in which they are produced and put to use in the market thus might be understood as the 'whole'. Nevertheless, the process of analysis always starts with the single words, concepts, categories and rhetoric devices that are used in the texts that are to be analyzed. To gain insight into the discursive practices through which people make sense of their life and achieve social order, or to understand the structure and effects of cultural discourses, a set of textual data that gives access to those cultural forms and practices needs to be carefully analyzed. On the level of detailed textual analysis, therefore, the 'whole' also needs to be defined as the corpus of texts (the transcripts of focus group talk, or a set of media texts, for example) that constitute the data for the study. Moreover, the data also need to be contextualized to the particular historical and local discursive space in which they have been produced. This context also forms some sort of a whole against which the texts and the details of the texts have to be considered. The parts and wholes, therefore, are not only transformed in the process of analysis but in different phases of the process of interpretation different entities constitute the parts and wholes that are to be analyzed.

To illustrate our point of view we describe how the iterative process of making interpretations can take place in the context of data that consist of narratives on green consumerism (Moisander, 2001). The specific aspect on which the researcher first focuses in reading the narratives is the rhetoric and metaphoric expressions that are used to describe the green consumer and to discuss green consumerism in general, such as 'to make a difference' and 'voting with the dollar'. These expressions represent or are related to particular discursive practices that are used to construct particular representations of green consumerism. The categorizations and expressions that consumers use, when describing social and cultural categories, such as the green consumer, are not something that they as individuals invent by themselves. They are rather available to, even imposed on, them in their culture. Studying these sorts of discursive elements in the data, contextualizing the emergent understandings into wider systems of meaning and culture, it is possible to gain insight into the ways in which green consumers are discursively 'governed' in the marketplace through particular cultural discourses and discursive practices. The representation of the green consumer as a person who wants to 'make a difference by voting with the dollar' reflects the predominant individualistic, economic discourse on sustainable development, for example. Importantly, these discourses and practices are grounded in wider economic and political structures and practices; and therefore, the iterative back-and-forth analysis must be extended beyond the mere narrative data.

Goal of interpretation

The dialectical and iterative process of hermeneutic interpretation does not produce fact-like statements or causal explanations of human behavior. Neither does it aim to produce interpretations that merely repeat and 'strengthen' some prevailing ways of seeing and understanding phenomena. Rather, its very purpose is to produce *different* interpretations: to engender some shift, change, or expansion of the horizon or frame of reference of the interpreter (Arnold and Fischer, 1994: 60). To understand is to understand differently (Schwandt, 2003: 303).

The existing stock of knowledge produces a world with which members already seem to be acquainted. It is the arbitrary nature of this semblance of everyday familiarity that is to be unsettled in the process of analysis. The researcher should challenge the taken-for-granted views on reality and thereby provide people with opportunities to become aware of new possibilities, new ways of interpreting in the world. This line of thinking purports, hence, to produce some *change* in the ways in which people – the researcher and her/his audience – see the social world, to unsettle the obvious and to show it in a new light.

This sort of ethos entails a readiness to critical self-reflection – but also an acknowledgment of the limits of such reflection, as we have pointed out. This sort of ethos is widely agreed upon within cultural studies. As Alasuutari notes:

> Analyzing empirical materials qualitatively, approaching them from different perspectives, is basically a means of reflection and self-reflection aiming at new insight about the cultural premises of social life. (1996: 382)

In cultural studies, therefore, the questions that motivate research, and the institutional frameworks and the disciplinary rules that produce these questions are recurrently critically scrutinized, discussed and debated.

The relevance of such an analytical goal for marketing and consumer research is well described by Arnold and Fischer (1994: 56, 66). As they state, the incorporation of these ideas into marketing and consumer research would enable researchers to draw more consciously, critically and powerfully on their own pre-understanding of the market phenomena that are under study. These sorts of insights can also extend into people's lives, since an interpretation of a text involves the explication, the clarification and the working out of the possibilities of our existence. It would also increase researchers' sense of moral ownership of the research they do.

On the whole, in analyzing cultural discourses and discursive practices, the researcher provides a basis for critically challenging the representational security of taken-for-granted realities. Elaborating on the constitutive processes that produce and sustain particular realities, researchers caution people to remember that the everyday realities of our lives are realities that we *do* (Gubrium and Holstein, 2003a). As Ian Hacking (1999) has argued, the point in making these sorts of claims is primarily to raise consciousness. Social facts and their meanings are not fixed, inevitable and 'natural'. Rather, they are products of a history of social events and forces, all of which could have been different. It is hoped that this will encourage – in a sense liberate, as Hacking argues – people to question the status quo; to incite people to start looking for different alternative ways of viewing the world, representing themselves and others, and maybe also to contest or negotiate undesired stereotypical, culturally shared meanings. As Christopher Falzon has argued:

> [by] freeing ourselves from the illusion that there is some absolute standpoint, and recognizing that all our concepts of knowledge, truth, and action are 'local' or historically specific, we will help open up a space for diversity, for otherness, for other forms of life. (1998: 3)

Analytic procedure

Now that we have elaborated on the interpretive framework and basic assumptions about interpretation, we turn to consider the procedures of data analysis in the cultural perspective that we have outlined in this book. In that perspective, the interplay between cultural discourses and discursive practice is given particular attention.

Analytic bracketing refers to an analytic procedure suggested by Jaber Gubrium and James Holstein (2003a: 234–6) for analyzing the interplay between discursive practice and cultural discourses. In the process of analysis, the researcher intermittently orients to everyday realities as both the products of discursive practice and the discursive resources that the available cultural discourses provide. The focus of analysis thus moves back and forth between these dimensions. At one moment the researcher tries to be indifferent to the discursive structures of everyday life so as to be able to document the ways in which these structures are produced through discursive practice. Then, in the next analytical move, the researcher temporarily defers, or 'brackets' – but not forgets – her or his interest in the practices to focus primarily on the structures. The principle of the bracketing, in this context, refers to an act of temporarily suspending ontological judgments about the nature and essence of phenomena so that the researcher can focus on the ways in which they are discursively constructed. The idea in analytic bracketing, in other words, is to oscillate indifferently between these realities of everyday life.

Analytic bracketing is, therefore, enduringly empirical in that it does not take the operation of discourses for granted. When the analysis is conducted in an appropriate and rigorous manner it displays the sorts of realities that are constructed in particular marketplace contexts, and the particular ways in which these realities are constructed.

The suitable point of departure for this sort of analysis is hard to designate. It is impossible to suggest that you should begin with one or the other side of cultural practice. Rather, as we have earlier discussed, you should be sensitive to the ways in which the data 'speaks to you' – and start with that. The techniques that we outline in the remainder of this section may enable you to make your data speak. We first discuss some conceptual tools for close reading of cultural texts, and then we discuss some more general useful tools that have been developed in qualitative research.

Conceptual tools for close reading of cultural texts

The process of interpretation is usually based on a close reading of the texts that are to be analyzed. Although the specific techniques may differ, in cultural research interpretation is always grounded on a close reading and careful analysis of the 'language' of the 'texts'. In this section we present some concepts that can be used as some manner of lens to do a close reading of a set of textual data. We also hope to illustrate how a set of theoretical concepts, developed in cultural studies, can be used to 'open up' the data for interpretation. In the following sections, we focus particularly on explicit or implicit norms, categorizations, stereotyping and rhetoric strategies, as concepts that may help the researcher to pay attention to the particular textual features of the text and to interpret the ways in which meanings are produced.

Explicit and implicit norms

It is sometimes fruitful to start the analysis by focusing on implicit and explicit norms referred to in the texts. This may help you to get a preliminary overall idea of the moral and political themes that the texts deal with.

Normative statements in the text imply that people perceive that there is a social norm and some sort of a conflict involved (Alasuutari, 1996). Norms are not treated as descriptions of the causes of action. Rather, the focus is on how people use norms to provide some of the orderliness, and proper orderliness, of the activities they observe (Silverman, 1993: 82). Normative arguments such as 'children should not be allowed to eat candy daily' imply that the subject is aware that there are other possible ways of perceiving the issue, or he or she recognizes that there is a temptation to behave in some other way. Therefore, when analyzing normative statements in market-related social texts it is necessary to ask why there is a norm governing the issue at hand and why these norms are referred to in the given situation.

Categorization and vocabulary

Many contemporary constructionist scholars have called attention to the systems of categorization that people use in constructing meaning (e.g., Potter, 1996; Silverman, 1993). They emphasize, as Potter (1996: 177) has argued, that it is through categorization and choice of words that the specific meaning of people, objects and phenomena is constituted. Categorization is not, therefore, any banal naming process, in which a word or category is assigned to the object that has the appropriate properties. Rather, it plays a central role in the ways in which marketplace realities are constructed. Therefore, in conducting a cultural analysis, it is useful to pay close attention to the categories and choices of words used in the texts under study.

It may be argued that choice of vocabulary and word forms results from and reflects an implicit choice of approach or a point of view that is based on conventional reason. Davies and Harré (1990) have argued that the words the speaker chooses inevitably contain images and metaphors that both assume and invoke the ways of being that the participants take themselves to be involved in. However, when producing descriptions and accounts people may not be aware of the assumptions associated with specific words nor the power of the associated images to invoke particular ways of being. As Davies and Harré (1990) point out, they may simply regard their words as normal for the way one talks on this sort of occasion.

For example, people are generally represented with reference to some wider social and cultural categories to which they belong. Such categories can take many forms. A person can be represented as a 'mother' or a 'daughter', depending on a situation. On some other occasion she can be categorized as a 'well-known lawyer', 'a mother of two young children' or 'the blonde next door'. In any case, our understanding and ideas about who a person is build up out of the information we accumulate from positioning this person within different orders of typifying categorization (Hall, 1997b).

Elaborating on Harvey Sacks' ideas, Silverman (1993) has focused on description as a socially organized activity, bringing forward the idea of culture as an apparatus of descriptive categories and category-bound activities through which descriptions are properly produced. Discussing this descriptive apparatus, he points up a number of issues that seem relevant also here, for carrying out the analysis of the discourse on green consumerism. The following aspects and properties in particular Sacks sees as relevant in the 'inference-making machine' or descriptive apparatus that underlies social texts:

- **Categories**: What types of categories are used in descriptions? As different categories describe different aspects of the person, the use of a particular category constitutes very definitely how we are to view that person. Therefore, when analyzing the text it is necessary to pay attention to the many implications that a choice of a particular label or category carries with it.
- **Collections**: Which collection of categories does the description call in? Which categories does such categorization exclude? According to Sacks (in Silverman, 1993: 81), each identity is heard as a category from a collection of categories (Membership Categorization Device, MCD). For example, 'mother' is from the collection of family-related categories; 'teacher' from occupation-related categories. To choose a category from a particular MCD to describe a person, thus, excludes him or her from being identified with some other category from the same device (for example, if mother, then not father).
- **Consistency rules**: Which are the other complementary or relevant categorizations that the chosen categorization implies or is consistent with? When one category from a given collection has been used to categorize one population member, then other categories from the same collection may be and often are used on other members of the same population. For example, when environmentally responsible human beings are categorized as 'green consumers' the relevant other actors associated with green consumerism are easily categorized in terms of the collection of 'market actors'.
- **Category-bound activities**: What are the activities that the chosen categorizations are taken to imply? Since many activities are associated with certain membership categories, in a taken-for-granted manner, identifying a person's activity provides for what his or her social identity is likely to be. In other words, things are read off the activities in which people engage (Silverman, 1993: 740). Moreover, it is possible to establish a negative moral assessment of people by describing their behavior in terms of performing or avoiding activities that are inappropriate to their social identity. How we define an activity is morally constitutive of it.

Overall, categorization is an important discursive practice through which people construct reality. Certain things (behaviors, characteristics) are known or taken for granted about any category, and categories can usually be read off the activities in which people engage. Therefore, people may try to avoid the normally category-bound implications of certain activity-descriptions and categorizations. In order to be able to escape these normal category-bound implications, people need to counter by accounting for why the category should not be read in the usual way in the particular situation in question. Sometimes there may even be a battle over which category is used. According to Sacks (1992, cited by Silverman 1993: 83), people are conscious of the descriptive categories they use more generally, as people can be held responsible not only for descriptions, but also for the inferences that can be drawn from them.

Consequently, categorization is a fundamental rhetoric strategy and a means of constructing reality; descriptions are recipient-designed for others, aimed at controlling the impressions others get. Any descriptive categorization formulates some item, person, or event as a particular entity with specific characteristics. Categorization defines certain activities and subject positions as normal and acceptable, and others as abnormal and immoral. Categorizations are not innocent, as Hall (1992a), among others, has pointed out.

Stereotyping, difference and otherness

The question of 'difference' and 'otherness' has been central in anthropological studies and it has come to play an increasingly significant role in constructionist studies, especially those informed by post-colonial and feminist theory. Paying close attention to the ways in which difference and the 'Other' are produced in people's accounts of marketplace phenomena may offer useful insight into the nature of the subject positions that is given to different market actors in the dominant cultural discourses.

The role of difference and the 'Other' in the construction of reality may be seen as ambivalent, both positive and negative. Difference and the generalized Other are considered necessary for the production of meaning, the formation of language and culture, as well as for the construction of social identity (Hall, 1992a, 1992b; Woodward, 1997). But at the same time, as Hall (1997b: 238) has pointed out, difference is 'threatening, a site of danger, of negative feelings, of splitting, hostility and aggression towards the "Other"'. Moreover, the binary oppositions through which difference is produced may be viewed as over-simplified, reductionist and value-laden, one pole of the binary oppositions usually being the dominant one, as numerous feminist scholars have insisted. Marking difference, therefore, always involves a relation of power.

On the one hand, it can be argued that construction of difference is an important discursive practice because meaning is relational and often depends on comparing and contrasting between opposites. Difference and binary oppositions are crucial for the everyday construction of meaning because people understand the world by assigning objects, people and phenomena to different positions or categories within the general classificatory systems that are relevant in the culture in which they live. To do that, they need to be able to establish a clear difference between the things they classify. Green consumerism, for example, may well be generally understood not so much in terms of certain 'green characteristics', but rather by distinguishing it from and contrasting it to the conventional conceptions of consumption. On the whole, then, if culture is conceived as being produced through production and exchange of meanings in systems of representation, then the marking of 'difference' may be seen as an important constitutive element of the ensemble of shared meanings and the associated social order that we call culture.

On the other hand, difference is often represented through stereotyping, that is, through discursive practices through which something is represented by reducing it to a few simplified characteristics or essentials, fixed in nature (Hall, 1997b: 257). Stereotypes typically display a strategy of splitting, dividing the normal and the acceptable from the abnormal and the unacceptable, excluding or expelling everything that does not fit or which is different. Stereotyping is associated with a practice of closure and exclusion; it symbolically fixes boundaries and excludes everything that does not belong. Stereotyping can, therefore, be viewed as a disciplinary technique that produces specific subject positions from which the normalizing discourses operate. As Hall has argued:

> [stereotyping] sets up a symbolic frontier between the 'normal' and the 'deviant', the 'normal' and the 'pathological', the 'acceptable' and the 'unacceptable', what belongs and what does not or is 'Other', between 'insiders' and 'outsiders', Us and Them. It facilitates the 'binding' or bonding together of all of Us who are 'normal' into one 'imagined community'; and it sends into symbolic exile all of Them − 'the Others' − who are in some way different − 'beyond the pale'. (1997b: 258)

Consequently, the discursive production of normalcy (what is accepted as normal and what is considered abnormal) through stereotyping has a powerful role in constituting subject positions, possibly even serving to fashion the whole of society according to a specific world view, value system, sensibility and ideology (Hall, 1997b: 259). Stereotyping, thus, can be seen as an important signifying practice through which symbolic power is exercised.

Therefore a focus on stereotypes and the ways in which difference and the 'Other' are represented in people's accounts of marketplace phenomena may offer useful insight into the nature of the subject positions that is given to different market actors in the dominant cultural discourses. Analyzing this, the following questions may be relevant (Hall, 1997b):

- What sort of dimensions of difference can be detected in the texts?
- How is the representation of difference linked with questions of power?
- What sort of binary oppositions and distinctions is the discourse structured by?
- Through which types of discursive strategies are 'otherness' and 'difference' produced?

Rhetoric strategies and tools

In constructionist accounts of social behavior it is often emphasized that rhetoric is a pervasive feature of all use of language and interaction (Potter, 1996). According to this line of reasoning, people use various types of rhetoric devices in their everyday communication and interaction to arrive at mutual understanding. Most descriptions and factual accounts of objects, events and phenomena may be seen as inherently evaluative, involving public positions that are inseparable from current controversy, conflict and dispute associated with the available competing discourses. In everyday communication people take a position in public discourse, each position being either explicitly or implicitly related to its counter position. As a result, the factual accounts and descriptions that people produce are usually rhetorically organized, involving a stance against what are perceived as counter-positions of the public position that they have assumed.

Jonathan Potter's (1996: 107–8) elaboration on the rhetorical tools people use to construct meaning in descriptions and accounts of events and phenomena provides a set of analytical tools for a systematic study of the discursive production of social texts. According to Potter, description and construction of facts are usually carried out using various forms of *offensive rhetoric*, to undermine alternative descriptions, and different forms of *defensive rhetoric*, to safeguard against possible discounting and undermining of the account offered. Specific versions of descriptions and factual accounts are thus built up and others undermined using these offensive and defensive rhetoric tools through *reifying discourses*, which construct versions as solid and factual, as well as through *ironizing discourses*, which undermine competing or alternative versions of the given accounts.

Moreover, descriptions often involve managing what Potter calls a *dilemma of stake*, or the fact that anything that a person says or does can be discounted as a product of stake or interest. Referring to vested interests is a powerful way of undermining what people say or do and, thereby positioning them in a negative way. Therefore, anticipated criticism of having a stake, and thus low credibility in the issue, is countered and headed off by using various types of defensive techniques and by stake management, the purpose of which is to work up an appearance of neutrality, accountability and reliability of the speaker.

A rhetorical analysis of the ways in which particular accounts of marketplace phenomena are constructed in text and talk using different defensive and offensive rhetoric tools may provide valuable insight into the cultural practice of the marketplace. An analysis of the ways in which the texts are rhetorically organized to produce particular views, to counter anticipated alternative views and to resist being countered, for example, may provide information about the nature of the different cultural discourses that are available in the culture. Potter (1996) elaborates on a number of rhetorical techniques that can be analyzed:

- **use of nominalization,** how verbs are nominalized to avoid endorsing a particular view of the responsibility of actions;
- **use of agency-obscuring and agency-promoting verbs,** how verbs with a different degree of opacity, with respect to the way they make explicit agency and intention, are used;
- **ontological gerrymandering,** how descriptions are specifically manipulated by selecting and formulating an area, by choosing particular descriptive terms and argumentative arenas, that are advantageous for the argument being advanced, and by ignoring other potentially relevant areas;

- **extrematization and minimization**, how 'extreme-case' formulations are drawn on to justify, accuse or argue conclusions;
- **normalization and abnormalizaton**, how abnormality is constructed in the text by using contrast structures, and how listing (three-part listing) is used to construct and present events and actions as normal, generic and representative;
- **stake inoculation**, how potential criticism about having a stake is headed off;
- **stake confession,** how criticism is disarmed by a confession of having a stake, as if the speaker had already taken into account his or her personal interests;
- **subtle stake management by qualification**, for example, subtly displaying disinterest precisely at the point where it could be a particular issue by various forms of qualification (for example, displaying uncertainty, searching for someone else's formulation, citing, giving exceptions);
- **category entitlements**, how the facticity of accounts is built up by representing the speaker as a member of a category who is generally treated as knowledgeable in the given context;
- **footing practices**, how the appearance of neutrality or accountability of the speaker is worked up by presenting some factual account as their own (close footing) or distancing themselves from it (distanced footing); and
- **externalizing devices**, how the account or description is constructed as independent of the agent producing it, by resorting to empiricist discourse (for example, passive voice and objectification), and by constructing consensus and corroboration (for example, presenting the view as being widely shared).

You can find more details on these rhetoric devices in Potter's book. Our aim here is only to illustrate the sorts of conceptual tools that can be used as lenses for doing a close reading of a cultural text.

Techniques for managing the process of analysis

In the cultural perspective we discuss here, the process of data analysis revolves around the two facets of cultural practice, cultural discourses and everyday discursive practices, in an attempt to produce a comprehensive and contextualized picture of the ways in which discourses do their work in the marketplace. To accomplish this analytical goal, researchers can apply the various methods and techniques that have been developed in the field of qualitative research. In this section, we discuss a number of such analytic techniques and practices.

Coding

Sometimes even somewhat mechanistic operations, such as coding, may serve as a fruitful catalyst for insightful analysis. In particular, in the beginning of the analysis, operations such as coding allow – or rather force – the researchers to familiarize themselves with the data. The essence of coding is to identify units of data that have something similar about them. Importantly, the coding should not be considered as an end in itself, but as an operational tactic that helps to see something interesting in the data.

Also, tabulations and cross-tabulations may be helpful in the process of familiarizing oneself with the data (Alasuutari, 1995: 116–32). They encourage, in particular, a systematic exploration of similarities and differences in the data and help the researcher to detect features that are missing.

In practice, much of the coding and tabulation is currently conducted using particular software packages designed for analyzing qualitative data. In this book we shall not discuss the computer-assisted analysis of qualitative data (see for instance Silverman, 2000: 154–72, or software developers' homepages for downloading free demonstration copies, if you are interested). We acknowledge that software packages may offer significant benefits, but we also give a word of warning. The specific features of the program may start to shape the way you conduct your analysis. The packages are always based on particular methodologies (such as grounded theory). Therefore you should be aware of the methodology that underlies the program, and in any case, use the software imaginatively, not mechanically!

De-familiarizing

De-familiarization is a way of distancing researchers from the taken-for-granted aspects of what is seen, allowing them to view it more analytically. Methodological textbooks provide some useful techniques and procedures for de-familiarizing (e.g., Alasuutari, 1995: 133–42). These techniques are often indebted to the classic work of C.W. Mills on 'sociological imagination'.

What Mills refers to as the sociological imagination consists, first and foremost, of the capacity to shift from one perspective to another – its essence is the combination of ideas that no one expects to be combinable (Mills, 2000: 211). This requires an almost playful attitude towards the data to be adopted. Such playful viewpoints, incorporating juxtapositions of similarity and difference, enlarge our vision and permit us to see patterns in the data that are not readily apparent. Even an attitude of playfulness toward the ways in which phrases and words are defined often loosens up the imagination (p. 212). Look up synonyms for each of your key terms in dictionaries in order to know the full range of their connotations. This simple habit may prod you to elaborate on the key terms of the problem and hence to immerse yourself into the phenomenon.

Another way of trying to make the familiar look strange is to make an attempt to find a point of comparison and to get a comparative grid on the materials. You may orient your comparison historically. If you think of shopping in the twenty-first century, bear in mind similar activities in different periods. Or spatially, think of how shopping is organized in localities that are different from the ones you are interested in. Often you get the best insights by considering extremes. For instance, if you study the mature market, consider also the baby market; if you study free time, consider also work. The imagination can sometimes be released by deliberately inverting your sense of proportion. If something seems very minute, imagine that it is simply enormous, and ask yourself: what sort of a difference does it make? (pp. 213–15.) You may also contrast your data with existing literature to find contradictions and thus generate insightful findings (Alasuutari, 1995).

Moreover, familiarizing yourself with strange theoretical constructs and perspectives, which differ from the tradition you are accustomed to, may help you to de-familiarize with the phenomenon and open up your horizon of interpretation. This practice may help you to see and challenge the theoretical assumptions embedded in your research question, and to realize how different assumptions might provide a fresh perspective on what is going on in the data. That is, it may help the researcher 'to raise havoc with our settled ways of thinking and conceptualization' (Marcus and Fischer, 1999: 138).

One practical form of defamiliarization is to form an interpretive group that consists of a number of people engaging in a process of interpretation through conversation (Thompson et al., 1989: 140–1). In practice, it often consists of researchers who have similar interests and share a set of cognitive goals and values, but who, in many important respects, have different ideas about research and the topic under study. Individual members of the interpretive group may therefore question the presumptions and taken-for-granted ideas that the other members have. When a particular interpretation is put forth by a member of a group, others respond to it by asking follow-up questions and by making their own alternative interpretations. Through these processes, an interpretive group may foster dialogue and render pre-understandings visible.

Importantly, this methodological procedure is not a means of avoiding the 'biases' of single individual interpreters. Rather, the goal of an interpretive group is to take up and make use of different perspectives and thereby enhance creativity in producing insightful interpretations. This sort of a procedure may be important because the perspective of a single researcher easily becomes sedimented: he or she may pay attention only to certain aspects of data while failing to see other aspects. Moreover, as Thompson and his colleagues point out (1989), the group can have an energizing effect on the interpretive process. It is a means of sharing the burden of interpretation. Analytical workshops may be needed because a single researcher, working alone, may well be overwhelmed by the interpretive task.

Writing

Researchers interpret as they write and in this sense writing may be thought of as analytic in its own right (Richardson, 2000). The analytic value of writing lies, first of all, in its ability to facilitate the dialogue between the text and the researcher. When researchers first familiarize themselves with the data, for example, the first step in working on the vague and intuitive preliminary ideas that they get is to write them down, to name them and to give them form. Often a mere taking of a note can be a prod to start thinking more carefully (Mills, [1959] 2000: 197). Writing can therefore be a fruitful way of giving concrete forms to ideas and thoughts that seem elusive, and to transform them into preliminary interpretations that can be further elaborated and refined.

Moreover, writing is also a practical device in the iterative process of the hermeneutic circle. By writing about specific elements, you may try to write some account of the whole, and in this sense, writing practices make you move back-and-forth in your data. In particular, trying to write a draft of the entire report may be helpful in trying to figure out 'the whole'. This trial affects the content of your earlier interpretations, makes you revise them and produce a new interpretation. In this sense, the mere craft of structuring and arranging the emerging insights through writing may release the imagination, as Mills remarks ([1959] 2000: 216).

Therefore, as the bulk of qualitative methodological textbooks recommend: write throughout the process of analysis, keep records, memos, research journals, try to write 'the whole', design a structure of your study and so forth. These practices not only facilitate the analysis but preserve the construction of your interpretive process and your inference-making. Quoting Wolcott (1990: 20), 'you cannot begin writing early enough'.

Moreover, in the process of trying to make sense of the data, it may be fruitful to employ a different mode of writing. By 'different' we mean different from the conventional mode of academic writing. As you change the means through which you interpret the world, your interpretations may also change. You see the phenomenon differently. Laurel Richardson employs the term 'creative analytical practices' (CAP) for various forms of writing, such as poems, novels, or short stories, but also for other forms of representations such as visuals, performances, or other artistic means. The key idea in employing these sorts of practices is that by changing the style of writing about your phenomenon you also change your angle towards it, and thereby get a different perspective on it. In doing so, these creative practices may illuminate previously unseen features of the phenomenon and thereby lead to interesting insights. They offer one way of bringing a social imagination to the setting that is to be analyzed.

For instance, if you are conducting an ethnographic study on creative team work in an advertising agency, you could try to write a play, based on your fieldnotes and insights that you have gained through fieldwork, to figure out 'what's going on in the field'. What sort of a horizon of interpretation does it open up (compared to the horizon offered by the marketing literature on creative team work in advertising agencies for instance)? what does the phenomenon look like now? What features of the phenomenon does this form of interpretation highlight and obscure?

These creative practices, and the practice of writing more generally, enables the researcher to have an ongoing conversation about what they know and how they know it. Through writing researchers can construct interpretations and then question how those interpretations have come about.

EXERCISE 6.2   Getting familiar with data

Familiarize yourself with your data by reading and re-reading it thoroughly. Read the data with a question in mind: 'What's going on in the data?' You may also try to break the surface of the data by coding it in some preliminary, even mechanical, manner. Or you may focus on the use of rhetorical tools, such as metaphors.

(Continued)

After this, you will probably have some sort of an idea, presumably vague, of the nature of the data, and perhaps also of some features that attract your attention. Then, apply some creative analytic practice in order to figure out what you have learned from the data. You may for instance try to consider your phenomenon as a play to be performed at a theater. What sort of play would it be? Who would be the actors? What would happen on the stage? What is the audience like? What would happen backstage? After writing this down, submit your 'play' to a reflexive analysis. What made you write like that? What does it imply? How does it differ from other sorts of 'plays'?

This sort of exercise is likely to focus your attention on the very essence of the phenomenon under study. Instead of a play, you can take any other form of creative analytic practice – poem, novel, TV program, performance, and so forth.

Note

1 In hermeneutic philosophy, however, it is maintained, in particular, that understanding that is gained through a hermeneutic circle is not a mere procedure or method for producing interpretations, but a way of being in the world.

FURTHER READING

The following textbooks offer informative and focused discussions on the process and techniques of qualitative data analysis. Silverman's books also provide a set of valuable exercises for students.

- Coffey, Amanda and Atkinson, Paul (1996) *Making Sense of Qualitative Data: Complementary Research Strategies.* Thousands Oaks, CA: Sage.
- Silverman, David (1993) *Interpreting Qualitative Data: Methods for Analysing Talk, Text and Interaction.* London: Sage.
- Silverman, David (2000) *Doing Qualitative Research: A Practical Handbook.* London: Sage.

C.W. Mills offers helpful techniques through which to nurture scientific imagination and de-familiarize oneself from the data. See particularly the Appendix 'On Intellectual Craftsmanship' in:

- Mills, C. Wright ([1959] 2000) *The Sociological Imagination.* New York: Oxford University Press.

For a good discussion on the intertwined role of writing and analyzing see:

- Richardson, Laurel (2000) 'Writing: A Method of Inquiry', in N.K. Denzin and Y.S. Lincoln (eds), *Handbook of Qualitative Research.* London: Sage. pp. 932–48.

7

Analysis in Practice

CHAPTER SUMMARY

This chapter offers two case examples of cultural analysis in practice:

- The first case is concerned with illustrating the process of conducting an analysis. It shows how the analyst proceeds from vague ideas to grounded interpretations through a constant dialogue and iterative back-and-forth movements.
- The second case example illustrates the ways in which discursive practices can be analyzed by using the conceptual tools for close reading that we presented in Chapter 6.

Introduction

Throughout the book we have emphasized that the process of data analysis and interpretation is not a simple mechanical procedure but a fairly complex interpretive process that requires creativity and imagination. A mere technical training in analytical methods will not produce creative insights, as Susan Spiggle (1994) among others has remarked. Nevertheless, in qualitative research, creative insights seldom occur without a great deal of routine work. Speed and urgency are the enemies of good research, as ethnographers tend to stress. 'It requires patience to be surprised,' writes Joost van Loon (2001: 281) for example. Therefore, it is important to begin the analysis as early as possible – as soon as you have produced or collected the first piece of your data set (see Silverman, 2000: 119–52).

Overall, to come up with insightful ideas you also need to have a truly fierce drive to make sense of the world (Mills, 2000: 211). This drive is needed because the process of data analysis is time-consuming, and because it typically involves a great amount of frustration and uncertainty – in the beginning you do not know where you will end up and what you will discover. Uncertainty is not an issue to be settled, but to be lived with, and preferably, to be enjoyed. And, as Lofland and Lofland (1984) remark, working systematically at an analysis and maintaining the faith that it will all come together in the end, provides joyful and rewarding moments. As ideas gradually come together and discoveries are made, the process also results in intellectual growth and professional development of the researcher.

In this chapter we offer you two case examples, based on our own work, which illustrate how some of the principles and techniques that we have discussed in this book can be put in practice. The objective is to give you an idea of the sort of procedures, practices and techniques that the process of analysis and interpretation involves, as well as to illustrate the sort of cultural knowledge that can be produced through these analytical procedures. Since the process of analysis is not a mechanical procedure, it is impossible to describe step-by-step how we have arrived at the interpretations or how exactly we have used the different methods and techniques to learn about the phenomena that we have been interested in. But we hope that by describing what we have done and what we have learned in a detailed manner, we can show how these methods and techniques work in the context of cultural marketing and consumer research.

The first case is concerned with the *process* of conducting an analysis. It is a case written by Anu Valtonen, who aims to illustrate how the researcher proceeds from vague ideas to grounded interpretations through a constant dialogue and iterative back-and-forth movements. In doing so she also exemplifies the ways in which theory and data may nurture each other, and how both the theoretical frame and the emerging interpretations are produced through the interpretive process.

The purpose of the second case example, a piece of analysis taken from the work of Johanna Moisander, is to illustrate the ways in which discursive resources and practices can be detected and analyzed through a process of focused close reading. More specifically, it focuses on the concepts, categories, metaphoric expressions, justifications and explanatory models that people use, as well as the subject positions that they give and take when constructing their accounts of particular social groups and forms of consumer identity, for example.

Case 1   The process of interpretation

The study

This case is based on a study that addressed one socio-economic category, free time (Valtonen, 2004a). As a wide range of previous studies on time indicate, temporal categories in general and the category called free time in particular have become contested in current society: people experience constant time pressures and increasing problems to manage fuzzy time lines, for instance. Despite this, consumer researchers have generally accepted the notion of free time without critical reflection. To begin to address this gap, the study carried out empirical fieldwork in Finland in order to gain everyday evidence of the complex nature of the ongoing re-negotiation of free time, and in particular, in order to achieve an understanding of the multiple ways in which various consumption activities and artifacts play a role in this negotiation. Put differently, the study is primarily interested in how the contested category called free time is managed, maintained and shaped in the arena of consumption.

One particularity of this study is that it deals with a phenomenon that is part of the researcher's everyday life. Therefore, the example also exemplifies particular techniques and methods through which the researcher sought to de-familiarize herself from the taken-for-granted everyday world. It therefore also exemplifies the ways in which the researcher's pre-understanding and attendant horizon of interpretation may change during the process.

Starting with loose theoretical underpinnings

In starting the dissertation I (A.V.) was theoretically informed by the stream of cultural research that assesses culture through cultural categories. I was also informed by attendant ontological and epistemological assumptions that stress the constitutive nature of categories and their linguistic nature. Put briefly, in this line of thinking it is thought that categories such as 'free time', 'child' or 'marketer' are constitutive building blocks of the social world. The categorization organizes the flux of everyday life into recognizable form, making it meaningful to people. Once the myriad phenomenon of everyday life is subsumed under a delimited number of shared categories, they create the sense that the life-world is familiarly organized (Gubrium and Holstein, 2003a: 217–18). The way these categories are recurrently used and practiced – for example, how free time is actualized through practices such as changing casual clothes and having a glass of wine – simultaneously sustains the category and gives it particular meanings.

Leaning on these sorts of theoretical ideas, the attendant methodological strategy was to produce cultural talk in order to be able to see the categories in use. Focus groups were chosen as the primary method because they were supposed to produce talk appropriate for the purpose of the study, that is, time-related story-like accounts of everyday life. As we already referred to this study in discussing focus groups in Chapter 4, the discussion guide was designed based on the pre-understanding of the topic and on the expertise gained by working as a qualitative market researcher. Basically, respondents were asked to tell about their everyday life, how their normal day goes, how they spend their weekends, holidays and spare time and so forth. The discussion centered upon general cultural categories and a wide range of probing questions was asked for each category to get an in-depth view of them.

Starting to familiarize with the data

At the start of the data analysis, I had quite a general notion on what I would like to look into in the data. I was interested in free time as a cultural category with a presumption that it is under negotiation at some level. With this rough aim in mind, I read and re-read the transcripts several times in order to become familiar with the data and in the hope of starting to see something interesting in them.

I decided to **code** the data with the help of the NVivo software program in order to break down the seemingly obvious surface of the data. This procedure produced one interesting observation. In describing the ways in which they spent their free time, respondents recurrently referred to a door: for instance, they would mention how they wish to forget work matters when 'closing the door' of the workspace. This feature, the door, caught my attention and led to an intuitive, yet vague thought, that 'here's something interesting'. The data were speaking to me.

Due to this small observation produced by the coding procedure, I was able to 'think through the data' when reading the work of anthropologists Arnold van Gennep and Victor Turner, who consider the door as a master symbol in the construction and management of status transfers of various kinds. After having familiarized with this line of theorizing I returned to the raw data and paid closer attention to the ways in which the door was actually present in the data. I also decided to observe those discursive practices that are played out at the door – when people leave the workspace, arrive at home – and the ways in which consumption activities relate to them, in order to get a more comprehensive and grounded understanding of this seemingly mundane phenomenon that thus far had seemed merely mundane.

Otherwise, however, I found the computer-based coding somewhat mechanical. It seemed to capture thinking instead of liberating it – as if I had to think in the same way as some software engineer – and it seemed to break the data into such small bits and pieces that it was purely confusing. Therefore, I looked for some other ways to approach my data. I took to carrying out **a metaphor analysis**. The analytical technique of metaphor was chosen because the substance topic of time is highly abstract by nature and abstract issues are commonly comprehended metaphorically, as Lakoff and Johnson (1980) have pointed out. However, metaphoric analysis produced a quite obvious finding: 'time is money'. This prevailing comprehension is certainly not a novel finding and it seemed somewhat hard to find anything interesting to be further considered in this regard.

The data did not speak to me in this case – until I familiarized myself with the cultural studies literature and had discussions with colleagues familiar with it. In trying to understand the underlying spirit of cultural studies I realized how I should address this 'finding' in a fruitful manner. Instead of believing that time *is* money, I should ask, how has the comprehension 'time is money' come about? In what sort of system of representation is it understandable? What does it exclude? Posing these sorts of questions, which are offered by the horizon of cultural studies, enabled me to see the data in a new light.

Now I could see that the comprehension 'time is money' is a product of the discourse of economics. This discourse offers an understanding that time, like money, is a resource to be spent, saved and allocated efficiently; an understanding that has been current since the industrial revolution. The power of the economic discourse partially lies in its ability to be 'seen but unnoticed', in its ability to appear as the only possibility while other possibilities are outside the plausible realm. But now I was able to ask: what is left outside? Aren't there any other plausible ways to comprehend time? Familiarizing myself with the literature on time opened me up to see that there are other sorts of systems of representations that offer a different way to understand and structure time. For instance, a system of representation can be identified that is not based on money, but on the cyclical and repetitive production of the life course. Returning to the data, I could identify this system of representation, in the context of Christmas, for instance. This in turn drew attention to the ways in which these different, partly overlapping, partly competing systems of representation are played out and shaped in everyday consumption practices through which people attempt to manage and structure time.

Dialectical interpretation

In reading data descriptions that at first sight appeared 'normal' to me, I tried to see something interesting in them by using a couple of techniques. Moreover, I tried problematizing them – both the raw data and the coded data – by the logic of question and answer. By taking a somewhat child-like curious attitude I approached the data by wondering: What do the respondents actually say? Why do they talk this way and not another way? What is this piece of data all about? I looked for answers not only from the data, but also in the theoretical literature, from the surrounding, everyday world, and from my own experiences. This process in turn produced new questions with which I returned to my data to see whether they provided answers. It made me also look for new data that might provide clues as to what was going on in the data. In this way, I gradually built up a body of observational data and other cultural materials, and also a body of interpretive comments, which were submitted to analysis. This is, hence, one practical application of the 'hermeneutic circle' in which the use of analytical work shops of various kinds also played a crucial role.

Such reflective back-and-forth questioning was possible since during the analytical process I continually wrote memos, drafts, working papers, and summary sheets. And I returned to my writings, reading them in a reflective way: what is my writing all about? In this sense writing constituted an integral part of the analyzing process.

Let us further illustrate this kind of dialectical analytical process by two examples. The following questions – taken from my research journal – illustrate the kinds of questions that emerged when I read my data. Roughly put, I generated questions on two levels: in terms of contents of the discussion (what respondents actually talk about) and in terms of single expressions (like 'ashamed', 'going away').

Why do urban workers in an information society use agrarian language when they describe their work, like doing spadework? Every group talks about sleeping, why is that? Why didn't I probe more into sleeping, why did I exclude it? Free coffee seems to be important for the respondents, and, of course, free drinks, but well, what's new in that? Why should it be new – what makes me think that way? They actually talk about conversations, that is, what they talk about during coffee breaks and in pubs, what does it mean? Is this what Douglas refers to as speech rituals? They talk a lot about Friday, and when they do the tone of the conversation changes: why do they laugh when they talk about Friday? Why do they keep questioning what free time is? Why do I hear it all the time, also in seminars?

Why do they use words like must, ashamed, necessity? This is about free time, isn't it? The word 'away' is repeatedly there – a kind of synonym for free time? They create another world, interesting spatial expression. Christmas is associated with death. Is there any other context where death is talked about? If free time is not solely a happy time, what then? What makes me think it should be a happy time?

The following example in turn attempts to illustrate the ways in which the whole research process is submitted to analysis. It is a story about one presentation of my on-going study. This event made me realize not only the tremendous strength of some cultural boundaries, but also how cultural boundaries become visible in various contexts. It also shows how the boundary between researcher/researched becomes questioned in this kind of analysis where the phenomenon under study is constantly present.

> I enter an empty classroom and I am worried about whether anybody will attend the seminar where I am supposed to give a presentation. I am glad to notice that people are arriving. When the time is quarter past, I start my presentation: 'Welcome everybody. I shall present my on-going PhD study that addresses free time as a cultural category.'
>
> The presentation continues pleasantly, and there is also quite a vivid and open discussion. Suddenly I notice that I am going to run out of time and I say: 'Well, I shall close my presentation by describing briefly how my respondents talk about Christmas. The younger respondents, in particular, seem to view it as time for duties and musts rather than as free time. They frequently used the phrase 'family hell' when they talked about Christmas. They referred to divorces and re-marriages being common. It is also interesting that the discussion about Christmas evoked a discussion about death. In my secondary data set, there is also an interesting account: 'Sometimes, I feel that I cook for dead people.'
>
> After saying this there is complete silence in the audience. I think that I was unclear and I repeat what I had said. Then one man raises his hand and says: 'But after all, it's good to have families, we all have family … there might be new kinds of families, friends can be families.' Others join the discussion speaking up for Christmas: 'It's so nice to have Christmas, isn't it?' No one says a single word about death.

What happened? What caused the silence? How might the reactions of the audience be understood? Why was family commented on and defended while there was silence about death? Reflecting on this afterwards, I realized that in my presentation I had crossed two profound cultural boundaries: that of (nuclear) family and that of death. Family represents something sacred in our culture, something not to be insulted; death in turn represents a taboo, something not even to be talked about. The reactions of the audience made me clearly realize what cultural boundaries are about.

Finding appropriate theoretical constructs

In this way, little by little, I realized that the complex phenomenon I was interested in may be best captured through the notion of symbolic boundaries. This notion is at the heart of the work of Mary Douglas, a pioneer of an anthropology of consumption that has explored the ways in which culture becomes created, sustained and shaped in the arena of consumption (Douglas, 2002; Douglas and

Isherwood, 1996). Simply put, symbolic boundaries refer to the ways in which cultural categories become separated from each other, differentiated. Boundaries become manifested through a set of symbolic artifacts, such as casual Friday clothes ('Dress-Down Friday') which separate and symbolize the boundary between work-week and week-end.

Douglasian analysis begins from the premise that all cultural life is in constant tension between control and resistance, orders and disorders. This tension is reflected in behavior, interaction rituals, normative systems and social structure, all of which are visible in the rules, communication systems and artifacts of particular culture. It commonly takes seemingly mundane events, even repulsive ones, and reproduces them in a way that exposes broader social processes of control, taming, power imbalance and the symbolic mechanisms that impose one set of preferred meanings of behaviors over others.

In particular, a cultural analyst following this perspective starts to read cultures from the viewpoint of the disorder. He or she takes a look at issues that do *not* fit into the assumed order, are out of order, fall in between classes, are defined as marginal, or merge with each other. These issues represent threat and danger, but also simultaneously potential for something new. They both fascinate and cause anxiety. To use a common term, these issues are 'dirty'. And where there is dirt, there is a system. That is, when something becomes interpreted as 'dirty' – as deviant – there must be some system and attendant set of rules that defines this entity as 'dirty' (Douglas, 2002). In identifying issues that represent order or disorder, clean or dirty, the analyst pays attention to certain cultural clues in the data. Examples include such clues as shame or pride; what is reasoned and explained, or what is considered evident and taken-for-granted. Moreover, issues that are silenced or tabooed stand at the center of such analysis. Understanding those systems in use is a general goal of an analyst.

This sort of theoretical perspective led me to acknowledge and capture the peculiar tension involved in the phenomenon under study, the contested category called free time. Through the construct of a symbolic boundary a particular horizon of interpretation opened up that enabled me to pose new types of questions and begin to see something new in the data. This horizon made visible that there is actually a great deal going on at the boundaries. It made visible that the boundary between work and free time is, actually, merely one part of the phenomenon. Besides, there may be identified a morally loaded boundary between dirty and clean free time, and the boundary between sleep and awake, all of which play a part in the ways in which people attempt to construct and manage a category understood as free time. Accordingly, the consumption activities and artifacts involved in this sort of construction and management go beyond the use of new technological devices 'that cause the fuzzy boundary between work and free', as the prevailing discourse seems to suggest.

Techniques of de-familiarization

In the present study, the requirement for seeing the everyday world in a new light is complicated by the point that I am doing research 'at home'. I am both historically

and locally situated within the very processes being studied and my own perceptions about the phenomenon are determined by the culture and language I live
in and with. That is, I see the world through the same categories as my respondents. This is likely to cause a problem of over-familiarity, which is said to become
particularly crucial when one studies everyday life (Coffey, 1999). As ethnographers have pointed out, the researchers inhabit a kind of in-between world, simultaneously native and stranger. They must become close enough to the culture
being studied to understand how it works, and yet be able to detach from it sufficiently to be able to report on it. A common suggestion regarding detaching
is that one should cultivate strangeness and distance. Here, the primary role of
cultivating strangeness is given to the theory and critical self-reflection.

First, as discussed, relying on the field of anthropology – a 'strange' discipline
for a trained consumer researcher – helped me to see not only my own world,
but also the consumption world in a new way. Academic boundary crossing
enabled new questions to be asked of the familiar data. Moreover, the reliance on
anthropological classics like Douglas, Turner and van Gennep transferred me to a
strange position in terms of time and space. When I associated myself, for instance,
with the Leles in the 1950s and took a look at my own world from that position,
my world changed. Suddenly, a huge number of symbolic boundaries appeared in
my life. The daily commute started to look like a fascinating status transfer. Weekly
cleaning routines, that thus far were boring, became an interesting and even fascinating boundary practice. The everyday world turned out to be a tensioned site
of good and bad, clean and dirty, order and disorder. Thus, the 'strange' theoretical position provided me with the joy of being surprised in my own mundane life.

Moreover, and importantly, familiarizing myself with the feminist literature was
of tremendous help in the process of learning to see beyond the obvious. Due to
the overall critical spirit infused in feminist literature it provided a fruitful intellectual stance to re-think, re-consider and re-define my taken-for-granted world.
It also pointed me towards noticing that cultural categories are far from neutral
and innocent and to consider the politics involved in them.

One further fruitful method of detachment may be mentioned: the world of
the arts. The basic themes of my study, time and freedom have been widely dealt
with and questioned within various spheres of the arts. For instance, reading *Don
Quixote* nicely reminded me that the theme of freedom does have a long and
widely shared history. Or, reading *One Hundred Years of Solitude* with its peculiar
temporalities forced me to question time.

Thus, these techniques of estrangement help to get some analytical distance
from categories I live in and by. They let me perceive many aspects of my culture
that had previously been invisible to me. That is, they made me change my pre-
understanding and to see differently. However, I do not attempt to claim that I
stepped out of cultural categories, but that I became aware of them and their silent
power. Neither do I want to claim that the world I am living in is thoroughly
familiar to me. It does have strange passages that provide fruitful 'ruptures' for
analysis. This came out in the focus group situations: for example, I do not have
children so I felt somewhat strange in the group of mothers and fathers with small

children; or, in the group of teenagers, I was the strange old researcher. On the whole, the question of strangeness and familiarity is rather complex conceptual machinery, as Coffey (1999: 22–3) points out.

Case 2   A close reading of cultural texts

The study

The second case example is taken from a research project that focused on environmental policy-related social marketing and the representation of the 'consumer' in marketing literature (Moisander, 2000a, b, 2001; Moisander and Pesonen, 2002). One of the objectives of the study was to identify and study the culturally standardized or institutionalized discourses that people draw on when representing green consumerism. This was done in an attempt to gain a better understanding of the ways in which the institutionalized discourses of green consumerism guide and constrain the representation of green consumers and green consumption in text, talk, images and signifying practices.

The texts

The data of the study discussed here consist of written accounts of green consumerism, which were generated using a projective technique. A group of business students, attending a course on consumer behavior, were asked to write a 1–2 page description of a 'green consumer'. Two different orientations were used. The wordings of the orientations were the following:

1   Imagine that you are an environment-friendly green consumer. What do you value, what do you pursue, what is important for you in your own life, society, and the world? Describe your values, beliefs, and feelings as thoroughly as possible.
2   Imagine that you are an environment-friendly green consumer. What is it that you do **not** value, what do you **not** pursue, what is not important for you in your own life, society and the world? Describe your values, beliefs and feelings as thoroughly as possible.

The aim in generating these descriptions was to obtain textual data on the cultural discourses that students call on when describing green consumers. It was presumed that when describing green consumers, students would be using the dominant discourses or systems of representation, negotiating, contesting and reproducing the culturally shared meanings associated with green consumerism.

I personally distributed the orientations, which were written on a sheet of paper, and students returned their answers by e-mail. The data so obtained consisted of 44 descriptions, based on orientation 1, of which 24 were written by female and 20 by male students, and 40 descriptions based on orientation 2, of which 26 were produced by female and 14 by male students. The length of the texts varied from 1 to 3 pages. An example of an account is given below in Box 7.1.

The writing task was given as a pre-assignment for a lecture on consumer motivation, and the texts were used in class, the following week, for group work on consumer motivation, and target group analysis for consumer marketing. In this context, a marketing discourse on green consumerism was thus offered to the students. The orientations referring to consumers (not people or citizens) and the context, a course on consumer behavior, would seem to have encouraged the students to think of green consumerism, particularly as consumption and green consumers as objects of marketing activities. However, by using a role-playing method (imagine that you are …), I attempted to position the students as consumers, not as marketing managers. Moreover, by designing the orientations so that they included a request to describe what is important for green consumers not only in their personal life but also in society, and in the world, I attempted to re-orient them to write more general descriptions, not just consumption-related descriptions. In fact, this repositioning seemed to work out well. Most of the texts produced addressed green consumerism as a general social phenomenon. Only a few texts took an explicit marketing manager's perspective. Nevertheless, it is clear that the context and the orientation offered the students the position of a consumer who expresses his or her values through consumption activities, as the marketing discourse expects.

Since marketing is generally seen as being based on satisfying consumer needs and wants, it would seem that the orientation and the context of the data generation encouraged students to try to think what sort of people green consumers 'really are', and not primarily what they should do and value. However, many of the texts presented the green consumer as an 'ideal type', a deeply committed 'true' green consumer. Also, the lack of commitment and inconsistency of people who consider themselves green consumers were recurrently referred to.

The orientation was designed to produce elaborate and many-sided texts about the cultural meanings associated with green consumerism by focusing on what green consumers are and are not perceived to value, pursue and consider meaningful and important. The orientation was first tested using a single version that focused on behavior, but it tended to produce fairly simple lists of environment friendly behaviors, which provided information mainly on the signifying practices associated with green consumerism. Therefore, an orientation with an explicit focus on values, feelings and meanings was designed in the hope of producing richer data on the non-behavioral discursive elements involved. Moreover, a negative orientation (that is, what green consumers do not value) was also designed because it was presumed that people tend to perceive the world in terms of opposites, defining the good and desirable in negative terms. However, to avoid imposing dualist thinking on the respondents, the questions about important and unimportant and the valued and unvalued issues were not included in the same orientation; instead two different orientations, distributed to different respondents, were used.

Finally, to encourage the students to produce well-thought-out and elaborate descriptions, the orientation included a request to 'describe … as thoroughly as possible'. Moreover, the assignment was an obligatory course requirement. The group work that was carried out on the basis of this assignment was graded, which would seem to have improved the students' involvement in carrying out the task.

EXERCISE 7.1   Selecting empirical materials for cultural analysis

Having read the description of the data collection procedures for the study discussed in Case 2, try to think of other possible empirical materials and other ways of generating cultural data for the study.

1   What are their advantages and disadvantages for studying how the marketing discourse on green consumerism guides and constrains consumers' everyday life?
2   Can you think of any naturally occurring textual materials that could have been used instead of generating cultural talk with a projective technique?
3   How about focus groups and interviews, would these methods offer materials with different perspectives on the phenomenon?
4   Can you think of any visual materials that could be studied to learn about the representation of green consumerism?

Analytical focus and procedures

In line with the cultural approach adopted in the study, the analytical focus was on the discourses that people draw on when representing green consumerism, as well as on the discursive practices through which these discourses are produced.

Instead of asking what a green consumer is or what the difference between green and non-green consumption is, the focus was on how 'greenness' as a subject position is constructed discursively. The purpose was to analyze the structure and content of the dominant discourses that constitute the idea of green consumerism, and the discursive strategies, techniques and tactics through which the difference between green and non-green consumers is produced.

The following constitutive elements of discourses were studied (Hall, 1992a, 1997a):

- the statements about green consumerism that give us knowledge about the phenomenon;
- the rules that prescribe certain ways of talking about green consumerism and exclude other ways; the rules that govern what is sayable or thinkable about green consumerism in the socio-historical context of the study;
- the 'subjects' who in some ways personify the discourse and the attributes that such subjects are expected to have, given the way knowledge about the topic is constructed at this time;
- how the knowledge about green consumerism acquires authority, a sense of embodying the truth about it; constituting the 'truth of the matter'; and
- the practices within institutions (marketing, government, etc.) for dealing with the subjects.

I first read and re-read the descriptions of 'green consumers' and 'green consumerism' to find related patterns in the data. I tried to identify differences and consistency or shared features in either the content or form of the accounts, focusing on possible constitutive elements of the discourses of green consumerism (presented above), and on the rhetorical or argumentative organization of the text (the discursive resources discussed in Chapter 6). Based on the observed patterns and organization of the text I formed preliminary ideas – 'hypotheses' – about the structure and content of the discourses called on in the texts, and about their functions and consequences. From the beginning, after just reading the texts through a couple of times, writing down notes about the claims, categorizations, images, stakes and norms that the texts drew from, it seemed clear that there were two or three partly overlapping discourses structuring the texts: one based on rational household management, one on political activity, and perhaps one on aesthetic/spiritual values and way of life. The elements of the aesthetic/spiritual discourse appeared to be associated with the other two discourses but it seemed, nevertheless, that it constituted a separate discourse.

To scrutinize and to seek linguistic evidence for the preliminary ideas, I carried out analytic induction[1] and deviant case[2] analysis. I chose descriptions of green consumerism that somehow seemed to be typical cases, that is, texts that personified the preliminary subject positions and discourses I had detected, and generated preliminary 'hypotheses' about the structure and content of the discourse they appeared primarily to call on. Then, one by one, I took more cases for closer examination and reformulated my preliminary understanding of the patterns in the texts when needed. I scrutinized deviant cases to ascertain whether (a) the deviant cases supported the provisional hypotheses or (b) the hypotheses were to be modified to allow for the inclusion of the deviant cases. I treated deviant cases as supportive if I could show that the initially established patterns and hypotheses exhibited an orientation in the text that involved the same discursive elements that produced the deviant cases. For example, if something in the accounts disclosed that a deviant discursive element was treated in the text as one involving a departure from the expected ways of representation or course of events, it was deemed supportive (for example, if it could be shown that some generally accepted idea about green consumers was contested). Where deviant cases did not show this orientation I treated this as an indication of a need to revise the original construction of the pattern in the data.

Hence, in analyzing the data and scrutinizing my interpretation I tried to focus on the following discursive resources in the text:

- the particular words that are chosen, the images and metaphors they contain, and the ways of being that they assume or invoke (Davies and Harré, 1990);
- the categorizations and distinctions made and used in the text (Silverman, 1993);
- the explicit and implicit norms referred to in describing 'green consumerism' (Alasuutari, 1995);
- stereotyping and the repertoires of representation around difference and the conceptions of the 'other' (Hall, 1997b); and

- the rhetorical organization of the text, the use of offensive and defensive rhetoric through reifying and ironizing discourses, and the stakes and conflicts of interests implied (Potter, 1996, 1997).

In reading and re-reading the texts I tried to focus on how any of these discursive resources would be used to construct descriptions of green consumerism, making notes of the words, categorizations, norms and stereotypical images and oppositions with which the descriptions were produced. Interpreting the 'functions' and meaning, and the images that the use of these discursive resources produced, I focused on the rhetorical and argumentative organization of the text. I tried to detect and analyze the use of different rhetorical devices in the texts to construct particular versions or descriptions of various aspects of green consumerism. On the basis of my notes of these observations and interpretations, as well as with some existing literature on the history of the environmental movement, environmental philosophy and green consumerism, I then gradually arrived at an interpretation of the content and structure of the discourses of green consumerism that the texts drew on.

In the following sections, a piece of textual analysis is presented so as to illustrate how a close reading can be done on cultural data with the help of these concepts and procedures.

Close reading of narratives of green consumerism

To illustrate how discursive practices can be studied I discuss one of the discourses identified in the study. It tended to represent green consumerism as some sort of a rational household management. This discourse tended to reify a version of green consumerism as rational and socially acceptable citizenry, and produced a subject position for the green consumer as relatively 'normal'. In the cultural context, where the texts were produced, the representation of green consumerism was clearly contested. Earlier, only radical political activists or 'hippies' were understood to be concerned about the environment. In the texts, therefore, the representation of a green consumer as an ordinary, rational and socially acceptable citizen was constructed by contrasting it to the two other, generally marginalizing representations.

Most of the accounts of green consumerism that were analyzed for the study called on an individualist and in a sense conservative reifying discourse of green consumerism as rational and morally responsible 'household management'. This probably has to do with the fact that in the cultural context where the texts were written, from the 1990s onwards, 'green consumerism' and sustainable development had been discussed and taught about in state schools. For this and a number of other reasons not presented here, it may be argued that the discourse labeled as 'rational household management' was, or at least was becoming, a dominant cultural discourse on green consumerism.

Before illustrating the ways in which this discourse was discursively produced in the texts that I analyzed, I present a piece of data which represents a typical case or portrait of a green consumer and which, to a considerable degree, personifies or represents the subject position that the discourse appears to produce (Box 7.1). The discourse could be discussed and elaborated on from many perspectives but here I focus only on a few ideas and interpretations, illustrating how they can be observed in the data.

Box 7.1   Data example: The reasonable and responsible green consumer

As a green consumer I value nature and the equilibrium of humans and nature. I feel that I can have an impact on the state of the world through my own consumption decisions and through my own choices associated with my everyday life. I hope that our environment stays clean and functional for future generations. I am not necessarily a *viherpipertäjä* [a pejorative expression for a green activist] shouting slogans at the barricades, but a logically thinking person.

I am vegetarian for many reasons. I do not approve of wasting resources, so the production of meat for food is unnecessary. Although in Finland there are sufficient resources, in China, for example, the situation is different. The Chinese imitate the Western countries and switch from rice farming to meat production. As a result, less food is produced and the poorer [people] starve. I understand that my choice can be an example for people who live thousands of kilometers away.

Moreover, I do not approve of the exploitation of animals. This is another reason for being a vegetarian, but it has also a more comprehensive meaning in my life. I could not even imagine myself dressed in furs, and I am opposed to fur farming in all of its forms. Foxes are not created for living in wire-mesh cages, or not even in small dirt floor farms. I nevertheless wear leather shoes and wool sweaters, because cows and sheep have been bred into domestic animals, and supposedly they do not suffer in captivity, like the foxes and the minks. I am, however, prudent when I use animal originated products. I choose the organic whenever possible, and I could not even imagine buying eggs produced in a poultry farm that coops up the chickens although they are a couple of marks less expensive, whenever there are alternatives. I will not, however, become a complete vegan because greenness is not a value for me as such; I do not want to make my life or others' life utterly difficult, but to make green choices in consumption when it is reasonably possible.

I try to choose organic products whenever they are available, and I also preferably choose domestic products. There are many reasons for choosing domestic [products]: to avoid unnecessary transportation, a belief in cleaner production, employment of farmers in Finland, etc. I choose organic [products] for the same reasons, but obviously especially because of the healthiness and cleanness of the products. For a vegetarian, the good taste of vegetables is also particularly important. Genetically engineered products I leave at the store, and I would not recommend the meat of animals that have been raised using hormones to anybody.

A domestic origin is also important for [products] other than groceries. It is important for me to support domestic employment and small businesses. I would rather pay for good service than use self-service. Neither do I want to buy products that have possibly been manufactured using child labor.

I would rather help the less fortunate of the Third World by contributing to different money-raising campaigns. On the other hand, I gladly welcome fair trade products; I am happy to be able to buy my coffee so that the producer also gets a good reward for his/her work. In general I wish that people saw the consequences of their choices at the global level. The solidarity among people [should not be restricted to inside national borders].

Recycling is a natural part of my life. Biodegradables, glass, metal, paper, etc. are not at all difficult to separate from the rest of household waste. For us city dwellers recycling has been made particularly easy – containers for biodegradable waste and paper can be found in the yard of almost every house, and the collection points for glass are not far away. I always try to choose products that have as little packaging as possible – why should one buy a package of coffee that has a separate layer of cardboard on top of the package itself? I keep a shopping bag with me because I do not want to have a huge armada of plastic bags to pile up in my home.

I do not throw my old clothes directly away but I try to sell them at the flea market. The money that I get is not the most important for me, but the idea that somebody can still use products that are useless for me. Reuse is an even better alternative than recycling.

I admire people who have moved to rural self-sustaining collectivities. It would be great if I myself could produce what I consume, without additives and fertilizers. I am not, however, ready for such radical changes – I do not even want to live in the countryside. Nevertheless, I appreciate people who have made such a choice.

I am ready to take part in boycotts to make large corporations respect the environment. I avoided French products after the nuclear testing and I still avoid Shell. But then again, I do not need gas stations because I am against the use of private cars. In the city, public transportation is significantly much handier than a car, also when traveling to other cities. Air traffic is the most problematic of all – on one hand I enjoy traveling and getting to know new cultures, on the other hand I am aware of the enormous emissions that airplanes produce. But, it is very difficult to get to far away countries in any other way but flying.

Greenness is largely an attitude of life that is based on intellectual deliberation. Although vegetarianism is a fad among many young people, for an adult person it is a conscious choice to ensure his/her own and others' wellbeing. I read a lot, so I am aware of the far-reaching consequences of my different decisions. Making green consumption choices is not the most important [value] for me, but adhering to certain principles I can maintain

(Continued)

(Continued)

my consumption such that I can look at myself in the mirror in the morning. For me it is particularly important to be able to respect myself – not so much to be admired by others. I do not rant and rave, foam at the mouth, to my friends about a better world, but rather I try to influence with my own example. When a suitable occasion occurs, however, I can try to influence my neighbors with arguments that appeal to reason. (Female)

INDIVIDUALIST MORAL DISCOURSE OF 'MAKING A DIFFERENCE'   The discourse is constructed on a reductionist moral framework that emphasizes the primary importance of individual commitment and of a contribution to sustainable development. In the texts, this can be observed in the clichéd expressions of 'adding one's mite to the pile' or 'doing one's bit', as if green consumers were brave little ants constructing a better future, or to 'small streams forming big rivers', as if individual acts would add up in some fairly unproblematic way. Excerpts 1 to 4 illustrate how the primary importance of an individual consumer is discursively constructed in the texts (emphasis added).

Excerpt 1:   *In environmental protection, my objectives would not be set as high as many others' [objectives], I would only just* add my mite to the pile, *and I would be happy to be just another ant among others. Even the biggest and most enthusiastic ant cannot build an anthill by itself, but a large number of little workers, striving towards a common goal, can achieve miracles. I would not get frustrated even if I faced hardship, and I would help other, frustrated people to concentrate their forces correctly. (MaleLM000)*

Excerpt 2:   *Contributing to the development of the well-being of nature and society is important. Happiness in life is also a result of being conscientious, caring about others and nature, and being considerate. I believe that everybody can have an effect with his/her personal input.* 'Small streams grow into a big river.' *Every deed, big or small, is important. When one remembers this, it is much more difficult to forget one's decision, for example to recycle, or to cut down on [buying] over-packaged products. It is also necessary that environmental problems are recognized in the political circles, and that something is done to avoid them. This is an issue that ordinary citizens can influence by pooling their forces. (FemaleSV000)*

Excerpt 3:   *Environment-friendliness is part of my everyday life and it builds on small everyday things to which I am ready to commit myself. I want to* add my mite to the pile *to ensure a clean environment also for the future generations. (FemaleUK199)*

Excerpt 4:   *... one has to remember that many little streams form big rivers which run into the sea. (MaleJV000)*

As I will elaborate in the sections that follow, the individualist discourse tends to represent green consumers as hardy individuals and decent, or rather exemplary, citizens who tirelessly but with a relatively 'low profile' work towards sustainable development. It underlines the virtue of doing small but momentous deeds, guided by a rigid personal ethic, and motivated by a firm confidence in their ability to make a difference. The discourse can be described as individualist in the sense that it accentuates the primary importance of the individual and the virtues of self-reliance and personal independence in the pursuit of sustainable development.

MAKING A DIFFERENCE THROUGH RATIONAL MANAGEMENT AND CAREFUL MONITORING   In the 'rational household management' discourse on green consumerism, the possibility of social change and sustainable development is generally attributed to informed moral choices, and to tenacious and careful, even meticulous, monitoring of everyday consumption activities. In the texts drawing on this discourse, global social change, for example, was seen to 'always [start] with single acts' (also Excerpt 14) by the individual, as Excerpt 5 shows.

> Excerpt 5:   *A positively thinking green consumer is not yet discouraged but believes that change is possible. S/he considers it important and himself/herself believes in it, that change always starts from the individual. When individual people behave in an environment-friendly way the overall effect becomes significant. (MaleJL782)*

In the texts that drew on the rational household management discourse the ideal green consumers were represented as 'prudent and critical consumers', unconditionally taking the time and effort to become informed and to engage in various forms of consumption-related reducing, reusing and recycling activities. Most of the texts included long and thorough *lists of different environmentally responsible behaviors* in which green consumers customarily engage. The following, clearly ironizing excerpt illustrates the morale and commitment a green consumer must have in constantly and carefully, almost obsessively, monitoring his or her behavior.

> Excerpt 6.   *Not for the whole world would I buy any Hennes & Mauriz's clothes made in the developing countries by cheap child labor, by small, poor, Hindu children under compulsion, or get new clothes needlessly, for that matter. At no price, moreover, would I put meat in my shopping basket at the [meat] counter of S-mart, I would also rapidly pass the shelves of precooked foods, and head straight to the organic food shop. Pepsi Max is only a pair of words, repeatedly uttered by the TV-brainwashed youth of the Western welfare states, I could not even imagine pouring it down my throat. I drink green tea that, for sure, is not picked in the child-labor-fields of India. And buying it intelligently, I verify its ethically acceptable origin. Luckily, my handy vegan guide has a comprehensive list of all the products that one is allowed to buy at S-mart, and I do not constantly have to disentangle the origin of all foodstuffs and not necessarily even read the list of ingredients. (FemaleM-137)*

Surprisingly, the significance of the individual and the meaningfulness of constant monitoring of choices and behaviors were barely questioned explicitly in the texts. Many texts, however, implied that sustainable development also requires political agreements, thus contesting implicitly the belief in the individual, as Excerpt 7 illustrates (also Excerpt 14).

> Excerpt 7:   *In environment friendliness, as in everything else, one has to use common sense. People should not constrain their lives with meticulous rules and regulations, but it is important to tackle the correct problems. The definition of major courses of action is the start of sustainable development. (MaleAT417)*

THE RESPONSIBLE GREEN CONSUMER: CIVIC DUTY FOR FUTURE GENERATIONS   The notion of *self-control* appears to be a central moral theme in the dominant individualist discourse of green consumerism. The discourse has a certain type of Puritan undertone, and tends to associate immorality with excess and surplus, and morality with moderation and self-restraint. Thus, the individualist discourse tends to represent green consumers as being *guided by more or less rigid moral and practical rules*. In this discourse, the motivation for being green seems to be attributed largely to a sense of duty and personal responsibility for environmental quality and for the well-being of future generations that go *beyond the pleasures of conspicuous or 'binge consumption' and self-indulgence*. Moreover, the individualist discourse tends to impose a norm on green consumers to *serve as an example* to the other, not yet enlightened, consumers. Green consumers are also expected to involve others and inform their peers about environmental issues, but in a moderate, non-preaching manner (see again Excerpt 14).

The following two excerpts illustrate how these ideas are produced. In Excerpt 8, the text presents a rational argument for green consumerism. The respondent feels that if she values an unpolluted environment, and if she believes that one person can make a difference, the only rational moral conclusion is that she must engage in environmentally responsible behaviors to fulfill her duty. In the second excerpt the writer underlines the exemplary nature of green consumerism and the association of morality with moderation and self-restraint.

> Excerpt 8:   *As a green consumer I value clean nature and fresh air. I appreciate even small attempts to cut down pollution and littering. I believe that only a single person has a big influence on the balance of nature, and that the input of every human being has an impact on the state of the environment. For that reason, I do my best to put as small a burden on nature as possible; I recycle, separate waste, and use environment friendly products, etc. This way I can feel that I am fulfilling my duty for a better environment. (FemaleKT000)*

> Excerpt 9:   *The green consumer does not seek acceptance for his/her behavior in his/her environment but s/he wants to act as an example … Fame and glory cannot be achieved with fancy things or materialistic wants but with the right and exemplary conduct. (FemaleAJ142)*

Hence, in the individualist discourse, self-control and a sense of environmental responsibility are seen as civic virtues, standing in stark contrast to the predominant 'irrational' and corrupted mood of contemporary 'throw-away' consumer culture with its indifferent and self-indulgent consumers demanding simple, conveniently packaged and easy solutions. The following excerpts (Excerpts 10–12) illustrate the image of contemporary Western consumers and consumer culture that the individualist discourse produces.

> Excerpt 10:   *Nowadays people consume absurd amounts with no consideration for nature. The only thing they think about is their own belly button, their own pleasure, which they want to get as fast and as easily as possible. Nature is overcharged because of the conceit of human beings. (FemaleTH061)*

> Excerpt 11:   *We are so used to our easy life, surrounded by innumerable products and services, that rational thinking is becoming obscured. (FemaleM137)*

Excerpt 12: *The laziness and indifference of people are things that I dislike. Cars are driven to go only to the other side of the block because one is too lazy to walk or cycle, and the idea of the detrimental impact of exhaust fumes on the environment does not even come to mind. (FemaleTH130)*

Furthermore, the individualist discourse on green consumerism appears to draw from some sort of rational, 'Quaker' critique of the consumption culture, emphasizing the strictly instrumental value of products. The products green consumers buy and the clothes they wear must be simple, durable and practical, instead of wasteful, extravagant and ostentatious. The excess meaning and value ascribed to products, over and above their functional utility, is seen as false or as incapable of fulfilling 'true needs', thus merely distracting people from pursuing the right and sensible things in life. The following example from the texts exemplifies these views:

Excerpt 13: *I do not value material things and I do not gather unnecessary things around me. I only buy what I really need, and even then I choose the product carefully ... I am not looking for social prestige or acceptability from others, so products have only instrumental value for me. Because I do not search for social status through consumption, the brand of the product does not provide me with additional value either. Brands that symbolize success do not interest me; I get a feeling of being appreciated from other things ... In my opinion, a short span of interest, indifference, and selfishness with respect to both the environment and other people are characteristic of contemporary society. I do not run after success and mammon because I do not consider it sufficient to make life meaningful. (FemaleSM261)*

Hence, the discourse constructs a view of Western materialistic consumption culture as if it were merely an aggregate of the personal characteristics, that is, self-indulgence, lack of morals, and the behavior of individual consumers. There is no reference to the institutionalized and structural nature of the consumer culture and the ways in which it guides and constrains our everyday thinking, reasoning and behavior.

THE ROLE OF POLITICS AND BUSINESS As can be seen from the extracts given above, the responsibility for sustainable development in the dominant discourse is placed with the individual consumer whose role is primarily to 'vote with the dollar'. In fact, surprisingly few texts analyzed here referred to the role and responsibility of government and politicians in sustainable development. The two words generally used to describe the green consumer's expectations toward society, legislators and politicians are '*to wish*' or '*to hope*'. The green consumer hopes that 'environmental problems are recognized in political circles, and that something is done to avoid them' (Excerpt 2, above), and '[wishes] that environmental problems also received more attention at the societal level'(Excerpt 14, below). But, involving politicians is clearly just another task or good deed to be shouldered by the environmentally responsible individual.

Excerpt 14: *I wish that environmental problems also received more attention at the societal level. Especially in Western cultures, where the current way of life is largely guided by*

materialistic values, people's knowledge about the environment and about the importance
of environmental protection could be increased through legislation or through societal
advertising, for example ... As a person who has adopted a green lifestyle, I do not
merely try to change things through my own consumption and through personal con-
duct. I am also a member of some environmental organizations that aim to influence
some, according to my views, important issues at the societal level. In addition, I also
wish that my friends and the people close to me would adopt an environmentally
friendly way of life so I regularly try to remind them about the fact that global change
always starts with single acts. (FemaleJJ155)

However, as regards the political aspirations attributed to green consumerism,
the dominant individualist discourse appears to produce a version of green consumerism that is clearly reformist or accepts as axiomatic that the dominant social
paradigm and, thus, the status quo should be maintained. The texts drawing from
this discourse often headed off anticipated criticism and allegations of bigotry and
political radicalism by different techniques of stake management. *Stake inoculations*
such as the following were common:

Excerpt 15:   *I am not necessarily a* viherpipertäjä *[a pejorative expression for a green activist]*
              shouting slogans at the barricades, but a logically thinking person. (FemaleKJ546)

The role and responsibility of business in sustainable development is represented
in much the same way as the role of political decision-making. In the data, consumers were given the responsibility to patronize environment friendly companies, principally The Body Shop, and boycott the 'unfriendly companies',
especially multinational corporations and particularly McDonald's, Nestlé and
Shell. Green or sustainable marketing was hardly referred to directly, and when it
was, the responsibility was placed with the consumer:

Excerpt 16:   *The responsibility for the environment does not reside with the firms only – rather quite*
              the contrary. The firms using child labor, for example, would not exist if nobody bought
              their products. The same goes for polluting or otherwise environmentally harmful
              branches of industry, for example automobile and tobacco industry. In this context, the
              role of marketing remains somewhat ethically questionable. Consumer values should not
              only be theoretical, but should be evident in all questions related to buying decisions:
              what to buy, when to buy, where to buy, how to buy, and from whom to buy. There
              are many questions but they are easy to solve if one has defined one's values and one's
              role in society beforehand. (MalePJ149)

Moreover, with only a few exceptions (Excerpt 16) in the texts calling on the
individualist discourse of green consumerism, there was almost complete silence
about the possible *negative* role of 'normal' everyday marketing activities in sustainable development. Green-washing was discussed (Excerpt 19), and marketing
was recognized as a technology of social change (Excerpt 14), but its obvious role
in producing, reproducing and strengthening the dominant consumer culture,
which was nevertheless acknowledged as one of the causes of environmental
degradation, was not discussed. According to the marketing ideology, the texts

appeared to attribute environmental problems to the unsustainable needs and wants of consumers, which marketers merely satisfy.

Hence, the green consumer, especially in the Western market societies, is represented as having not only a central role and responsibility but also significant *power* in environmental protection, as the majority of the texts analyzed here argued. The following excerpt illustrates these views:

Excerpt 17:   *In my opinion, the ordinary consumer has very powerful weapons in the fight against the destruction of nature. It is evident that on a large scale the supply side, production methods, raw material choices, emissions from plants, and other factors that have an effect on the well-being of nature must be influenced. [But] by choosing products that are manufactured and processed in a way that is as nature friendly as possible and has as small a burden [on the environment] as possible, an ordinary consumer can influence production methods indirectly. Constantly seeking information on one's own initiative is important as is communication. (FemaleSM280)*

In most texts, moreover, it was taken more or less for granted that firms have a considerable stake in the contemporary 'consumption binge', and that they cannot really be expected to take responsibility for changing the dominant unsustainable consumption culture. Hence, firms were not so much expected to practice honest and open marketing communication, but rather, as one of the respondents put it, were *appreciated* for pursuing such practices. In other words, in the dominant individualist discourse reasonable green consumers are represented as not being entitled to have realistic expectations or to make demands for firms to be completely trustworthy in their green marketing activities, as the following excerpts indicate. Excerpt 19 is especially interesting for the subtle ways in which it ascribes responsibility to green consumers. While addressing the issue of green washing and the need to cooperate with environmental organizations, it suddenly brings up the role and responsibility of consumers, thus laying part of the blame for corporate green washing on green consumers who do not buy the environment-friendly products. Moreover, green washing is in a sense represented as operating according to the principle of 'doing small good deeds', as the consumers are expected to behave.

Excerpt 18:   *I appreciate firms that invest in 'greenness' more than laws and regulations require. (FemaleRA062)*

Excerpt 19:   *Many large firms have fortunately started paying more attention to environmental issues and they are developing environment-friendly products. If one could only get people to take an interest in these products. A bad thing, in this, is that many firms create an image of themselves as environment-friendly and thereby succeed in creating a positive image of the company, whereas in reality the environment friendliness of the company applies only to a small part of the production of the company. Firms should start cooperating with the leading conservation organizations. These organizations would surely have something to contribute to development, [adding to] the company's own research resources. (MaleVV850)*

To conclude, I wish to emphasize that this analysis on the ways in which the representation of green consumerism was constructed in the texts, represents only the early phases of an analysis that also aims to investigate the power effects of the cultural discourses and the ways in which they are to be resisted. The purpose here was only to illustrate how cultural texts can be read to find evidence of discursive practice.

Notes

1 Analytic induction refers to a procedure in which preliminary hypotheses are first generated from a small body of data, and then more cases are taken for closer examination and reformulation of the hypotheses. Examination of cases, redefinition of the phenomenon and reformulation of hypotheses are repeated until an omnipresent relationship can be shown (Peräkylä, 1997).

2 Deviant case refers to a case where some element of the suggested pattern is not associated with the other expected elements (Peräkylä, 1997: 210).

8

Criteria for Good Cultural Analysis

CHAPTER SUMMARY

This chapter elaborates on the criteria for good cultural analysis in the context of marketing and consumer research. It also serves as a summary of the view on cultural data analysis that we have been discussing in this part of the book. It is proposed that:

- insightfulness and relevance;
- methodological coherence and transparency;
- sensitivity to phenomenon;
- sensitivity to ethics and politics of interpretation, as well as
- communication and credibility are important evaluative criteria for cultural analysis.

Basis for defining criteria

There is considerable debate over what constitutes a good interpretation in cultural research. As discussed in previous chapters, data analysis cannot be thought to yield any single, final, correct, complete or definite interpretation. Rather, there are multiple possible interpretations, each of them being necessarily partial. Acknowledging this, the question arises whether it is possible to distinguish any particular interpretation as better, more correct, or more justified, than any other.

We aim to avoid the absolute relativist view that any interpretation is as good as any other. Instead, with Helen Longino (2002) we take the view that validity and justification of any interpretation is subject to epistemic norms of internal coherence as well as correctness based on empirical constraints (for a good discussion see Schwandt, 2003). In the same vein, we take the view that the scientific community plays a key role in defining the 'goodness' of an analysis: the emergent consensus of the scientific community confers greater authority for some interpretations than others. Ultimately, all standards of evaluation rest on a research community's agreement.

Moreover, as we discussed in Chapter 2, evaluative criteria cannot be thought of as any theory-free list. Rather, criteria arise from and are tightly interwoven with the philosophical and theoretical assumptions of the research, and accordingly, the criteria that we are proposing here draw from the basic assumptions that we have discussed throughout the book. Drawing on these premises we emphasize ways of generating interpretations that place a premium on the following features:

- insightfulness and relevance;
- methodological coherence and transparency;
- sensitivity to the phenomenon;
- sensitivity to the ethics and politics of interpretation;
- communication and credibility.

In the remainder of this section we elaborate on each of these criteria. They should not be treated as fixed criteria that would decisively determine the correctness and goodness of interpretations. Rather, by presenting one possible way of thinking about analytical criteria, we wish to promote further discussion on what constitutes a good analysis in the context of cultural marketing and consumer research.

To start, we wish to point out that a precondition of a good analysis is good data. By good data we do not refer to any particular form of data, but to data that are relevant with respect to the research question and the analytic methods applied. For instance, if you aim to conduct a discourse analysis based on interview data, interviews that contain only answers such as 'hmmm' or 'yes' or 'no' do not necessarily provide good empirical material for such an analysis. Another precondition of a good analysis is that it is rigorous and imaginative. That is, data must be fully and thoroughly worked with, not merely scanned through, and the data must be worked with imagination, not merely in a mechanical manner. Also, as there are plenty of ways of engaging with the data, and conducting analysis, the researcher should make principled, theoretically and methodologically well-informed decisions and explicit choices, as Amanda Coffey and Paul Atkinson (1996) aptly remind us. The skilled cultural researcher also communicates the findings clearly, and is attuned to the moral responsibilities he or she has as a researcher.

Insightfulness and relevance

First and foremost, a good analysis *develops disciplinary knowledge* on marketplace behaviour by offering *new theoretical insights* into the problem at hand. An insightful analysis challenges and unsettles particular features of the existing body of knowledge and in so doing turns attention to a new direction, thus opening up a new horizon for new questions to be asked. Put differently, a good analysis yields insight that leads to revisions in pre-understandings and in doing so it provides the joy of learning more about the phenomenon. In this sense, a good analysis urges change instead of adherence to the status quo.

For instance, a good analysis on a marketplace phenomenon may help readers to become aware of assumptions that are built into disciplinary positions, into ways of seeing and comprehending the market in a particular way. In cultural market research this means, for instance, that taken-for-granted pre-understandings of segmentation as a mere strategic and managerial tool are revised, as in a study of Lisa Peñaloza (1994). Her study illustrates the ways in which segmentation is a means through which agencies become created for people in contemporary society.

Obviously, defining something as 'insightful' is not theory or context-free. What is considered 'insightful' can be defined only against some previous theoretical debate in some particular research community: what is insightful in one literature and in one community is not necessarily so in that of another. Therefore, a good analysis is closely situated to the body of literature it seeks to develop, and it explicitly shows *how* the analysis contributes to this literature, what it provides that is new.

By situating and linking the analysis tightly to the existing body of literature, the researcher also shows its *relevance*. (Being relevant refers to being connected with what is happening, what is being discussed.) Besides the theoretical relevance, a good analysis may well be relevant for social policy-makers and for market practitioners, as we have discussed in the beginning of this book.

Relevance also refers to the appropriate *focus* of the analysis: that the study displays only those parts of the analysis that are relevant for the particular debate in question. Instead of reporting everything found during the analytic process, a good analysis reports particular features in a focused manner.

On the whole, hence, an insightful and relevant cultural analysis always presents a broad-ranging knowledge upon which it draws: it draws widely on previous marketing and consumer knowledge as well as from other knowledge relevant to the phenomenon. This is because 'no amount of routine analytic work will produce new theoretical insights without the application of disciplinary knowledge and creative imagination' (Coffey and Atkinson, 1996: 192).

Methodological coherence and transparency

Methodological consistency and general coherence may be viewed as some sort of general goals for a good cultural analysis. This means that a good analysis leans on a particular, well-chosen methodological perspective, respects it throughout the study, and produces interpretations from this particular perspective.

As widely acknowledged in contemporary cultural research, the interpretations that are produced are not considered to represent 'the one and only truth'; rather, they present one way of interpreting and making sense of the phenomenon. Therefore, anyone attempting to evaluate such an interpretation must accept that there may be a multiplicity of readings. Accordingly, it is of crucial importance that the cultural researcher makes his or her interpretive perspective as open and explicit as possible; from which stance are interpretations produced? The researcher should openly explicate his or her methodological and theoretical starting points and underlying ontological and epistemological assumptions.

Moreover, a good analysis reports and explicates the process of arriving at conclusions in a transparent way. An honest and open account of the actual procedures used for arriving at the conclusion adds credibility and trustworthiness to the study. This relates to the explicitness of not only the methods used but also of the analytical procedures. Whatever methods and procedures are adopted they should be documented systematically and with detail. In evaluating an analysis, hence, the reader should be able to detect *how* and *why* particular methods and particular analytical procedures were used.

A good analysis also provides relevant reflexive accounts of the research process and the researcher's place in it. This directive seems quite evident since the practice of reflexivity has nearly become an obligation in current cultural inquiry. By most accounts 'reflexivity is a deconstructive exercise for locating the intersections of author, other, text, and the world, and for penetrating the representational exercise itself' (Macbeth, 2001: 35). This directive means that a good analysis examines the researcher's own position in order to understand how it shapes the analytic exercises ('positional reflexivity') and/or the very exercises of textual representation ('textual reflexivity'). However, we wish to stress that the analyst should clearly explicate what is the *analytical value* of 'being reflexive' in that particular piece of study instead of merely 'being reflexive' because it happens to be a trendy topic in current methodological debates. That is, a good analysis answers explicitly the question: *how* does reflexivity serve professional analytic purposes?

Sensitivity to the phenomenon

A good cultural analysis shows fidelity and respect to the phenomenon under study. It is not based on following trendy analytical constructs, methods, or theories to apply them to whatever phenomena come to mind. Nor is it based on applying analytical methods in a factory-like manner, mechanically and efficiently. Instead, a good analyst puts considerable time and effort into trying to understand the particularities of the phenomenon. It is informed by a careful consideration of what sorts of methods and analytical procedures may best capture these particularities. Such an analysis seeks to find and create innovative ways of grasping the essential in the phenomenon under study, to learn the most out of it.

In other words, the analyst is attuned to specificities afforded by the text, and aims at listening to what the objects of their interpretation say, acknowledging that what they say will be different in light of the changing horizons of interpretations and the different questions researchers learn to ask.

Sensitivity to the ethics and politics of interpretation

Good cultural analysis of marketplace phenomena is also concerned with the ethics and politics of interpretation. This is because interpretation – and the whole process of inquiry–always is, in some sense, ideological, political and permeated with values. As Elisabeth Hirschman (1986: 238), among others, remarks: 'research inquiry is inherently value-laden because researcher values inevitably influence the choice of phenomenon, choice of methods, choice of data, and choice of find-ings'. Also, the researcher makes choices during the process of interpretation. Researchers cannot think of themselves as neutral analysts of the market. Rather, through the numerous choices they make, researchers exercise power. In producing particular interpretations, the analyst is inevitably taking sides. Therefore, it is a good research practice that researchers reflect upon the role and status they have in society, and in the settings where they carry out their studies, and think of the kinds of implications that particular interpretations may have (Schwandt, 2003).

Some research projects – especially those inspired by critical theory and feminism – explicitly locate the interpretive project within some emancipatory and transformative agenda. These projects are committed to the task of interpre-tation for purposes of criticizing and dismantling unjust and undemocratic social practices, so as to transform them. Different theoretical traditions and movements, however, take a somewhat different view on the question of what is the possibil-ity of an interpretive project producing a change in the society (Schwandt, 2003).

Moreover, we consider the ethical criteria important for evaluating the quality of cultural analysis of the marketplace. We wish to promote an analysis that produces *ethically sustainable knowledge* and which is produced through *ethically sustainable research practices*. Let us explain. Generally conceived, ethical research practices refer to particular standards and practices to be adopted towards others in carrying out our research. The methodological classes commonly take up the ethical dimension of doing research – issues related to privacy and anonymity for instance – and various institutions have developed explicit ethical codes to be followed in conduct-ing research. In these discussions, primary attention is often given to ethical issues concerned with the relation between the researcher and those researched.

Moreover, we wish to draw attention to ethical practices of the research community. That is, to ethics related to the ways in which researchers treat other researchers, colleagues, team-members and peers. This relation is of importance in the context of interpretation, since it is in the community that interpretations are produced, developed and evaluated. How do we as researchers treat other researchers? Do we acknowledge their work? Do we cause harm for our col-leagues by producing particular interpretations? Do we give credit to those who merit it, those who have, for instance, greatly helped us in producing interpreta-tions? How do we behave in conferences and seminars? Are we ready to help others or merely want others to help us?

On the whole, ethical dimensions are pertinent to how researchers conduct their work through all stages of the research process from project planning to disse-mination. We shall discuss the ethics of co-authoring in the last part of the book.

Communication and credibility

Finally, a good cultural analysis is well written. We discuss the topic of research writing in more detail in the following chapters, but here we wish to highlight the ways in which writing may be thought of as an important evaluative criterion for analysis.

First, skillful writing adds to the credibility of the study: readers should have faith in interpretations and inferences drawn from them in reading the analysis. The interpretations made by an analyst must be credible and the links between the empirical data and the claims made about them clear. Therefore, in writing you should try to make visible the inferential processes that connect the end product of research to its data, and evidence your findings with relevant empirical examples. But as we have pointed out, the empirical examples do not 'speak for themselves'; it is the relevant theoretical frame that makes them speak in a particular, and interesting, way. Therefore, a good analysis goes beyond merely reporting accounts of daily life. It does display the complexity of the phenomenon studied but it does it by displaying the structures-in-use. It exhibits both constitutive and contextual sensibilities drawing attention to the fine-grained details of daily life, but also showing links to the wider discourses.

In writing analysis that is also ethically sustainable you should not only pay attention to the respondents (for example, by considering anonymity), but also to those you have worked with (for example, in terms of references). Moreover, you should also consider the reader. It is good ethical practice to think of the reader and not to waste his or her time by providing insignificant descriptions, and badly written and poorly argued analysis. It is part of ethics to work with your expressive quality and seek to offer an analytical account that is persuasive, engaging, interesting, stimulating and appealing (Arnold and Fischer, 1994). This brings us to emphasize the rhetorical nature of an interpretation and communication. Rhetoric is argumentation aimed at the dialogic community and it covers all modes of discourse that aim at persuasion and conviction. The selection of alternative interpretations is, ultimately, a matter of argumentation and debate.

As we have highlighted the key role of scientific community and attendant dialogue in the practice of conducting market inquiry, we consider the communicative quality of an analysis as an important evaluative criterion. Briefly put, the researcher should take into account the audience in writing the analysis. Accordingly, the writer should address the intended audience with both a terminology and a set of ideas to which they can easily relate. As Arnold and Fischer put it (1994: 64), the interpretation should be comprehensible to the audience given their pre-understanding. It should show 'good will' by adapting to them and taking into account their world-view. Therefore, in writing for audiences that are less familiar with particular modes of analysis, for instance, be more explicit about what you do with data and how your conclusions are built up from your interpretations.

EXERCISE 8.1   Criteria for good analysis

Take one published study on cultural marketing and consumer research *or* an on-going study of your own, and evaluate it using the criteria outlined above. What do the criteria mean in that particular study? Does the study meet the requirements we have proposed?

Part 4

Writing Cultural Research

Throughout this book we have been discussing a range of market-related cultural texts and textual practices. Part 4 sets out to discuss the texts that cultural marketing and consumer researchers produce, and the textual practices that they use in the course of the research process. Our primary objective is to make our readers aware of a range of theoretical, methodological and ethical debates that concern research writing. In so doing, we aim to highlight the ways in which theoretical foundations and writing are inseparable.

We begin by discussing the debate on 'the crisis of representation'. At the heart of this debate there is the question of how researchers can adequately represent the results of their work to others. In Chapter 9, we elaborate on this question, highlighting issues such as: What does it mean for marketing and consumer researchers that writing is no longer considered an unproblematic activity that produces neutral accounts and transparent reports of the world that is being studied? Why should researchers carefully consider for whom they speak, with what voice, and to what end? What are the legitimate ways of knowing and telling? What is actually the role of writing in the process of doing research?

In Chapter 10, we move on to discuss questions related to writing up the final research report or paper. Although we are open to divergent styles of writing, we take the view that the aim of academic research writing is, first and foremost, *to put forth arguments*. We also draw attention to the key role of the audience in research writing, and discuss the ways in which writing – and reading – takes place within particular research communities. We also take up the issue of co-authoring and the ethical issues concerning authorship credit and authorship order, which we consider important especially for doctoral students. To close the book, we discuss the art of publishing cultural marketing and consumer research – and the peculiar power games it may involve.

9

Writing in Cultural Research

CHAPTER SUMMARY

In this chapter we take up the topic of *writing* in cultural research. We argue that writing constitutes a key research activity throughout the research process, and that writing cannot be characterized as a neutral and unproblematic activity. We elaborate on these views through discussing the problematics of research writing from the following perspectives:

* the process of writing – writing as a method of inquiry;
* the poetics of writing – ways of representing research; and
* the politics of writing.

Introduction

Writing is a key activity of any researcher. Researchers are professionals who must write whether they like it or not. Ultimately, the advancement of their professional careers is based on their scholarly production, and that means writing, as Harry Wolcott reminds us (1990: 11). In contemporary cultural research, writing is, however, much more than just a craft skill needed to 'write up' final results and to climb the career ladder. The so-called crisis of representation – uncertainty about what constitutes an adequate depiction of social reality – has turned researchers' critical attention to research writing as a discursive practice and to the methodological issues involved (Clifford and Marcus, 1986). In this chapter we set out to discuss some of these issues and draw attention to the multiple choices and options that research writing entails.

The primary objective is to problematize conventional understandings of research writing. We encourage you to reflect critically on the styles and strategies of writing that you use when discussing and communicating your research results. In our experience, people – students and senior scholars alike – often mimic, fairly unreflectively, the sources they use when working on a research paper. This is sometimes a good strategy because particular research communities and journals often adhere to particular writing conventions, which researchers need to accommodate if they wish to have their papers published and their ideas taken seriously. Such default writing strategies, however, are not necessarily well suited for all audiences and for all theoretical contexts. Therefore, in this chapter we wish to put forth the idea that research writing is to be based on informed and explicit stylistic and rhetorical choices.

As we puzzle through the problematics of writing, three intertwined issues are at the forefront: *process* of writing, *poetics* of writing and *politics* of writing. We start with the process of writing. That section is concerned with the roles that writing plays in different stages of the research process, and how it may be viewed as a method of inquiry. Then we turn to discuss the poetics and politics of writing. The poetics of writing refers to different textual practices and ways of representing research as well as to the particular views of knowledge and science that inform those practices. The politics of writing, in turn, refers to the idea that all texts are implicitly or explicitly political because they construct and reproduce certain views of social reality. In practice, poetics and politics are inseparable, but to highlight the various dimensions of research writing we discuss them separately. We start the chapter by briefly introducing the 'crisis of representation', which underwrites the intellectual background of the emerging debate on writing in cultural research.

Hence, in this chapter we are not concerned with craft skills of putting thoughts on paper. Rather, we are concerned with the consequences of putting consumers and other market actors on paper, and with the multiple ways in which this may be done. For practicalities of writing, there are several excellent 'how-to' books available, for instance Wolcott (1990) and Silverman (2000: 221–53). All the practical advice we give here, with Wolcott, is: Get the words down, you can always change them. Actually, you *must* change them, since texts can never be produced ready-made: 'Writing is first and foremost analyzing, revising and polishing the text', as Alasuutari (1995: 178) among others points out. Writing is – rewriting.

Writing after the crisis of representation

Over the past two decades, writing has become a central topic of theoretical and methodological discussion and debate in cultural research. A whole range of academic conventions of research writing are being challenged and rethought (Clifford and Marcus, 1986; Denzin and Lincoln, 2002; Richardson, 2000). This debate has been most vivid among ethnographers (Clifford and Marcus, 1986; Van Maanen, 1988), but also consumer and marketing researchers have been wrestling with it (Brown, 1995, 1999; Sherry and Schouten, 2002).

This debate is commonly known as the 'crisis of representation'. The crisis refers, briefly put, to an acknowledged uncertainty about what constitutes an adequate depiction of social reality. The crisis arose primarily from the acknowledgement that language does not reflect the world out there, but constitutes it. This led to the problematization of the very idea that qualitative researchers could directly capture people's lived experience. Many poststructuralist scholars emphasized that what researchers refer to as 'lived experience' is actually created in the social texts that they write. Research writing was therefore better understood as a discursive practice through which researchers not only made sense of social reality but also created it.

Acknowledging this, researchers are forced to draw attention to the ways in which various sorts of textual practices create particular views of social reality and silence others. As it is realized that the power to name things is the power to create particular meanings, writing can no longer be understood as a neutral or innocent scholarly activity. Research writing is rather an activity that involves different forms, relations and effects of power. Therefore, the ethical and political issues related to writing, reporting and publishing have become central.

Moreover, the crisis of representation has turned researchers' critical attention to the academic writing conventions and to the view of science they have come to rely on and sustain. As a result, new alternative forms and genres of presenting research results have been explored and suggested. And currently there no longer appears to be any single way – nor a 'right' way – to stage academic texts. Researchers rather face a range of options. They can present their work through fiction, drama, performance, or poetry, for example (Denzin and Lincoln, 2002; Ellis and Bochner, 2000; Sherry and Schouten, 2002).

These new forms of representation have emerged as a response to a set of questions that cultural researchers typically encounter when trying to write their research in a way that is in line with their theoretical and philosophical assumptions. As cultural research is based on the assumption that people live in a world that is constantly being produced and reproduced, a question arises whether or not the linear language of science is particularly suitable for representing the on-going circuit of meanings. Also, as the purpose of cultural research is neither to measure nor testify but rather to subvert and re-evaluate, it seems justified to ask whether many of the typical conventions of scientific reporting, which are generally geared to objectifying and naturalizing our accounts, should be problematized. How should we represent tacit knowledge or the visual world in a research report? And finally, how can we communicate and represent power relations? What sort of power relationships are being reproduced in the texts that we write? Does our writing reproduce a particular system of domination, and how could we hope to challenge that system?

Many of the new forms of research writing and representation that have emerged in recent years may be understood as an attempt to find new ways of producing and communicating knowledge that enhance the diffusion of power in social life. The objective has been to create 'texts' that are vital and can make a difference in society. It seems obvious that conventional academic writing is not well suited for reaching wide audiences.

Through the debates on writing, the role and nature of research writing has thus been rethought and puzzled out. One further theme in this debate is the important role of writing throughout the entire research process. Writing is not a mere mode of reporting the results but rather an open strategy of discovery – a method of inquiry.

Writing as a method of inquiry

Research writing is most commonly associated with writing up the final account, the research report. The final written account is built up of smaller, less coherent bits and pieces of writing that are produced throughout the different stages of study. These bits and pieces are not only raw material for the final report but also an important way of gaining insights into the topic. As Laurel Richardson (2000) among others has argued, writing is not merely a mode of telling, but also a mode of knowing, a method of inquiry. This section takes up this theme.

The idea of treating writing as a method of discovery derives from the very nature of qualitative inquiry. In methodological textbooks, qualitative research is typically described as a set of stages, as a process of reviewing literature, analyzing data, obtaining results, drawing implications, and then writing up and publishing the study. It is usually emphasized, however, that qualitative inquiry is a continuous learning process during which the topic, viewpoint, focus, research questions and problem statement are under continual scrutiny. It thus requires continuous analysis throughout the different stages of the process. So, you the researcher have to analyze the literature, not just review it; you have to analyze the data as well as the theoretical constructs that you choose to use to 'open up' the data, and you also have to analyze the writing conventions of the particular scientific community that you decide to attend to. And you do this largely through writing – making notes, keeping a journal, writing working papers and drafts. In the on-going process of doing qualitative research, writing is therefore a practice that serves to advance the research process throughout the project. Writing may be reinterpreted as a way of finding a problem and also resolving it (Wolcott, 1990: 31–2). In this sense, it is as much a means of discovery and analysis as a form of communication. It is, actually, a form of thinking.

The interplay of writing and thinking has been widely discussed (Mills, 2000; Richardson, 2000; Wolcott, 1990). Writing provides, first of all, a way to gain access to the personal fund of tacit information, to that continually growing store of ideas that first appear as most vague, unsure, hesitant and intuitive. It is precisely these vague ideas that are to be worked out, for they are indispensable to originality in any intellectual pursuit – 'it is in such forms that original ideas, if any, almost always first appear' (Mills, 2000: 212).

The first step in working on these vague ideas is to give them form, to name them and write them down. Merely to name an item of experience often invites you to explain it, and to further elaborate on it. Therefore, you should not let them pass from your mind, but try to formulate them and to write them down. Writing offers a way to capture and give concrete form to sometimes too-elusive ideas. Once thoughts are on paper, they have a physical embodiment. This practice transforms vague ideas into data – into objects that can be studied, elaborated and rethought. As these objects pile up, they call for connections to be made and implications to be drawn.

This practice of writing down your vague and emergent ideas is also a reflexive practice in which you can critically assess the ideas that you produce. The notes you write invite you into conversation with yourself. We have emphasized throughout the book that research always involves reflexive thinking, and writing provides a concrete tool for such an enterprise. It offers a fruitful way to develop self-reflexive habits, since a mere taking of a note is often a prod to start to think of it more carefully. Once they are put on paper, you may take a look at the ideas and start to ponder: What is this all about? What makes me think this way and not another way? This practice is a way 'to keep your inner world awake', as Mills nicely puts it (2000: 197).

Writing – and attendant reflexive thinking – also offers a way of discovering gaps in your thinking. In this sense, it offers a way of tracking what you have understood and discerning what you need to find out next. In doing so, writing provides a concrete track of your research – and also a proof of your advancement, which is psychologically most rewarding.

All this involves getting into the habit of constant and controlled writing, be it in the format of a research journal, memos or fieldnotes. Importantly, academic writing is not a matter of waiting for inspiration, but instead of maintaining a habit. This habit helps you to develop your powers of expression and also enables you to engage in a dialogue with your peers and colleagues. The most important benefit of continuously writing and rewriting is, however, that you are obliged to review and critically assess your topic, research questions and emerging interpretations. Such a procedure is an indispensable means of keeping the intellectual enterprise oriented and under control.

Although writing occupies such a central place in the analytical and creative process of doing qualitative research, the very question of 'how to write during the process' has not received considerable attention in (general) textbooks on qualitative methodology. The practice of writing has perhaps been most thoroughly discussed – and problematized – in ethnographic literature. For ethnographers, as we have discussed, a great amount of data is produced by writing, and the quality of research ultimately depends much on these writings. Therefore in the methodological literature on ethnography, close and systematic attention has been paid to the issue of writing sensitive, useful and simulating fieldnotes, as well as to the ways in which researchers can reflect upon their own writing (e.g., Emerson et al., 1995). We recommend that the ideas discussed in this literature be seriously considered and taken into account in all qualitative research, beyond ethnography. It is good practice, for instance, to make notes immediately after conducting interviews and focus groups, and also to submit these notes to critical, reflexive analysis. What made you write the particular notes you did, instead of some other kinds of notes? What sort of view on the market and market activity is written in these notes?

Moreover, the question of 'how to write during the process' has been discussed by Richardson, who has introduced the idea of creative analytical practices (CAP)

(Richardson, 2000: 934–5). It means that the researcher may draw freely from literary and artistic genres of various sorts – poetry, drama, photography or performance – in doing research. The rationale behind this is that different genres may provide a different angle on the phenomenon under study and thereby open previously unseen views and aspects of it. In a way, these creative methods enable the researcher to have different 'takes' on the same topic. Science is one lens, creative arts another. It is worth stressing, however, that the very aim of borrowing from the realm of the arts is to nurture scientific imagination, and thereby to *contribute* to some theoretical body of literature. The aim is not to try to become an artist.

The same idea of leaning on the realm of the arts for the purpose – or in the hope – of nurturing scientific imagination is already present in the classic work of C.W. Mills. He discusses role-playing as one method for producing a variety of viewpoints on the topic in question. It means that the researcher may think of him/herself as a historian or technician, for instance, and ask: what would a historian or technician say in reading my piece of research? What would a historian say of my study on the role of trust in *e*-commerce? What would a biologist say of my interpretation on the role of pets and the pet market in contemporary society? The point is really to write down this imaginary dialogue, and to reflect upon it. As he suggests: 'You try to think in terms of a variety of viewpoints and in this way to let your mind become a moving prism catching light from as many angles as possible. In this connection, the writing of dialogue is often very useful' (Mills, 2000: 214).

Also, in marketing and consumer literature, an arts-inflected approach can be identified, which appears to draw on the classical debate between art and science. As a result of this approach, significant insights into marketing and consumption phenomena have been obtained by means of the tools and techniques of arts in general and literature theory in particular (e.g., Brown, 1995, 1999; Scott, 1994; Stern, 1993). Another result of this arts-inflected approach is the body of studies that have investigated the ways in which marketplace phenomena are represented in works of literature and arts (e.g., Holbrook and Hirschman, 1993). This latter stream of research highlights the rapprochement of arts and science. Consider, for instance, the ways in which contemporary forms of art – such as novels and movies – are replete with depictions of marketing artifacts, or the ways in which artists apply the machinations of marketing to make themselves known (Brown, 1995).

You may well utilize these sorts of existing examples as sources of inspiration in developing creative analytical practices that you find generative for your own style of thinking and for your particular piece of research. We conclude this section with Richardson's point that: 'even when writing an article in a conventional form, trying on different modes of writing is a practical and powerful way to expand one's interpretive skills, raise one's consciousness, and bring a fresh perspective to one's research' (Richardson, 2000: 931). Different modes of writing may prove to be helpful in overcoming the inevitable troubles of conducting cultural research. In any case, whatever mode of writing you are using – also the most conventional form may well be fruitful – it surely advances your study. Writing is an integral part of the entire research process, from the vaguest notes to the most finished texts. So, keep writing.

The poetics of writing

The poetics of writing is currently a topic of widespread interest and discussion among cultural researchers. The 'poetics' refers to the various ways in which research may be represented: it covers the questions of style and genre, use of rhetorical devices and illustrations, and so forth. More and more authors in various fields have discerned that conventional forms of academic writing seem increasingly insufficient as vessels for representing our understandings or for inviting action in the world. As a result, these authors have paid particular attention to questions of writing and have continued to explore new ways of writing, such as fiction, drama, performance and poetry, in research texts (for a review see Denzin and Lincoln, 2002; Ellis and Bochner, 2000; Richardson, 2000).

Most academic disciplines have been affected, to varying degrees, by the current debate on the poetics of research writing. Most forcefully, perhaps, ethnographers and feminists have questioned the standard methods of inquiry and introduced new methods and forms of representing social reality. The new ethnographers, in particular, have challenged the realist agenda inscribed in generally accepted tenets of research methodology (Clifford and Marcus, 1986; Van Maanen, 1988). Feminist scholars, in turn, have forcefully resisted the tendency of mainstream social research to present the masculine voice as the standard or as equal to humankind, introducing alternative modes of representation for a more multi-vocal view of reality (Coffey, 1999).

Something of this resistance is now surfacing in the marketing and consumer literature. Postmodern, poststructuralist and feminist researchers, in particular, have challenged the received notions of legitimate knowledge and truth, and the ways in which marketing knowledge may be meaningfully represented (Bristor and Fischer, 1993; Brown, 1995, 1999; Firat and Venkatesh, 1995; Fischer and Bristor, 1994; Sherry and Schouten, 2002; see also Thompson et al., 1998). John F. Sherry and John W. Schouten (2002), for instance, discuss the ways in which poetry may contribute to the consumer research (see Box 9.1), while Stephen Brown (1999) analyzes 'marketing poetics' of the published works of two prominent marketing academics, Theodore Levitt and Morris Holbrook, by applying techniques of literary theory.

Box 9.1   The poetics of writing in consumer research

To exemplify the idea of poetics of writing, we illustrate how one non-realist form of writing, poetry, may be utilized to tackle a consumption-related theme. In the *Journal of Consumer Research*, Sherry and Schouten (2002) discuss the ways in which poetry may contribute to consumer research. They position their study as 'cultural phenomenology', and from this position – which is fairly different from the position that we have taken here – they seek to

(Continued)

understand consumption experiences. The authors argue that 'to communicate the essence of some of our most meaningful consumer experiences,
the precise, linear language of science and academia may be, in and of
itself, unsuitable' (2002: 219). Instead, they suggest that using the insight
of poets one is able to produce a more comprehensive account of understanding. This is because poetry highlights emotions that are, according to
them, crucial to consumption experience: lived experiences and attendant
emotions may be captured and represented through poems. Poetry may,
therefore, offer insight into consumers' hearts and minds as the authors
put it. It may also offer insight into the researchers' interpretations; authors
use poetry as a vehicle for researcher reflexivity, and through poetry
researchers are able to record personal reactions, thoughts and observation during the fieldwork.

Therefore, following Richardson (2000), Sherry and Schouten use poetry
in two ways: as a strategy of discovery and as a strategy of representation;
to get insight into the consumption experiences, and to represent these
experiences. Moreover, as they emphasize, poetry evokes a kinship between
author and reader, and it may therefore be used as a form of cultural dialogue
connecting the researcher and researched and the researcher and the
reader (Sherry and Schouten, 2002: 220).

By examining and also challenging the various modes of marketing discourse,
these sorts of studies have made explicit the often implicit disciplinary writing
practices and the sort of marketing ethos that they sustain. In particular, they
draw attention to the fact that the style of writing and the rhetorical devices
used – the scientific style – are not trivial, 'merely rhetorical' matters, but discursive practices that reflect particular epistemological and methodological criteria. Form and content are intertwined. As Elisabeth Hirschman has pointed
out: 'the types of scientific style utilized by researchers within the field will necessarily affect the content and structure of knowledge generated about consumption' (1985: 225).

For example, if a researcher operates under the flag of objectivity and truth, a
typical discursive practice is to represent the researcher as an unattached and
objective instrument, for example, by using the passive tense and thereby hiding
the writer. If you do not subscribe to this comprehension of knowledge creation,
you may not wish to resort to such discursive practices. Also, to further illustrate
the point, in studies that adopt the atomistic world-view, which has dominated
the marketing discipline in the past (as we shall discuss in Part 5), theories are typically represented using over-simplified four-cell matrices (Brown, 1995). In the
same vein, studies drawing from the information-processing paradigm, which is
based on the computer metaphor, tend to present results in ways that resemble
computer language and program flow charts (Hirschman, 1985). Unless critically
assessed, these forms come to favor, create and sustain a particular vision of the
world and norms for appropriate marketing knowledge.

All in all, it is our contention that marketing and consumer researchers will benefit from considering new ways of writing and representing their research results. Trying on new styles and techniques, researcher-writers may become more conscious of the received disciplinary conventions of writing, which may sometimes work against the objectives of cultural research. Being informed about different ways of writing and about the questions of representation may also help researchers to make explicit choices concerning their writing, as well as to elaborate on the likely consequences of these choices. Moreover, as we have discussed, these new forms may be fruitful in expanding researchers' analytical and interpretive skills by opening up fresh viewpoints.

Finally, and importantly, although genre is often thought of in relation to the work of authoring, it also plays an important role in the work of reading, as Barbara Tedlock reminds us (2003). Academic marketing language is not necessarily most suitable for all audiences, not even for marketing practitioners, as Stephen Brown (1999) points out. Therefore, mastering divergent forms of writing and representing may increase the size of the audience for the research. For instance, using visuals in presenting results may be worthwhile if the audience consists of advertising and communication personnel whose professional identity is largely based on a developed visual literacy. In any case, over the course of a career, a researcher typically has to utilize a number of genres to create and communicate findings to and for different groups of people.

This need for diversity in styles of writing is further accentuated by the moral and ethical ethos that drives contemporary cultural research; the challenge is to disseminate research results widely and effectively in the hope of improving human welfare and the quality of life of all human beings. Also, in the field of consumer inquiry, there has been a call to conduct consumer research that is designed to improve the awareness and general welfare of consumers (e.g., Firat, 2001). This nicely highlights the importance of the questions of audience and style we have been discussing: how to write, how to represent and for which audiences, through what kinds of communication vehicles, publication outlets and modes of expression?

The politics of writing

The politics of writing has also become a focus of increasing interest among cultural researchers. The interest is largely brought about by the ever-more generally shared view that language is a constitutive force, and that the relationship between words and worlds is anything but easy or transparent (Richardson, 1990, 2000). It is acknowledged that research writing, the choice of words, categorizations and rhetorical structures, creates a particular view of reality, and not some other kind. The texts that researchers write are political in the sense that they portray the often internally conflicting interrelationships among people in a society and thus inevitably get entangled in networks and relations of power, which are always played out in the texts as people read them. Language, politics and power are therefore inseparable. In this section, we draw attention to the ways in which being attentive to relations and effects of power is important in writing marketing and consumer research.

To start, we provide an example of the ways in which the rhetoric of the marketing relationship – and the manner in which the marketer/consumer relationship has been theorized – entrenches certain power interests and represses others. Adopting a poststructuralist feminist perspective, Eileen Fischer and Julia Bristor (1994) examine the rhetoric of marketing literature, focusing on the ways in which exchange relationships between consumers and marketers are constructed in the language of marketing academe. In practice, they 're-read' textual descriptions of each phase in the evolution of the marketing concept, from production orientation to relationship orientation, paying particular attention to the gendered nature of marketer/consumer relationships and the associated power dynamics.

Their analysis shows that as a theoretical construction the marketer/consumer relationship is thoroughly gendered and parallels the typical cultural talk on male/female relationships. According to their analysis, the notions of patriarchy and seduction become woven into the dominant conceptualizations of exchange relationships – and these conceptualizations are usually uncritically accepted and taken-for-granted in the marketing and consumer research literature. Consumers are represented, for example, as displaying flirtatious behaviors associated with the feminine, such as 'favoring', whereas marketing managers are described as engaging in decisive purposive behaviors associated with the masculine, such as 'concentrating' and 'achieving' (1994: 324). Overall, according to Fischer and Bristor's, analysis, a deeply embedded notion in marketing theory is that consumption is the opposite of production. Consumption has typically been represented as distinctly non-productive non-work that is simply self-gratifying, rather than potentially value-creating. As they conclude:

> The relationship of marketers to consumers in the rhetoric of the marketing concept can be read as akin to the relationship between male warriors and the females who occupy a territory they seek to conquer. The marketer/warriors determine what the consumer/targets really 'need'. (1994: 326–7)

This sort of critical analysis of the political aspects of textual representation is relevant not only for academic work but importantly also for general marketing texts. Much of marketing output – both academic and practical – is actually textually mediated. Think of published articles, draft papers, data analysis, computer printouts, interview protocols, respondent representations, methodological guidelines, existing literature, textbooks, marketing brochures, Web pages, organizational charts, direct marketing campaigns and so forth. These marketing artifacts exist through several, by no means transparent or neutral layers of textual practices, as Stephen Brown remarks (1999: 2).

It seems worth emphasizing, however, that being attentive to or self-reflective of the politics of representation in research work does not boil down to politically correct writing. Values and ideological assumptions are brought into play throughout the research process. Already favoring one conceptualization of reality over another or choosing a particular topic or 'problem' to be investigated may have political implications. Particular values and interests embedded in the background assumptions that guide the research process shape the selection of legitimate research problems, central concepts and research designs. For example, the emphasis on consumer choice over constraints in traditional consumer theory directs attention toward the autonomous and rational choices and stable preferences of economic actors instead of external constraints and, thus, undermines the influence of institutional constraints in directing people's choices. Moreover, as there are usually a set of possible stories that you can tell based on your data analysis, selecting a particular story to tell is an important and by no means neutral decision. By choosing a particular story, a particular way of writing and a particular point of view, researchers come to privilege one ordering of social reality over others.

Another closely related dimension of the politics of writing deals with texts that are *not* written – the sorts of issues, viewpoints, voices, topics, markets, countries, areas, brands, companies and so forth that are not present in the research texts. There is also reason to ask, what kinds of market-related stories are silenced and with what consequences? What power relationships are then being reproduced or challenged? Very often, as Craig Thompson and his colleagues (1998) point out, these questions are passed over without critical reflection, since the implicit rules and conventions of our research community make us 'automatically' see and privilege specific topics, issues and problems. Research agendas and paradigms are infused with power, which guides and constrains the formation of research problems and the ways in which they may be studied and narrated. Therefore, we recommend that you reflect upon your choice of topic and paradigms at an early stage of your research. And when you write down your first notes, first drafts or first conference papers, you may find it worthwhile to ask yourself to whom you give voice in your writings.

In any case, it is important to pay critical attention to the ways in which the people that you study are represented in your texts. Research writing is a discursive practice that creates agencies for people in the name of science. For example, if you study the so-called 'mature market' there is a big difference whether you call these people 'seniors' and 'elderly people' or 'babyboomers' or 'gray panthers'. Each of these terms has a very different connotation with respect to agency, and the use of each term may also have very different consequences. The words and categories that the researcher chooses to describe the participants of the study inevitably contain images and metaphors, which both assume and invoke particular ways of being. Members of 'the elderly segment' are generally viewed as less active market actors who consume health care services and live in homes for the elderly. 'Babyboomers' and 'gray panthers', on the other hand, may invoke images of more active senior citizens who enjoy their retirement, for example, by traveling around the world.

Categorization, therefore, is an important discursive practice through which we construct reality. Certain things (behaviors, characteristics) are known or taken for granted about any category, and categories can usually be read off the activities in which people engage. Any descriptive categorization formulates some item, person, or event as a particular entity with specific characteristics. For example, in a business negotiation associated with a cooperative research project between a university and a company it may well make a big difference whether a person trying to get his or her ideas accepted is categorized, represented and discursively positioned as a 'doctoral student' of a participating professor or as a 'former executive of a multinational company' who is currently working on a PhD. As a former executive this person is most probably expected to have valuable views on the complexities of corporate strategy-making. But as a doctoral student she or he may be expected to serve the professor and the other participants as a secretary. Moreover, categorization defines certain activities and subject positions as normal and acceptable, and others as abnormal and immoral. Categorizations are not innocent. Sometimes there is even a battle over which category is used (for example, terrorist *vs.* freedom fighter).

Consequently, it is not merely the naming of people but the whole way in which people are described and represented in reports that has to be carefully considered. Putting people on paper involves, therefore, wider questions than that of merely taking care of their anonymity. The discourse in which we write our results is as important as the language of the texts of the fieldnotes we analyze. As Richardson (2000) reminds us, taking the view that no textual staging is ever innocent we must turn our attention to ourselves, who are doing the staging. How should we as marketing and consumer researchers use our skills and privileges as *authors*? Unfortunately, however, when producing descriptions and accounts of the participants of their study, researchers often do not come to think about the assumptions that are associated with the specific words and categories that they use. Nor are they aware of the power of the images associated with these words and categories to invoke particular ways of being. They simply regard their words as normal for the way one talks on these sorts of occasions.

EXERCISE 9.1   Writing about writing

As writing constitutes such a crucial activity in an academic career, it is worthwhile reflecting upon your own particular relation to writing. For that purpose, we recommend the exercise offered by Laurel Richardson (2000: 941).

Write a writing autobiography, that is, a story of your experiences as a writer. What is your personal relation to writing, to the practice of putting words down? In what kinds of different contexts do you write? How has your relation changed during your life-course? How do you consider writing in a business academy?

This exercise helps you to be more aware of the various institutional guidelines and constraints that underlie your writing. School and university, in particular, are often crucial institutional backgrounds, with their special discourses.

EXERCISE 9.2   'Political' re-reading of your own texts

Take a critical look at some of your own texts. Re-read the texts paying particular attention to issues related to 'politics of writing'. What kind of a view of the market/science/people is the work based on? Through what sorts of textual practices have you produced these views?

FURTHER READING

Writing Culture: The Poetics and Politics of Ethnography by James Clifford and George Marcus is a classic collection of essays that explore the status of texts and authors from a number of perspectives, taking also into account their political and ethical contexts. Although the focus is on ethnographic texts, the book is valuable for any researcher interested in the question of representation in writing up qualitative research.

- Clifford, James and Marcus, George E. (1986) *Writing Culture: The Poetics and Politics of Ethnography*. Berkeley, CA: University of California Press.

10

Writing up Cultural Research

CHAPTER SUMMARY

Chapter 10 discusses the principles and practices of writing up the final research report, from the perspective of cultural marketing and consumer research. It focuses particularly on:

- writing as an institutionalized activity;
- the structure and content of good research reports; and
- publishing cultural research on marketing and consumption.

Introduction

This chapter is concerned with writing up the final report and thereby engaging in a constructive dialogue with the scientific community. We start our discussion by considering the ways in which academic writing – and reading! – takes place within the institutions and discursive frameworks of academia. As we have repeatedly pointed out throughout the book, the scientific community plays an important role in the production of knowledge throughout the research process. A particular scientific community, the editors and readers of a scholarly journal or the members of your PhD committee for example, are often the crucially most important audience of your work. Therefore you need to write your texts specifically to this audience, bearing the specific writing and reading conventions of this particular audience in mind. Doing this, it is important to pay attention to and deliberate on the styles and techniques that you use to increase your credibility as well as to initiate discussion and debate within the community. In our view, this is a challenging task that requires continuous learning.

In this chapter, we also take up the sometimes challenging issue of co-authoring. Cultural research tends to be based on the idea that knowledge creation is a collaborative endeavor and collective achievement. It is based on continuous processes of organizational and individual learning within particular institutional and cultural settings. Therefore, co-authoring would seem to be a particularly fruitful way of doing research and writing research texts. Co-authoring, however, entails a range of ethical issues that we wish to take up. We wish to work towards open and mutually agreed guidelines that help scholars and students to make decisions about authorship credit and authorship order.

Then, we turn to discuss the structure and content of a good cultural report. Our discussion is premised upon the assumption that the style of writing of a research report or paper should be consistent with the philosophical perspective adopted in the study that the text reports on. Therefore, we discuss styles and techniques of reporting developed particularly in the field of cultural studies, which we see as fit for the theoretical and methodological perspective that we discuss in this book. We do this fully acknowledging that there is a whole range of available styles and different conventions that shape the ways in which research reports are to be written and structured.

As we have often repeated, the final report is a place to tell readers what you have found out, and you should do this convincingly, credibly and interestingly. This activity is commonly comprehended as a story-telling activity, but we wish to stress that it is not merely a question of telling a story. Rather, the challenge is to put forth an interesting and well-grounded argument. The very point of academic writing is to say something specific about a particular debate or phenomenon to a particular audience – be it the scientific community, practitioners or any other market actors. In this chapter, we discuss what such an act of argumentation means and entails.

Finally, by way of closing the chapter, we discuss the art of publishing. As marketing researchers, we consider publishing a marketing task, and as by now you should have realized, no market is ever innocent and free of power games. We draw particular attention to the particular gatekeepers of this market, the editors and reviewers.

Research writing

Research writing is a thoroughly *institutionalized* activity. One writes within, and against, specific traditions and disciplines, and for specific *audiences*, with the aim of *contributing* to a certain body of literature. Like all writing, research writing is also a *rhetorical* activity, shaped by stylistic conventions through which social science authors aim to articulate their ideas convincingly and credibly. Importantly, these conventions are not fixed but differ from field to field, discipline to discipline, journal to journal, and also from country to country.

Therefore, although in the process of doing research we may be 'free' to choose our writing methods, in drawing up the final written account we must acknowledge the prescribed conventions that in given fields and periods define the proper reporting style. This means that the voice with which you may speak and the rhetorical devices you may use depend on the scholarly community you are part of. The prevailing writing conventions hold power over researchers: conforming to these conventions increases your chances of getting your submissions accepted into core journals. Therefore, it is crucial to master these conventions.

Importantly, mastering the conventions also increases the probability of your work being understood. As we have discussed throughout the book, understanding is contingent on the discourses that are available to individuals. If the discourses that frame prevailing reading conventions are subverted, readers simply may not understand the text. You may even have personal experience of this. Many students complain that when they read the first pieces of cultural research they 'do not understand anything at all'. This is because they lack the basic concepts and vocabulary, and their reading is shaped by the logic of marketing discourse. Therefore, although genre is often thought of in relation to the work of authoring, it also plays an important role in the work of reading. As Tedlock (2003) reminds us, since the meanings that readers derive from a text are shaped by the discourse of the communities to which they belong, authors need to have a clear idea of which readers they wish to address.

Scientific research employs particular kinds of forms for creating, identifying, analyzing and organizing statements that can be classified as legitimate knowledge claims. Participants in a research community function as an interpretive community who expect several taken-for-granted conventions to be present in a 'credible' research report. Hence, the cadre of researchers who share a common paradigm read and write texts in terms of particular conventions and from a particular socio-cultural position (Thompson et al., 1998: 108).

It has been our aim throughout this book to offer such constructs as are conventionally employed in a cultural research community. They may appear somewhat difficult, we agree, but mastering their usage is necessary in order to be able to produce a 'serious speech act' within this scholarly community. Constructs do constitute an important part of the particular writing conventions that govern cultural research. These conventions may – and often do – differ from writing conventions that govern, in particular, positivistic research. We elaborate on these particularities in the next section. Before that, however, we take up one theme that should, in our view, acquire appropriate attention in debates related to institutionalized writing practices: co-authoring.

Co-authoring

Co-authoring is a common practice in contemporary academic research, and at its best, it results in a more creative, rigorous and comprehensive work than authoring by oneself. But co-authoring inevitably involves a range of ethical issues, not only in the case of collaborative publications with faculty and students, but also with peers. As we discussed in Chapter 2, high quality cultural research is sensitive and attentive to the ethical issues involved in research – it is a question of 'validity' in cultural research. Therefore, drawing largely on the article of Mark Fine and Lawrence Kurdek (1993), we highlight some ethical principles that may provide assistance in making decisions on *authorship credit* and *authorship order*. It is to these two issues that ethical dilemmas commonly relate. These dilemmas derive in large part from the very fact that in academic settings decisions regarding promotion and tenure are heavily influenced not only by the number of publications in peer-reviewed journals but also by the number of first-authored publications (Fine and Kurdek, 1993).

Therefore, the authorship credit and authorship order are far from trivial matters, but matters that should be carefully and openly discussed. We suggest here some ethical principles, and we hope that the issues raised, principles reviewed and recommendations made will help readers to engage in the process of making appropriate authorship decisions. We also hope that they will promote further discussion on ethical issues concerning authorship in academic institutions and encourage researchers to work towards common guidelines and policy statements.

First, we maintain that authorship decisions should be based on the scholarly importance of the contribution to the study. This means that mere possession of an institutional position, such as Department Chair, does not justify authorship credit. In the same vein, being dissertation supervisor does not automatically justify authorship credit. Instead, we take the view that it is the nature of the contribution that is made to the study which determines whether the authorship credit is warranted or not. Our basic principle is that authorship credit is warranted only for those who have made *professional contributions* to the study. The key issue, then, is to try to determine the term 'professional contribution' and to differentiate it from 'minor contribution', especially in the case of doing cultural studies.

To be included as an author on a publication, a researcher should make a professional contribution that is creative and intellectual in nature, and that is integral to completion of the study. As professional contribution we consider issues such as developing the research design, integrating diverse theoretical perspectives, developing conceptual frameworks, engaging in the fieldwork, contributing to data analysis, interpreting results, and writing portions of the manuscript. As minor contributions we consider such as tasks as inputting data to qualitative software, typing recorded interviews, proof-reading, literature search, or minor contribution to fieldwork (for example, conducting a couple of interviews without taking part in the design of the questionnaire or the fieldwork in general). These sorts of tasks often take time and effort, but nevertheless, they may be regarded as supportive.

Importantly, authors must jointly decide what combination of professional activities warrants a given level of authorship. By necessity, there will be some variation in which activities warrant authorship credit across differing research projects.

Collaboration between two professionals can – basically – occur on an egalitarian basis, but collaboration between faculty and their students is inherently unequal due to the very nature and purpose of the relationship. Supervisors should help students further their careers by including them as authors when their contributions are professional by nature, and give them what they deserve. One common problem is that the faculty takes authorship credit although it was earned by the student. That kind of case may be considered an 'intellectual theft'. But neither is the opposite case fair: if students are granted undeserved authorship credit, it falsely represents the students' scholarly expertise.

As Fine and Kurdek (1993) suggest, it may be relevant to consider authorship relative to a competence continuum. This view, which serves to assist future students, means that for the same level of authorship credit one should expect greater professional contributions from collaborators who have more competence than from those who have less competence. But, it is also important to notice that scholarly talents are not necessarily distributed in terms of institutional positions. Students may have considerable talents in one or more activity and this should be reflected in authorship decisions.

In any case, the faculty and students should have the opportunity to mean-ingfully participate in the process of determining authorship credit and order, although they are not equal in power, status, competence and expertise. This also concerns authorship decisions related to publications based on dissertations. Basically, if the article is based primarily on the student's dissertation, he or she is to be listed as principal author on a multiple-authored article. This is because the dissertation represents original and independent work by the student, and there-fore, the first authorship should be reserved for him or her. However, there may be cases where the originality and also independence may be questioned (for instance, if the dissertation is part of a larger research project where the disserta-tion task is more or less given). Moreover, the increasingly popular article-based dissertations, where the dissertation itself includes several authors, further compli-cates the issue.

On the whole, we advocate early, thorough and systematic discussions that lead to explicit agreements with all authors. These agreements, however, do not necessarily need to take the form of signed informed consent forms – authorship papers. But, it seems important to acknowledge and accept that these initial agree-ments may need to be renegotiated during the research process. This is because scholarly projects in general, and cultural studies in particular, often take unex-pected turns that necessitate changes in initial agreements. If, for instance, the project requires further data-gathering or revision of the original theoretical framework, this may require additional professional contributions beyond those initially agreed upon.

Writing good research reports – composing good stories

In cultural research, the objective of the final research report or paper is not to describe the entire research process and the results thereby obtained in a chrono-logical order. Rather, the objective is to put forward an argument by telling a theoretically sophisticated and empirically well-grounded story about the phe-nomenon that you have studied. In this section, we aim to give some practical advice on how to compose such a story. We proceed by first discussing some general principles and then elaborate on the content and structure of each of the main sections or chapters of a research report (that is, introduction, literature review, methodology, data analysis, conclusion and references).

With several other authors (Richardson, 1990, 2000; Silverman, 2000), we take the view that scholarly texts may be treated as stories: they are premised upon a narrative structure, they employ narrative devices, and their scientific frame itself is a metanarrative. During the history of qualitative research a range of possible story types have been presented, such as the analytic story (Silverman, 2000), or mystery story (Alasuutari, 1995). We consider a research report as *an argumentative story*. It means that each part of the research report, from the structure of the study to the choice of data extracts, should develop your argument.

In writing the research report, hence, you become the story-teller. You say something interesting to someone you expect to be interested in what you are doing. Therefore, the very first step in writing the final report is to determine the story that you wish to tell. Commonly, there are several arguments that you can form on the basis of your analysis. Therefore, there are usually also several stories that you can tell about your study. Often, however, it suffices – and is more efficient – to concentrate on one story only with one main argument in a single report or paper. Choosing this story is a critical task and you may wish to think of the choice fairly pragmatically, in terms of which particular story is most likely to be relevant and interesting for your audience, or which story makes a strong contribution to some particular literature to which you wish to contribute. In any case, the argument that you wish to put forward does not have much value unless it is presented and targeted to a particular scientific community and positioned in relation to a particular body of knowledge.

Moreover, to make sure that the story advances a strong argument, it is good to work out a coherent structure for the report. First, you outline the macrostructure, for example by developing an expanded table of contents or a mind map for the report. It helps you to get a good overall picture of what you are doing as well as to proportionate the different parts of the report. Then you work out the microstructure by organizing the chapters, sections and paragraphs in more detail. Having the plot of your story structured in this way helps you to concentrate on building a convincing and insightful argument throughout the twists and turns that the story takes in the different parts of the research report.

Title and abstract

Considering the structure and content of each chapter and section, it is good to take the anticipated reader's point of view. The title and abstract of the research report or paper is undoubtedly the first texts that the potential audience of your work is exposed to. The title, in particular, plays a crucial role in a sense that it may be the only thing the reader sees, for instance, in the list of references or when making library inquiries. Therefore, it should contain the sort of keywords that situate the work within the theoretical debate to which the study is intended to contribute. For instance, 'brand' if the aim is to contribute to the brand literature, or 'value generation' if that is the focus of study. Trying to come up with the title of the research report or article is, actually, an analytical activity through which the author is trying to figure out the very key point of the study. It is therefore good to try to think of the title early on, during the research process. Creating a title that catches the attention of the readers always requires several trials, and re-trials.

In the same vein, abstracts are important because the reader often makes the decision whether or not to read the report or paper solely based on the title and the abstract. The form and length of abstracts vary from journal to journal (and conference to conference). Some prefer more 'summary-driven' while others favour more 'results-driven' types of abstracts. We are in favor of a more 'result-driven' type that focuses on research findings, conclusions and contributions.

List of references

The *list of references* is often the next part of the research report or paper that the reader scans through, as it provides a quick and fairly reliable guide to the writer's disciplinary or professional orientation. It also tends to tell quite a bit about the depth and up-to-datedness of that orientation (Wolcott, 1990). Therefore, the list of references plays an important role in inviting the anticipated readers' attention. In the same vein, the ways in which these references are actually then used in the text also convey important meanings to the reader. Therefore, it is necessary to consider, throughout the process of writing, whether or not the particular references that you use and the ways in which you use them advance your argument. Does the list of references tell your story? Is it comprehensive? Is it relevant with respect to the problem statement? Are the key authors of the topic included? What is the time frame of references? Is it representative of your theoretical and methodological position? Have you referred to those scholars that you hope will read your paper? Have you referred to those that have offered assistance to you during your study, for instance by giving valuable comments? And finally, and perhaps most importantly, do the references and citations that you integrate in the text itself provide clarifying information on the premises of your argument, and justification for the conclusions that you make.

Introduction and conclusions

Moving on, the readers of the research report – much like the readers of any story – usually expect to find a clear narrative structure that they can follow. A good story is generally expected to have a beginning, a middle and an end. In academic stories, the beginning and the end are the parts that are often read first. Only after reading them do people decide whether they want to read the middle. In academic story-telling communities, the skill of writing good *introductions* and the *conclusions* is thus crucially important. Nevertheless, the introduction and conclusion section of a paper often prove to be illustrative of the overall quality of the work that is being reported in the paper. Bad papers often consist merely of a middle part but lack a beginning and an end. In other words, the authors concentrate on reporting the problem and on the ways in which it was solved, but forget to introduce their problem and situate it in some relevant academic debate. They also forget to talk about the broader relevance of their findings to particular academic communities. To avoid this problem, you may find it useful to consider the entire research report in terms of an hour glass structure. This often-used metaphor highlights the ways in which the beginning (upper part) and the end (lower part) are not only wider by their nature, but also crucial for the very functioning of the report.

The introduction, in particular, plays a key role in inviting readers' attention. It should capture the reader's attention by presenting the topic and problem, the key body of literature, as well as the contribution of your study. The introduction is a place where you should present and sell your story. It should provide answers to questions that are in the reader's mind: Why should I read this study? What shall I learn from reading it? What new does it offer to what body of knowledge?

In the *conclusion* section or chapter, you should explicitly state the theoretical contribution of your study. This means that instead of writing a summary of your study, you must underline the significance of your findings to the research community you have chosen for your intended audience, and perhaps also to the relevant discipline more generally. How do your findings contribute to a particular body of knowledge? Moreover, you must consider broader implications of these findings for fellow scholars, practitioners and policy-makers.

Literature analysis and conceptual framework

Scientific research always builds upon existing literature, and that requires that you present earlier research in your report. This part of the report is often referred to as a literature review. We question, however, the relevance of a separate literature review chapter in the final report. As Atkinson et al. point out: '[t]here are few if any genres of scholarly writing that are less life-enhancing than the literature review' (Atkinson et al., 2001b: 1). Academic research is not about reviewing and paraphrasing. It is about building strong arguments. As the word 'review' insidiously tends to guide researchers indeed to perform a *review*, we feel that it is better to think of the 'literature review' in terms of a *literature analysis*. That is what you are supposed to do: to analyze the literature. We also take the view that there is necessarily no need to write a separate chapter on literature analysis. Analysis of prior knowledge is a basic constitutive element of argumentation in all chapters. Literature needs to be analyzed, for example, when the research problem is nested in the introduction and when analysis is situated in regard to existing literature.

Nevertheless, the choice of appropriate literature is an important one. The existing literature needs to be drawn upon selectively and appropriately, considering what is the relevant literature with respect to the problem at hand among the intended audience. You do not have to refer to everything that has been written about your topic before, but rather to pieces of existing work that are essential for justifying your story.

Where and how then to present the *theoretical framework and theoretical constructs* of the study? In our view, there are several options. As we have maintained that all knowledge claims are perspectival, produced from a particular theoretical perspective, we consider it is essential to make this perspective as clear as possible. This means that the author should specify and present the theoretical foundation and theoretical constructs that she or he is using. This may well be discussed in a separate chapter, if needed. But, it is important to understand that the purpose of a separate theoretical chapter is *not* to offer a theoretical frame that is then 'tested' with the empirical data. Instead, its role is to provide the perspective from which the world under study – and the empirical data – is assessed. It is evaluated on the basis of findings, that is, whether or not the theoretical frame being used enables the researcher to produce insightful findings.

However, presentation of the theoretical perspective does not necessarily require a separate chapter. It may also be integrated within the written report. We offer one example of this strategy by referring to a study conducted by Soile Veijola and Eeva Jokinen (1994). Their article 'The Body in Tourism', published in *Theory, Culture and Society*, is concerned with the notion of body in the context of leisure studies. Methodologically, it is an ethnographic study and the fieldwork took place in a typical Mediterranean tourist resort. The authors argue that the notion of body is neglected in the sociological literature on tourism and that this is a considerable neglect, since the body constitutes a core part of the very idea of being a tourist.

Instead of making a separate theoretical part and a separate fieldwork description these authors infuse the two. Actually, they make the theory and the fieldwork description interact in the report. The whole story is written in the form of a dialogue, a dialogue between empirical observations and theoretical literature. For instance, the authors take up an empirical ethnographic observation related to the body – such as sunbathing or dancing – *and* juxtapose it with chosen excerpts of previous sociological literature on tourism that neglects the body. In doing so, they concretely draw attention to the prevailing conceptualization of a tourist as a disembodied and sexless being, one which the previous literature has adopted. Methodically, authors actually relocate or transfer the academic texts on tourism to the very context of being a tourist. As they say: 'We have *rewritten* the chosen texts into tourist events and encounters, into the duration of time and sexed body, into being and writing *there*, in the temporal space of tourism' (1994: 149).

In the chapters on analysis, we emphasized the dialogic nature of interpretations and the need to have a constant and close dialogue with data and theory in order to produce insightful findings. The above-mentioned mode of writing is in line with such a mode of inquiry. But, we wish to emphasize that if you choose to write 'differently' and 'creatively', your choice should present some *clear added value to the argument* you wish to put forth.

Methodology

How about the chapter on *methodology*? As we have repeatedly emphasized in this book, methodological considerations are not merely something that take place and are reported in the chapter or section on research methodology. Methodological questions must be addressed throughout the research report. The study must be based on a set of methodological principles and commitments that informs the ways in which the social world under study is approached and analyzed throughout the research process. The purpose of the methodology chapter, nevertheless, is to explicate these principles and commitments as well as to elaborate on the methodological choices that they involve. Doing this there is one important thing that you should do. You need to *position* your methodological approach within the field of relevant research methodology. This means, for example, that you not only state that the study is based on interviews and thus describe the way these interviews have been carried out. It is important that you also specify the particular methodological perspective to interviews that you take, locating your approach to interviews in the wide range of possible ways of conducting and applying them.

To give an example of methodological positioning, we refer to Lisa Peñaloza's (1994) article on Mexican immigrants, published in the *Journal of Consumer Research*. (We discussed this article also in Chapter 3 as an example of critical ethnography.) In the vignette offered in Box 10.1, we quote a piece of text, the introductory paragraph from the section on methodology entitled 'Ethnographic study', from the article. We suggest that you read the quotation and pay particular attention to the ways in which Peñaloza positions her study first in the methodology of ethnography, and then in relation to a particular tradition within ethnography implicit in the reference. She briefly discusses the previous use of ethnography in consumer research, and then moves on to discuss more thoroughly the specific ethnographic variety that she applies in her study (for the references used in the quotation, please see the original article). Also pay attention to the ways in which the choice of this methodology is argued to be appropriate. This is what you tend to find in good methodology chapters, a well-justified argument that specifies why the methodologies and methods used in the study are relevant for the particular piece of research at hand.

Box 10.1   Example on methodological positioning

'Ethnographic research techniques were selected for this research because of their long-standing tradition of studying 'other' cultures and cultural phenomena (Clifford, 1988). In recent years ethnographic studies have made significant headway in the field of consumer research as researchers have gone to the field to investigate consumers' experiences and to explore the social significance of consumption (see, e.g., Arnould 1989; Belk 1991; Belk, Wallendorf and Sherry 1988; Hill, 1991).

'This research is positioned in the emerging tradition of critical ethnography (Clifford and Marcus 1986; Rosaldo 1989; Thomas 1993). Critical ethnography, like more traditional forms of ethnography, is characterized by the use of participant observation data collection techniques and interpretive analysis. It differs in its concern with issues of subjectivity and relationships

(Continued)

of power affecting both the researcher(s) and those under investigation. Concerns of critical ethnographers included (1) relations between the researcher and the researched, (2) the agency of those being investigated, i.e. how people were treated during the course of the study, how they were represented in the written account, and whether the study incorporated their interests, and (3) the importance of situating our work within the global economy'.

Source: Peñaloza (1994: 35)

The discussion on methodology should be written with a particular audience in mind. The less familiar the intended audience is with the methods, methodologies and theories that you use, the more elaborate and detailed your discussion on methodology needs to be. In disciplines and communities where different forms of cultural research have become well-known, scholars no longer need to discover and defend their methods, nor do they need to provide exhaustive reviews of literature on standard procedures such as participant observation or interviewing. Instead, they need to consider whether there is something new and original in the use of the established methods, and elaborate on that – not on the basic, well-known procedures. Many contemporary management journals, for example, currently request that methodology be elaborated in detail only to the degree that it is new. Therefore, we recommend that sometimes it is a good idea to consider carrying out some of the more detailed discussion on methodology in appendices and end notes. This allows you to concentrate on what is truly essential for your argument in the methodology section or chapter, and thus make your story more readable and your argument more transparent.

We also wish to stress that in cultural research, methods are not standard techniques or tools that can be employed mechanically to analyze any suitable data you may have. In a sense, they need to be 'reconfigured' for every piece of research. The methods that we have discussed earlier in this book are generally flexible in nature: they can be applied in a great many ways and within various sorts of theoretical and methodological frameworks. In the methodology chapter, the critical task, then, is not only to argue *why* you have chosen your methods but also *how* you have used your methods. This should be discussed and argued in regard to your problem: how have the data and methods helped you in solving the problem?

Overall, the chapter on methodology should not only present the data set and the data-gathering procedures but also specify and elaborate on the interpretive framework that is employed in the study. By interpretive framework we refer to the principles and procedures of interpretation, and the general theoretical view of interpretation that is adopted in the study. Moreover, it should briefly cover the ways in which the whole study and interpretations have emerged and evolved during the process.

Data analysis

Writing the chapters that deal with *data analysis* is a critical task in qualitative research. We wish to stress at the outset that you should write and organize the data analysis chapters in a way that develops and presents your argument. Depending on the nature of your argument this may take several forms, and therefore we find it somewhat difficult to offer definite structures and guidelines for writing data analysis. One form of story-telling may be suitable for one sort of argument, another for another kind.

The starting point is, however, that in writing the final data analysis chapters you should know what your message will be (though it will often be developed during the final writing process!). Then you should present it to readers convincingly and interestingly. Answers to the questions of how to convince readers and what is found interesting largely depend on scholarly conventions and vary in different disciplines and traditions. The way ethnographic research reports, for instance, are often written – involving detailed and lengthy descriptions of the field setting – may be found convincing and interesting among ethnographic scholars, but somewhat 'boring' among other scholars. Therefore, you should keep your audience in mind when writing up your analysis.

The audience is important not only in evaluative terms – defining standards and norms for writing analysis – but also in more practical terms. You should consider the way academic stories are commonly read and work towards a reader-friendly story. Importantly, it is your job to tell the story, not the reader's task to try to figure out what the story might be. In the chapters on data analysis, this means, first of all, that you need to communicate only the essence, only that part of the analysis that is relevant for the argument. Avoid data overload, that is, do not to give exhaustive descriptions of all of the interesting points found out during the data analysis. That will confuse the reader – who will most likely soon become an ex-reader. One way to help the reader to follow your story is to use headings and subheadings in a way that communicates your story. That is, instead of naming them as 'data analysis' you may name them in terms of your findings.

One further reader-friendly strategy is to work out a consistent microstructure of the data analysis chapters. For that purpose, we draw on Silverman (2000: 244–8), who suggests that each analytical chapter should have three sections: introduction, main section and conclusion.

The *introduction* is some sort of scene-setting of the chapter, serving as an introduction to the particular theme of the chapter. It commonly explains the general areas that the chapter discusses and how they relate to the overall topic and argument of the study. It also provides a brief overview of what is in the chapter.

The main section concentrates on the proper data analysis. It presents data extracts and interpretations drawn from them. Importantly, the point is not to amuse the reader by offering some 'nice real-life data extracts' but to make an argument based on these extracts. Every chosen data extract should have a place in your argument. Therefore, you should top and tail each data extract, to use Silverman's expression, that is, to connect it to your story. This often means that you also make connections to previous studies, to the previous literature. The purpose is not to show that you know the literature, but to *use* the literature in order to develop your argument. The contextualization is one way to convince the reader: it makes your story more relevant when you tie it to the larger themes that are relevant for your argument.

One practical rule for writing the main sections – there may be many of them depending on the nature of your argument, but some three to five is commonly enough – is that if they contain more data extracts than your interpretive text, you should rewrite them. This is often a sign of poor data analysis, and more analysis is needed. The data do not speak for themselves, you should make them speak.

This means that you should make explicit the interpretive framework through which you make the data speak. Only then, the readers may be able to assess the quality of your interpretations and judge your claims. As we have discussed earlier, the data may be interpreted in a variety of ways and you should make clear what is the theoretical and methodological stance from which you make your particular interpretations, and how you understand the very notion of interpretation. This stance, which is commonly explicated in separate theoretical and methodological chapters, is put into practice in the chapters or sections that report your analysis. Moreover, and importantly, you should make clear why the interpretation that you present – the particular story – is worth writing and reading.

The *conclusion,* then, is the place where the whole analysis is tied together again, and connected to the main points of the argument.

Finally, it is worth remembering that a well-argued and reader-friendly study will never be achieved at one go. Writing is re-writing. In elaborating whether you have succeeded in presenting your argument in an interesting and convincing manner, *feedback* is essential, as Wolcott points out (1990: 43–6). Good feedback on writing is hard to give and hard to take, however, mainly because there are so many dimensions on which feedback can be offered: whether one has identified the right story to tell, how well and convincingly it has been told, and so forth. When obtaining feedback, it is good to remember that not all reviewers are likely to have something to contribute to every aspect of your paper. It is also good to keep in mind that it may well be the case that the more critique you get, the more seriously your effort has been taken. And if you get good feedback, consider it a gift. A gift is, first and foremost, reciprocal, so you yourself should be prepared to give feedback to others.

Publishing cultural research on marketing and consumption

An important part of the academic work cycle is to publish your findings. We do not consider publishing as a mere means to advance your career but rather as a social responsibility that comes with the job. Researchers should disseminate their research (especially if they occupy state-funded positions). Most common publishing outlets are books and journals, and both are obviously needed and necessary. As the journals tend to be more valued in the academic power game, we focus the discussion on the challenge of publishing in peer-reviewed journals.

In considering the art of publishing, it may be helpful to think of it in market terms, as Stephen Brown (1999: 12) suggests. The publication market is currently highly competitive, and it also involves its own politics and power games. This market has its producers and consumers, segments and position strategies, publishers and channels of distribution, brands and brand extensions, stars and cows, leaders and followers, relationships and networks, as well as spokesmen and barriers to entry. Associate editors and reviewers, in particular, occupy a key position in determining whether attempts to enter the publications market succeed or not.

Therefore, we close the chapter by considering writing from the point of view of reviewers. We have stressed that in writing you should consider the reader. The reviewer is one of the most important readers in a sense that he or she plays a key role in deciding whether other audiences may have the opportunity to read your text. The reviewer is, in turn, part of a scientific community. In reviewing manuscripts for peer-reviewed journals, reviewers often adhere to particular rules and conventions that are – implicitly and explicitly – stated in the profile statements and guidelines of the journals. At the beginning of our book we mentioned a number of established and new journals that publish cultural marketing and consumer research. All of them have, however, different profiles. To exemplify, we take up two different descriptions of journals that both deal with consumption: the *Journal of Consumer Research* and *Consumption, Markets & Culture*.

- Founded in 1974, the ***Journal of Consumer Research*** publishes scholarly research that describes and explains consumer behavior. Empirical, theoretical and methodological articles spanning fields such as psychology, marketing, sociology, economics and anthropology are featured in this interdisciplinary quarterly. The primary thrust of *JCR* is academic, rather than managerial, with topics ranging from micro-level processes (for example, brand choice) to more macro-level issues (such as the development of materialistic values).
- ***Consumption, Markets & Culture*** focuses on consumerism and the markets as the site of social behavior and discourse. It encourages discussion of the role of management and organizations in society, especially in terms of production, consumption, colonialism, globalization, business performance and labor conditions. Combining theories of culture, media, gender, anthropology, literary criticism and semiology with analyses of business and management, the journal is international in its scope and iconoclastic in its aims. The editors consider marketing to be the ultimate practice of postmodernity, blending art and commerce and requiring the constant renewal of styles, forms and images. Educating readers about the conscious and planned practice of signification and representation is, thus, the journal's primary aim; its second is to take part in inquiring in and construction of the material conditions and meanings of consumption and production. (Notes for contributors, CMC 6: 1, 2003)

In order to succeed in publishing, it may be crucial to understand the meaning of these sorts of descriptions, and what they imply in terms of writing. Therefore, the first task in the process of writing papers that you wish to submit for publication in academic journals is to analyze the profile and conventions of the particular journal in which you wish to publish. We have been emphasizing the importance of an analytical attitude throughout the research process, and it applies to the game of publishing as well. To help you to practice your sensitivity in detecting the profiles and conventions of different journals, we propose that you do the following exercise. We want the exercise to help you recognize the important role that scientific communities play in the game of publishing.

EXERCISE 10.1   Analyzing academic writing conventions

We recommend that you undertake this exercise in small teams, because it is somewhat laborious, and because you are likely to get more out of it if you can discuss and share your views.

Choose two established journals that are relevant for your work but represent different disciplines; take one from the field of marketing, the other from the field of cultural studies (e.g. *Journal of Consumer Research* and *Cultural Studies*).

Analyze the journals, focusing on the editorial statements and the articles of the last few issues. What sorts of topics are featured? What is the key rationale of the journal? Consider the topics and debates included. Examine carefully the lists of references. Who seem to be the key authors? Which other journals are referred to? What does this tell?

Then turn to examine stylistic conventions. Consider the representational style. What sorts of illustrations, tables and charts are favored? How is the researcher represented? Look at the structure of the articles, both at the macro and micro level. Consider each chapter. In the introduction, for instance, how is the topic introduced? How is the relevance of the topic presented? What sort of rhetorical devices are favored, for instance? Is relevance defined in terms of money? Go on examining each chapter, and try to analyze the argumentative path. Does it differ from article to article, or from one journal to another?

Finally, consider the ways in which you should write differently if you intended to publish in those journals.

FURTHER READING

The following two books consider writing as a craft and provide an excellent elaboration on the issues researchers typically face in writing up qualitative research:

- Richardson, Laurel (1990) *Writing Strategies: Reaching Diverse Audiences.* Newbury Park, CA: Sage.
- Wolcott, Harry F. (1990) *Writing Up Qualitative Research.* Newbury Park, CA: Sage.

Part 5

Defending Your Research Report

In the previous chapters, we have made an attempt to explain what it means to take the sort of cultural approach to qualitative marketing and consumer research that we have taken in this book in different phases of the research process – what sort of empirical materials are considered appropriate, how data are to be analyzed and what is the purpose and role of different methods in the production of cultural knowledge, for example. Next, we shall discuss the basic assumptions of cultural research in more detail, focusing on the more scholarly, philosophical questions that may be raised by reviewers and members of PhD committees for example. Our discussion is organized around a number of questions and answers.

Our answers to the questions that we take up form the interpretive framework through which we discuss qualitative marketing research in this book. We consider it important to elaborate on the elements of this framework in more detail because in different frameworks, qualitative methods may well play very different roles in the production of knowledge, and also the nature of knowledge that is sought with the methods may be different. Qualitative methods (for example, personal interviews, focus groups, techniques of data analysis) are generally understood and used differently in different philosophical frameworks.

Our objective in this last part of the book is primarily to offer resources for making explicit and well-informed methodological choices throughout the research process. As we have repeatedly argued, it is necessary to specify the interpretive framework that guides your research project. We also hope that these questions and answers provide resources for responding to the often misplaced critical questions that students who do cultural research sometimes encounter in research seminars and conferences where the audience is not entirely familiar with the basic assumptions of the cultural approach.

11

Theoretical Legacies and Philosophical Questions

CHAPTER SUMMARY

Chapter 11 discusses the conceptual and philosophical foundations of cultural marketing and consumer research in more detail. The objective is to draw attention to theoretical legacies of ACP (analytics of cultural practice) and cultural research, as well as to historicize the cultural turn in marketing and consumer research.

Is there a theory on cultural marketing and consumer research?

It is our contention that theory and methodology are inextricably linked. Methodologies and methods are no more than ways of expressing particular paradigmatic perspectives and theoretical positions. So, as we discuss qualitative methods and methodology in the context of cultural marketing and consumer research, the question inevitably arises: Is there a particular paradigmatic perspective that characterizes the cultural turn in marketing? Or is there possibly even a specific theory with a distinct methodological approach that informs cultural marketing and consumer research?

In the field of consumer inquiry, Eric Arnould and Craig Thompson (2005) have recently offered the term 'consumer culture theory' (CCT) to capture the core theoretical interests and questions that define the new, still emerging research tradition. They characterize CCT as 'a family of theoretical perspectives that address the dynamic relationships between consumer actions, the marketplace, and cultural meanings'. Acknowledging that the body of literature focusing on these relationships represents a 'plurality of distinct theoretical approaches and research goals', they argue that CCT scholars nevertheless 'share a common theoretical orientation toward the study of cultural complexity that programmatically links their respective research efforts' (Arnould and Thompson 2005: 868).

We largely agree with Arnould and Thompson and find their paper important, in many ways, for further development of the field. Here, however, we wish to call attention to the variety of paradigmatic, theoretical and analytical perspectives that the body of research they refer to entails. We find the existing literature on the cultural complexity of marketplace phenomena fairly heterogeneous, and sometimes also lacking an explicit, coherent theoretical and methodological perspective to support the empirical work. In research practice, cultural marketing and consumer research still sometimes appears to be too unformed, eclectic or philosophically 'messy' to be called a distinct theoretical approach.[1] The conceptual foundations and philosophical underpinnings of the different streams (or rather authors) of 'cultural consumer theory' are many (Arnold and Fischer, 1994) and not necessarily very clear (Moisander, 2001).

In our view, it is therefore difficult, if not impossible, to describe the cultural approach to marketing and consumer research in terms of a single theory or an umbrella-like paradigm. Cultural marketing and consumer research is best understood as a range of somewhat different but more or less converging or parallel approaches to studying marketplace behaviors as cultural phenomena. As a particular, distinct research approach it constitutes itself at a number of theoretical and methodological levels, and thus takes different forms depending on the selections made at each level.

Therefore, we believe that to support theoretically sophisticated research in the field (which also makes empirically well grounded research possible), there is a need to specify and outline a set of clear, philosophically coherent theoretical positions for cultural research on marketplace phenomena. Rather than insisting on philosophical purity of research, we wish to emphasize that *all marketplace knowledge is perspectival*, something that is always constructed from a particular perspective with particular interests (Arnold and Fischer, 1994; Longino, 2002). Taking a particular perspective on consumption, for example, we interpret and represent consumers in particular ways, and thus also help to assemble particular forms of subjectivity for consumers (Miller and Rose, 1997). Therefore, it would seem to be good epistemic practice to explicitly deliberate on the perspective taken and on the interests pursued. The paradigmatic assumptions, particular theoretical perspectives and epistemic virtues that inform and guide research practice need to be explicitly specified, and thus submitted to inter-subjective evaluation and constructive critique within the research community (Longino, 2002).

Moreover, qualitative methods (for example, personal interviews, focus groups, techniques of data analysis) are generally understood and used differently in different philosophical frameworks. In a sense, specific methods *are* different in different methodological perspectives. In the traditional 'positivistic' approaches to qualitative research, for example, personal interviews are seen as a means of obtaining facts about external social reality, whereas in the more contemporary, 'postmodern' approaches to qualitative research interviews are generally viewed as one form of social interaction or conversation in which both the researcher and the respondent have an active role (Gubrium and Holstein, 2003b). Different perspectives may thus prescribe different roles and purposes for particular qualitative methods in the production of knowledge on the marketplace. And also the nature of knowledge, which is sought after with the use of various qualitative research methods, may be understood differently in studies that employ different methodological perspectives.

In this book we outline and discuss only one of the many possible ways of doing qualitative marketing and consumer research, which reflects recent theoretical developments, debates and research interests in the field of cultural marketing and consumer research (e.g., Belk et al., 2003; Bristor and Fischer, 1993; Joy and Venkatesh, 1994; Firat and Venkatesh, 1995; Holt, 1997; Peñaloza, 2001; Thompson, 2004; Thompson and Troester, 2002). Based on an analysis of this emerging stream of cultural research, we define and elaborate on a methodological perspective that we see as particularly well suited for studying the cultural dynamics of the marketplace – and thus for cultural marketing and consumer research. We call this approach *analytics of cultural practice (ACP)*.

What is ACP?

ACP (analytics of cultural practice) (Moisander and Valtonen, 2005), the approach to cultural marketing and consumer research that we have chosen to elaborate in this book, is inspired and informed particularly by the work of Jaber Gubrium and James Holstein (2003a), Ian Hacking (2004) and Gale Miller (1997).[2] Building on the arguments of these scholars as well as on a range of recent literature on cultural studies and cultural marketing and consumer research, we discuss qualitative methods in this book primarily from this perspective.

ACP draws from two basic interpretive analytics for studying the cultural complexity of marketplace phenomena: (1) ethnomethodologically informed analysis of *everyday discursive practices* through which social reality is constructed and social order achieved within an existing institutional and cultural structure (Potter, 1996; Potter and Wetherell, 1987) and (2) analysis of *culturally standardized or institutionalized discourses*, which is based on more poststructuralist and Foucauldian ideas and considerations (Dreyfus and Rabinow, 1983; Foucault, 1978, 1980, 1983; Howarth, 2000).

These two analytics may be viewed as two slightly different orientations toward the study of cultural practice and the workings of culture in the everyday life of its members. In the analysis of everyday discursive practices, the focus is particularly on the ways in which people make use of the available cultural categories, rationalities, visibilities and representations to make sense of their life and to achieve social order. The focus could be, for example, on the ways in which consumers construct and perform their identity or engage in resistance towards the consumer society in their talk and through particular consumption-related practices. It is emphasized that culture, and the rules, norms and values it involves, is not something that is merely imposed on people but something that people 'do' and produce themselves in social interaction. The analysis of culturally standardized or institutionalized discourses, on the other hand, focuses primarily on the ways in which these cultural discourses and the networks of power/knowledge they entail come into being and are structured, and how they constitute the conditions of possibility for subjectivity and agency for the members of culture. The focus could be, for example, on the sorts of subject positions or forms of subjectivity that the dominant discourses on the European information society construct for various groups of people. It is emphasized that cultural discourses not only provide people with discursive resources but also guide and constrain meaning-making and social action.

Finally, it is important to note that ACP is not a theoretical framework in the traditional sense. It does not try to explain the state of matters in question or pose the question *why* individuals are doing and feeling the way they do. It is rather an analytics; it aims to describe the ways in which individual experience and social reality are represented and rendered intelligible in text, talk and signifying practices. It thus gives us a particular point of view to the study of marketplace realities as discursively produced and practiced in society. Marketplace behavior is analyzed within the context of people's everyday life and cultural practices instead of trying to explain it under the lens of some unifying theory (Firat and Venkatesh, 1995: 255). It is pre-theoretical in this sense (Gubrium and Holstein, 2003a).

What sort of assumptions about language and discourse is ACP based on?

Discursive approaches to studying human behavior, such as the one we specify here, are generally based on the assumption that language does not merely mirror reality; it operates performatively and constitutively; it is used to construct reality (Davies and Harré, 1990; Gergen, 1997; Hall, 1997a; Potter and Wetherell, 1987). Moreover, it is maintained and underlined that meaning is dependent on the frameworks of interpretation that are brought to it. Adopting this approach we, thus, tend to reject both the 'reflective approach' to representation, according to which representations reflect the true meaning as it already exists in the world, and the 'intentional approach', in which it is taken that words mean what the author intends them to mean (Hall, 1997a). Instead, we subscribe to the view that meaning is constructed discursively in social interaction, with the help and within the limits of available discourses and representational systems, using text, talk, sounds, images and signifying practices.

According to this view, objects of knowledge in themselves do not have a single, fixed and transparent meaning. Their meaning is contextual and contingent on the way they are represented – for example, on the ways in which people talk and think about them and how they are integrated into the cultural practices in particular contexts. Meaning is not looked at as a product of individual experience, for example, the intention or inner psychological experience of the speaker, as in many phenomenological approaches to marketing and consumer research. The meaning of an object of knowledge is rather a function of a system of discourse or some representational system that is brought to it. This is because people can grasp or understand things (objects, people and events) only through concepts and words or other symbols that signify those concepts. According to poststructuralist theories of language, these words and symbols get their meaning not from their reference to the things themselves (or to the concepts) but from their relations to all other signs in a representational system, which provides a way of talking, thinking and representing knowledge about these things (objects, people and events). When this system of representation changes, for example, when new signs are introduced into the system, the meanings of the signs that were already in use change. Therefore, words, symbols and objects of knowledge do not have a fixed meaning over time. Their meanings are produced, transformed and changed in and through systems and practices of representation.

To exemplify, let us consider the ways in which particular days of the seven-day week system acquire meaning. The specific meanings attached to days such as Monday, Sunday or Friday do not become understandable if they are assessed in isolation, as if they were isolated entities. Rather, these days acquire their meanings only in relation to each other, and these relations in turn are part of some system – the seven-day-week system. This system frames and shapes the way individual weekdays acquire meanings.

This illustrates the basic structuralist premise of a *systematic relation of difference*: elements are seen to acquire meaning in relation to other elements in a particular system; it is the difference between the elements that constitute meaning (De Saussure, 1983). The idea of relational difference should not therefore be understood in terms of simple oppositional pairs, as the early structuralists inspired by Lévi-Strauss tended to do. Rather, it is the representational system as a whole, its underlying rules, logics and values that must be taken into consideration when cultural meanings are assessed.

These ideas about language can be extended to cultural practices more generally. The key idea underlying this extension is that actions and practices are linguistic signs. Like words, they signify things beyond themselves by means of metaphor and metonymy for example. Metonymy means, simply stated, that a part can stand for the whole. The name Picasso stands for his paintings, for instance, or the name of one weekday, Friday, stands for a whole set of particular practices related to it. Metaphor, in turn, means viewing something 'as if' – seeing something in terms of something else. It entails a comparison of two domains, and typically, an abstract domain such as 'time' is conceptualized in terms of more concrete terms.

Accordingly, we may comprehend the course of a week in terms of a journey (Lakoff and Johnson, 1980).

Meanings attached to weekdays, then, are encoded not only to the ways in which days are named but also to the ways they are practiced in the course of social life. Think of Friday. It is not only a linguistic category but a category that becomes produced through a set of cultural practices – funny Friday talks, leaving work early on Fridays, after-work beers to kick off the weekend etc. – and consumption and marketing activities are tightly involved in these practices. Think, for instance, of casual Friday clothes, 'Thank God it's Friday' postcards, funny Friday e-mails, and so forth. In the same vein, Sunday is given particular meanings through a set of practices, or actually, through regulating and prohibiting some practices, for example, government regulation of retail opening hours.

Moreover, a particular system of signification, such as the seven-day-week system, gets its meaning in relation to other representational systems, and as part of the more general systems of discourse that are brought to it. The seven-day-week system, for example, is tightly connected to and is also subject to change in line with the prevailing and emerging cultural discourses on work, religion and economy. In the Western market economies, for example, the current discourses of workforce or labor market flexibility, particularly the talk about 'efficiency' and 'efficient economy', have contributed to changes in the ways in which 'Sunday' is understood and practiced. While the Christian religious discourses on work and leisure would seem to govern people to devote their Sundays to relaxation with friends and family, the current economic discourses may well make people talk about 'feeling guilty' if they fail to do anything 'smart' on a Sunday – because they do not allocate their scarce time resources efficiently (Valtonen, 2004a). There thus appears to be a contest over the 'appropriate' ways of spending Sundays, for instance, both at the individual level (can I work a bit even though it is Sunday?) and societal level (should shops be allowed to be open on Sundays?).

Therefore, cultural meanings are not fixed but contextual and subject to change. Although representational systems tend to be somewhat persistent, meanings are constantly contested and negotiated in processes and practices of social interaction and representation. As Lawrence Grossberg ([1986] 1996: 157) argues, 'the meaning is not in the text itself but is the active product of the text's social articulation, of the web of connotations and codes into which it is inserted'.

From this perspective, language is understood to enter into the very constitution of 'things' (Gergen and Thatchenkery, 1997; Hall, 1997a). It operates through institutionalized use of language and language-like systems (Davies and Harré, 1990), representational systems (Hall, 1997a) or discursive formations (Foucault, 1972). These *discursive systems or frameworks*,[3] are seen as clusters or formations of ideas, images, and signifying practices (Hall, 1992a: 291) that involve configurations of assumptions, categories, logics, claims and modes of articulation (Miller, 1997: 32). They provide people with coherent interpretive frameworks and practices for representing or constructing knowledge about a particular topic or practice. People's experience of their social identity, in terms of gender, race, class and age for example, can only be expressed and understood through the categories and meanings available to them in the discourses that are made relevant in specific situations (e.g., Katila and Meriläinen, 1999).

Available discourses, therefore, guide and constrain the way that a phenomenon, person or topic can be meaningfully discussed and reasoned about, and define acceptable and intelligible ways of conduct with respect to it. As Gale Miller (1997: 33) has noted, 'discourses are conditions of possibility that provide us with the resources for constructing a limited array of social realities, and make other possibilities less available to us'. Therefore, different discourses produce different social realities, and within the different, discursively constructed realities different kinds of people reside, different relationships prevail and different opportunities are likely to emerge (1997: 32). Language can therefore rarely if ever be regarded as a value-neutral medium of communication. Rather, it is considered as the key repository of cultural values and meanings (Hall, 1997a).

Consequently, the methodological perspective to cultural marketing and consumer research that we specify here is based on a presumption that discourse is through and through infused with forces and relations of power. Following Michel Foucault (1977, 1978, 1980), power is seen to work through discourse, constituting a matrix of understanding, which produces what is considered 'true' and 'normal', thus helping to set rules, norms and conventions by which social life is ordered and governed. Quoting Foucault, it is maintained that:

> power produces knowledge ... that power and knowledge directly imply one another; ... there is no power relation without the correlative constitution of a field of knowledge, nor any knowledge that does not presuppose and constitute at the same time power relations. (1977: 27)

Therefore, it is emphasized that discourse empowers and dis-empowers, and that the use of language and the production of knowledge have important social and political implications (Gergen, 1998; Potter, 1997).

Accordingly with these assumptions of language and representation, in empirical research people's descriptions of the world are not seen as 'outward simulacres of an inner mirror', reporting their private observations and perceptions, as Kenneth Gergen and Tojo Thatchenkery (1997) have argued. It is emphasized that neither interview data of narrated experience nor people's verbal responses to survey questions, for example, merely reflect people's subjective experience or cognitive representations of objects, events and categories pre-existing in the social and natural world. Rather, they are viewed as 'social texts' that construct a particular version of those things. Such texts are treated as complex cultural, social and psychological products, constructed in particular, context-specific ways to carry out relationships and to constitute what is a real, true and good in a particular community (Gergen, 1997; Potter and Wetherell, 1987). By the same token, institutional documents are constructed according to conventions that are themselves part of a documentary reality – and to make things happen (Atkinson and Coffey, 1997: 61).

Hence, as Jonathan Potter (1996: 108) has argued, descriptions and factual accounts have a double orientation. They have an *action orientation*, in the sense that they are used to accomplish an action, and they have an *epistemological orientation* in the sense that they are constructed in particular ways in order to build up their status as a factual version. Accordingly, it is generally presupposed, for example, that attitudes, descriptions and preferences are not necessarily stable and consistent over time in some de-contextualized manner. Rather quite the contrary, it is acknowledged that depending on the functions to which language, talk and text are put, there may be considerable variation in people's accounts.

What does it mean that things are studied as texts?

Methodologically, much of cultural research draws extensively from *literature studies*, adopting methods of textual criticism for reading cultural forms other than literature, as well as from *structuralism,* in its interest in the systems, the sets of relationships and the formal structures that frame and enable the production of meaning. Drawing essentially from Ferdinand de Saussure's theory of language[4] and signifying systems, it is based on the assumption that language has relevance beyond linguistics because language and signifying systems reveal the mechanisms through which people make sense of their world. As language gives us a particular version of reality, objects or sites of analysis can be looked at as texts. And the structures of those texts can be analyzed to gain an understanding of the wider cultural structures and practices that produce them. In ACP, therefore, texts are studied for the cultural forms they realize and make available. Text is a site where cultural meanings are accessible to us, rather than a privileged object of study in its own right (Turner, 1990).

Accordingly, culture is thus analyzed as a text, based on the model of *textuality*. Here the term 'text' does not refer to a site where meanings are constructed at a single level of inscription – writing, speech, film, dress – or even less to a single artifact, a text. It works as an interleaving of levels. If something is analyzed as text, this 'text' involves practices, institutional structures, flows of knowledge, different relations and forms of power, and the complex forms of subjectivity and agency they entail. It involves legal, political and financial conditions of existence, as well as a particular multilayered semantic organization. And at the same time this text exists only within a network of intertextual relations (Frow and Morris, 2003: 509.) Consequently, the methodological perspective that we discuss here is based on an understanding that culture must be studied not only in language but also in its material forms – in the institutions, visibilities and social practices through which people organize their lives.

A key characteristic of this sort of analysis is a focus on cultural *discourses as systems of representation*, in which meaning is produced through language and signifying practices (Hall, 1997a). These systems consist of the words, concepts, ideas, images, classifications, norms, values, role expectations and signifying practices that are used to refer to and represent knowledge about objects, people and events of all sorts. They provide a way of talking and thinking about a particular topic in a particular historical and local context, and they are linked up with particular social practices. They also partly constitute the conditions of possibility for agency and subjectivity in social life.

How do you account for material practices in ACP?

Discursive approaches to cultural research are sometimes criticized for ignoring the material conditions of everyday life. It is important to note, however, that here the terms 'discourse' and 'discursive' do not refer to something that is merely ideational, linguistic or linguistically structured. In the sense that we use these words, they refer to cultural practice, through which people's everyday realities are constructed and social life organized. Discourse is not only an ideational unity, such as a configuration of meanings, values and representations. It also entails practices. It involves linguistic practices, such as particular ways of talking about and referring to things, people and incidents, as well as 'material practices', such as appropriate ways of behaving in particular social settings and situations. As such it also entails social practices that guide and constrain communication and social interaction between people. Moreover, these cultural practices are parts of more general social and institutional arrangements that are sustained and managed with particular forms of knowledge, techniques and visibilities, that is, visible material objects and spatial arrangements. Knowledge of these institutional and material arrangements is also highly relevant for understanding cultural practice.

Sometimes a distinction is made between discursive and material practices or between cultural and material practices. We, however, do not make such distinctions. We tend to agree with Stuart Hall (1997a), who has argued that all material practices are *signifying practices*; they have communicative elements and make sense only through their cultural representations. In the context of contemporary Western consumer society the distinction between discursive and extra-discursive or between cultural and material seems particularly unclear. In an empirical setting where everyday life is increasingly commodified or at least revolves around markets (products, brands, marketing and the exchange of goods and services), most material practices (like shampooing your hair, or eating) involve complex signifying practices, which are informed by and make sense in the context of particular cultural discourses. Actions and practices may thus be read as linguistic signs. Like words, they signify things beyond themselves by means of metaphor and metonymy, as we pointed out above. This makes it increasingly difficult – if not meaningless at times – to disentangle the cultural from the material, as Margaret Wetherell (2001: 391) notes. Material culture is an essential part of 'culture'. And from the perspective of marketing and consumer research, in any case, it is interesting to study how material practices and objects acquire their culturally mediated representations and how these representations guide and constrain marketplace behavior and interaction. Therefore, when we talk about 'everyday discursive practices' we do not refer only to linguistic practices, such as talking, writing and communicating, but to all the cultural practices through which social reality is constructed and social order achieved. Nevertheless, analysis of cultural practice focuses on all of these signifying practices as discursive forms, as texts and as objects of discourse, which can be analyzed using a selection of ontologically commensurate concepts and methods adopted from linguistic and literary theory (Howarth, 2000: 10).

How do you see structure and agency in ACP?

The methodological perspective that we propose here is a discursive approach to cultural marketing and consumer research, and it is based on the assumption that social reality, what is real and meaningful for people, is culturally constructed. Does this mean that people are powerless dupes whose behavior is causally determined by cultural structures?

In our perspective, much of the debate on structure and agency draws from a false dichotomy between determinism and autonomy (Butler, 1990, 1993; Pulkkinen, 2000; Sawicki, 1994). There is no reason to view agency either in terms of a choosing individual or in terms of social structures and systems that determine human behavior. As Margaret Wetherell and Janet Maybin (1996: 222) have argued, since the person, consciousness, mind and the self are social through and through, it makes little sense to ask what is determined from the inside and what is determined from the outside. The dualist view of agency, either in terms of individual choice or in terms of social structures and systems that determine human activity, fails to address the complex, insidious and diffuse ways that social realities and subjectivities are constructed, contested and transformed. Therefore, ACP questions and rejects the assumption of an authentic core self, but at the same time retains the idea of agency and resistance.

Cultural discourses and social reality are produced by people in social interaction but simultaneously these cultural discourses constitute the conditions of possibility for that cultural production of social reality. The relationship between cultural discourses and everyday practices of meaning-making and construction of social reality is thus *reflexive*. They mutually constitute each other. In other words, accounts and descriptions of social reality constitute that reality in a particular cultural context while they are simultaneously shaped by that context. Cultural discourses and their everyday mediations must therefore be viewed as reflexively interwoven with talk and social interaction (Gubrium and Holstein, 2003a).

The analytic focus therefore is on the *interplay*, not the synthesis, of discursive practices and cultural discourses. They can be viewed as parallel, complementary methodological approaches focusing on the interactional, institutional and cultural factors of socially constituting discursive practices and institutionalized or culturally standardized discourses (Gubrium and Holstein, 2003a; Hacking, 2004; G. Miller, 1997).

Moreover, the methodological perspective on which we elaborate in this book is based on a recognition that human activity at all levels always takes place within and over concretely 'contested terrain', as Grossberg ([1986] 1996: 154) has argued. The meanings and discourses that shape and organize social life are actively transformed, reconstructed and contested not only at the institutional or disciplinary, political, and cultural level, but also at the small-group level in everyday social practices and interaction (Davies and Harré, 1990; Hall, 1997b; Potter and Wetherell, 1987). As Stuart Hall (1997a) has argued, meaning is always being negotiated and inflected with new situations; it is often contested, and sometimes even bitterly fought over. At the level of everyday interaction, people can be seen to constantly try to 'bend what they are given to their own needs and desires, to win a bit of space for themselves, a bit of power over their own lives and society's future' (Grossberg, [1986] 1996: 154).

What is the conception of subjectivity in ACP?

Questions of subjectivity are important because the ontological assumptions that we make guide the ways in which we do research in very concrete ways. Discussing personal interviews, Gubrium and Holstein, for example, argue that:

> [t]here is always a working model of the subject lurking behind the persons assigned to the roles of interviewer and respondent. By virtue of the kinds of subjects we project, we confer varying senses of epistemological agency upon interviewers and respondents. These, in turn, influence the ways we proceed technically, as well as our understanding of the relative validity of the information that is produced. (2003b: 30)

ACP relies on poststructuralist or postmodern conceptions of subjectivity. Being a subject is acknowledged as 'the condition for and instrument of agency' (Butler, 1997: 10). But accordingly with the poststructuralist assumptions about language and discourse, it is not conceived of merely as the 'agent' who performs the action but, rather as the 'subject' who is also 'subjected' or subordinated to various cultural practices and material conditions. The subject is thus viewed as being constituted through representational systems and discourses. It is the product of interplay between cultural discourses and everyday discursive practices, as discussed above.

It is taken that subjectivity is largely a product of the individual's *positioning* within a system of representation or discourse in a field of power. Subjectivity is conceived in terms of multiple and changing *subject positions*, which people take and are given, possibly also subvert and resist, and which are produced or made available by the discourses that are called on in different situations and historical contexts.

At the level of social practices, this positioning is taken to be both interactive, that is, what one person says positions another, or reflexive, that is, people position themselves, but rarely intentionally or consciously (Davies and Harré, 1990; Potter and Wetherell, 1987). Nevertheless, the position that an individual becomes assigned to is viewed to largely determine the conditions of possibility for acting and constructing reality. As Bronwyn Davies and Rom Harré have put it:

> [a] subject position incorporates both a conceptual repertoire and a location for persons within the structure of rights for those that use that repertoire. Once having taken up a particular position as one's own, a person inevitably sees the world from the vantage point of that position and in terms of the particular images, metaphors, storylines and concepts which are made relevant within the particular discursive practice in which they are positioned. (1990: 46)

To illustrate, from this perspective, environmentally responsible consumption could be conceptualized and analyzed in terms of the multiple subject positions that people take and are given to as 'green consumers', and which are produced through discourse (Moisander, 2001). The analytic focus, then, could be on what kind of subject positions the dominant discourses of green consumerism produce for the 'green consumer'. What are the cultural institutions and appropriate procedures (acts, gestures and desires) for being a green consumer? This approach to subjectivity would seem to discourage approaching green consumerism as a question of 'natural being', for example, as a natural inclination to care and take responsibility or as an inherent or socially acquired essential anarchist predisposition to rebel against society. It shifts the focus to the complex processes of knowledge and discursive power that produce the subject positions associated with green consumerism. It also denaturalizes and politicizes the notion of the consumer as an autonomous, choosing individual who is responsible for the environmental protection that the dominant economic discourse of the markets seems to produce and naturalize. Doing this, it would also appear to question perhaps one of the most important foundational premises that legitimize the regulatory harmony of the markets in sustainable development.

Such a non-essentialist position with respect to the theory of agency would, thus, seem to postulate a discursively variable construction of self and action, emphasizing the fluid and constantly transforming nature of subjectivity as a site of agency and subversion (e.g., Grossberg, [1986] 1996; Braidotti, 1994). An interesting non-essentialist conception of the subject that has emerged from the critical postmodern and poststructural discussion on subjectivity might be called a migratory or *nomadic subject*, which Grossberg describes as:

> a subject that is constantly remade, reshaped as a mobilely situated set of relations in a fluid context. The nomadic subject is amoeba-like, struggling to win some space for itself in its local situation. The subject itself has become a site of articulation with its own history, determinations and effect. ([1986] 1996: 166)

Consequently, subjectivity is viewed as distributed, emergent and contextual rather than singular, independent, self-contained and self-generative. The subject is not conceived as consisting of one single 'true self', to be described once and for all, but of multiple selves, or as a continuously changing and fluid history of relationships. Wetherell and Maybin, (1996: 226), for example, have argued that it is best understood as distributed, being the sum and swarm of participations in social life, contextual or different in different relational settings, and emergent in the sense that it is continually constituted in different social sites. They argue that in any highly differentiated industrial society, movement across different social sites from home to work, for example, embroils the person in different contexts and, thus, creates different identity possibilities. Each of these communities has its own claims and its own identity pathways. There is, thus, not one self-emerging but multiple and sometimes contradictory configurations.

To sum up, ACP is based on the assumption that people are significantly limited and constrained by available discourses and the subject positions they offer. Discourses and systems of representation create the possibilities of what we are and what we can become. They construct places from which we can position ourselves and from which we can speak, as Kathryn Woodward (1997) has argued. But, within the limits of, and enabled by their discursively constituted subjectivities, people are assumed to have the capability of shaping their lives. They may well contest the identities and subject positions that are given to them and the associated moral orders that they are subject to. Therefore, in different social situations people are positioned and they position themselves differently. Consequently, when studying social behavior, the focus of interest is above all on the specific configurations of the systems of representation in which the subjectivities that individuals take are continuously and repeatedly produced, reproduced and resisted.

What's wrong with the 'humanist' subject?

Problematization of the prevalent modernist conceptions of the transcendental centered, 'humanist' subject has been a central theme in postmodern and poststructuralist critiques of philosophy and social theory. In much of social scientific research, particularly in psychology, the subject tends to be depicted as a unique individual who has an essential inner core or center – for example, 'that self which one truly is' (Rogers, 1961) – largely sheltered from social and cultural forces. Such conceptions of the subject are often labeled 'humanist' as they tend to entail a belief in the humanist premise that there is an essential 'human nature' – that is, the universal essence of human beings that is an attribute of all individuals – which can form the basis for moral judgments and actions.[5] Research premised upon these views of the subject has tended to conceptualize human beings – be it consumers, managers or researchers – as fairly autonomous agents whose mind is capable of independent thought and action (Atkinson and Silverman, 1997; Burkit, 1998; Gergen, 1998; Hall, 1992b). In the poststructuralist critique of social inquiry, which informs much of contemporary cultural studies and also the methodological perspective that we elaborate on in this book, many of these assumptions have been rejected as highly problematic. The 'humanist subject' is criticized particularly for the overly individualistic and essentialistic[6] assumptions that it involves. For most poststructuralist critics, and for us, questions of subjectivity and human nature are not simply philosophical or theoretical issues. They are inextricably linked to *political questions,*[7] as we shall argue and elaborate in the following sections.

On the one hand, for poststructuralist critics the subject as a transcendental, centered 'knowing subject' and the individualist forms of explanation that it entails are epistemologically suspect. Much like in contemporary social epistemology (Longino, 2002; Rolin, 1999, 2002), the 'autonomous' subject of knowledge, for example, a researcher, as a detached, neutral, interchangeable spectator, is rejected, arguing that knowledge always reflects the particular perspectives of the subject. Also, the subject as a meaning-giving self and the focus on what is 'experientially real' for that self is rejected or at least bracketed. The idea that individuals have priviledged access to their inner thoughts and feelings as primary sources of knowledge is problematized. (Think of all the people who pay psychiatrists to find out and make sense of how they feel!) It is argued that the subject is always structured and constituted by a culturally and historically specific network of practices. Therefore, the subject cannot be the starting point for our knowledge of the world (Oksala, 2004).

On the other hand, the autonomous humanist subject is not only theoretically faulted or epistemologically problematic, however. The humanist view of the centered subject is also criticized for entailing an overly individualistic conception of human agency in the sense that it places too much emphasis on the individual and on the virtues of self-reliance and personal independence in social and political life. In marketing and consumer research, for example, this conception of the subject seems to have directed attention either to intrapersonal processes of the mind (for example, motivation and intention) as causal antecedents of overt behaviors or to subjective experience and personal structures of meaning as sources of knowledge about the world.

In positing the primacy or centrality of the subject in the production of meaning and social reality, social scientists and marketing scholars have generally produced fairly reductionist views of social life, in which social phenomena and social problems have been explained as outcomes of individual behaviors and decisions. Adhering to some sort of methodological individualism, researchers have thus grounded their theory on social and cultural phenomena in individual action. To illustrate what we mean by this, we quote Jon Elster, who argues that:

> [t]he elementary unit of social life is the individual human action. To explain social institutions and social change is to show how they arise as the result of the action and interaction of individuals. (1989: 13)

In the context of social marketing research related to environmental protection, for example, environmental degradation, which is arguably a complex social and political problem, has been studied primarily as a fairly simple problem of 'socially conscious' or 'ethically responsible' individual choice (Moisander, 2000b).

Such individualistic conceptualizations and understandings of subjectivity, agency and social phenomena may be viewed as problematic – particularly in the context of social problems – because they tend to place little emphasis on, or even fail altogether to recognize, the historical, political and social limits and conditions of life. Moreover, this view of the subject as a stable core self with an essential human nature that is responsible for its moral judgments and behavioral choices is likely to hide the interests and power relations through which this 'self' is continuously being constructed and governed. It may therefore sustain the particular configurations and relations of power that are at work in forming and shaping the subjectivity of individuals in different contexts (Butler, 1990; Gergen, 1998).

As Judith Butler (1990), among others, has argued, the coherence and continuity of the person are not logical or analytic features of personhood, but rather socially instituted and maintained norms of intelligibility. Poststructuralist thought, therefore, tends to reject the notion of a core self, and emphasizes the need to deconstruct the humanist assumptions about subjectivity, shifting the focus of inquiry to the complex discursive processes and conditions in which subjectivities emerge, are produced and reproduced.

Consequently, the poststructuralist view of subjectivity is very different from the prevailing conceptions of the subject in the field of marketing and consumer research. It seems important to stress here that the difference between the post-structuralist cultural research and mainstream marketing and consumer research is *not* mainly on the different degree of emphasis each gives to the social and cultural factors in determining consumer behavior. While much of the earlier critical sociologically oriented 'interpretive' marketing research has tended to focus on various economic, political or socio-cultural structural and contextual factors, as 'social facts' or variables that *impinge upon* or *influence* the core human self, the more poststructuralist streams of contemporary cultural studies increasingly reject the idea of a prediscursive core self altogether.

Why is the focus in ACP always on the political aspects of marketplace activity?

From the discursive perspective that we take in this book, marketplace behavior and interaction are inherently political in nature. In one way or another, they always act upon the actions of others, and thus entail the exercise of power (Foucault, 1983). As cultural practices, marketing and consumption may therefore have multifarious effects on social reality and social relations. From this perspective it is important to critically analyze the roles and positions that different market actors take and are given in the relations of power involved in processes and practices of consumption and production.

Marketing and consumption are constituent parts of the systems of representation and power/knowledge where the facts, norms, values and role expectations that regulate and organize social life take form and are contested. These systems both constrain and enable writing, speaking, thinking and doing and thus constitute the conditions of possibility for subjectivity and agency (Butler, 1990, 1993, 1997; Foucault, 1978, 1980, 1983). As Dawn Currie's (1997) study on advertising and teenage consumers shows, advertising and marketing communication, much like women's magazines, are implicated in women's social subjectivity. Exerting cultural leadership in struggles surrounding what it means to be a woman, they shape particular consensual images and definitions of femininity. Nevertheless, as she argues, women do not necessarily passively internalize the scripts marketers and advertising professionals write. Gender is an accomplishment that is sustained through ongoing, everyday practices that resonate with or react against the dominant definitions of what it means to be a woman.

Moreover, marketing techniques are designed to act upon the actions of others, to modify the conduct of consumers and other significant stakeholders, such as shareholders, employers and business partners. Marketing may therefore be viewed as a form or technique of *government* (Foucault, 1991; Dean, 1999; Rose, 1999). The term 'government' here does not refer so much to the political or administrative structures of the modern state but, rather, to 'conduct of conduct' or to the ways in which the behavior of individuals or of groups can be led, directed and guided (Foucault, 1983). As Michel Dean defines the concept:

Government is any more or less calculated and rational activity, undertaken by a multiplicity of authorities and agencies, employing a variety of techniques and forms of knowledge, that seeks to shape conduct by working through our desires, aspirations, interests and beliefs, for definite but shifting ends and with a diverse set of relatively unpredictable consequences, effects and outcomes. (Dean, 1999: 11)

Marketing as a form of government, therefore refers to more or less considered and calculated practices that are destined to act upon the possibilities of action of other people, particularly consumers, by structuring their possible field of action (Foucault, 1983). To analyze marketing as a form of government is to analyze those practices that shape, sculpt, mobilize and work through the choices, desires, aspirations, needs, wants and lifestyles of consumers and other market actors.

However, according to Foucault (1980), governing people is not a way to force people to do something. It is always a versatile equilibrium involving complementary and conflicting techniques; techniques that impose coercion and processes through which the self is constructed or modified by the subject. Importantly, government thus also involves self-guidance and self-regulation.

Peter Miller and Nikolas Rose (1997) discuss marketing as a distinctive mode of mobilizing the consumer, assembling the subject of consumption. Through institutionalized apparatuses as diverse as advertising, market research, delivery and pricing strategy, marketing creates a vast network of formal and informal techniques for the production of what we might call consuming subjects. As Miller and Rose argue, marketing entails not so much the invention and imposition of 'false needs', but a 'delicate process of identification of the "real needs" of consumers, of affiliating these needs with particular products and in turn of linking these with the habits of their utilization' (1997: 6). Making up the consumer entails simultaneously making up the product or brand and assembling the little rituals of everyday life that give meaning and value to the product or brand. Marketing thus is not so much about influencing or persuading consumers to buy certain products but rather about orchestrating the everyday life of consumers in a way that their 'lifestyle' links up a particular complex of subjective tastes and allegiances with a particular product. Marketing as a technique of government may therefore be understood as a set of cultural techniques for the production of particular modes of being.

The struggles between marketers and consumers are thus not only about what is supplied in the market and at what price, but also about meaning and about the acceptable and desirable modes of being and forms of political society (see e.g., du Gay et al., 1997; Joy and Venkatesh, 1994; Moisander, 2000a; Thompson and Troester, 2002; Valtonen, 2004b). This contestation involves not only open conflict and domination but also more insidious relations and mechanisms of power as well as subtle, insinuating forms of resistance, for example, through practices of government and self-government (Foucault, 1983, 1991).

The different ways in which firms and marketers exert power and exploit consumers have been extensively discussed among the Marxists and critical marketing scholars (e.g., Hirschman, 1993). Also, from a more postmodern perspective, Fuat Firat and Nikhilesh Dholakia (1998: 60) have argued that marketing is a leading force in the signification and representation of values, perceived needs and preferences of the consuming masses.

In the field of consumer research, several authors have also documented the ways in which consumption can involve various forms and modes of *resistance* (Holt, 2003; Thompson and Haytko, 1997). Using the symbolism embodied in brands and practices of consumption, either referring to it or resisting it, consumers make sense of their world, construct their identities, express their selves, and come to take a stance in current moral and political issues. Sometimes this happens in an active, conscious and goal-directed manner, for example, when green consumers boycott multinational corporations or when they actively shape their consumption-related behaviors and their self according to certain political or religious principles (Moisander, 2001; Moisander and Pesonen, 2002).

Often consumption-related resistance is not, however, very conscious, deliberate, or rational. In many marginal subcultures and postmodern tribes, for example, resistance is strongly based on iconic brands. As Holt (2003) has argued, certain brands such as Harley–Davidson are generally associated with resistance to the dominant middle-class lifestyle. As iconic brands, they can be used to solve acute tensions that people feel between their own lives and society's prevailing ideology. These brands therefore have political authority, particularly for those whose way of life contradicts the values of the dominant culture. Such a brand may maintain this authority even when the myths that it encapsulates lose their significance as important cultural models.

Sometimes the contestation concerning the aesthetic, ethical and social meanings of brands and products is brought about by economic, cultural and societal transformations, quite independently of individual consumers' activities. In such a case the political dimensions of consumption may remain implicit and unknown – both to consumers themselves as well as to marketers and market researchers. For example, when the traditional values, norms and ideals lose their relevance as a result of social, economic and cultural transformations in some domain of social life, the meanings of products and brands relevant for that domain also become problematized (e.g., Conroy, 1998). This seems evident, for example, in the market for processed baby foods, where the representation of the ideal mother is being contested and re-negotiated in the media through public discussion on the use of commercial baby foods (Mirjami Lehikoinen, personal communication). As a result, whether or not they like it, producers of baby foods are engaged in struggles surrounding what it means in our society to be a woman and an ideal mother.

How does the cultural approach differ from other interpretive marketing and consumer research?

In many respects, ACP differs from the earlier interpretive approaches to qualitative marketing research, particularly from 'existential-phenomenology' (Thompson et al., 1989) and naturalistic-humanistic inquiry (Belk et al., 1988; Hirschman, 1986), and to some extent also from critical theory (Murray and Ozanne, 1991; Murray et al., 1994, cf. Hetrick and Lozada, 1994).

These interpretivist approaches, as they are appropriated and practiced in marketing and consumer research, tend to focus on the *individual*, whereas the focus of interest in cultural marketing and consumer research – as we define it – lies on analyzing *culture and cultural practices*. The methods developed in the earlier interpretive approaches to qualitative inquiry may undoubtedly offer valuable techniques for gaining insights into the meanings that consumers attach to products and services. But many of the theories employed in these studies, particularly concerning the intra-personal psychological constructs and processes that motivate behavior (such as extended self, self-identity, personal or personalized structures of meanings, etc.), are to some extent paradigmatically incommensurable with and thus not suitable for the methodological perspective on cultural research that we specify in this book. Much of the earlier research on consumer culture has tended to rely on some version of the 'humanist subject' for example.

ACP rather focuses on the discursive and socially constructed aspects of consumption. It focuses on culture and cultural practices as texts and refrains from relying on the 'knowing subject' and from trying to understand the intra-personal psychological constructs of individual consumers. The analytical focus thus shifts from 'tapping into people's minds' as if to reveal their true feelings, thoughts and views, to the specific ways those phenomena are represented or produced discursively in text, talk, images and behavior, as well as to the effects that these discursive practices have for different market actors.

In this sense, ACP is very different from the phenomenological-hermeneutic approaches to qualitative consumer research that have been very popular among interpretive marketing scholars during the past twenty years. It is more in line with the critique of Douglas and Isherwood ([1979] 1996), who highlight the thoroughly social and cultural nature of consumption, the 'liberatory postmodernism' of Firat and Venkatesh (1995), and the poststructuralist feminist critique of consumer research introduced by Bristor and Fischer (1993), which denies that objective knowledge can be obtained by experience and argues that it is socially constructed by historically, socially and politically shaped discourses (1993: 524). Methodologically, the approach also draws from the structural approach of Levy (1981), semiotics of Mick (1986) and the integrative approaches to literary criticism (Stern, 1996).

What is the history of cultural marketing and consumer research?

The origin of the cultural approach to marketing and consumer research lies, perhaps, in the critical, philosophical and radical discussions and debates on mainstream marketing thought (Firat et al., 1987) that were initiated in the 1980s and early 1990s by the 'interpretive' marketing scholars. In the following sections we briefly discuss some of the topics and key concerns of theses debates.

Crisis of relevance and radical marketing thought

From the early advocates of more radical marketing thought to the contemporary postmodern critics, much of the discussion on alternative or radical perspectives to marketing thought has revolved around issues associated with an alleged crisis of relevance in marketing research. This lack of both social and practical pertinence has generally been attributed to a narrow focus and to a methodological inflexibility, which have characterized the prevalent research orientation in mainstream marketing, which the critics have customarily labeled 'positivist' or 'logical empiricist' (e.g., Arndt, 1985; Belk, 1991; Firat et al., 1987). Methodological ideals set by natural sciences have, more or less implicitly, guided marketing research towards testing restricted hypotheses with simple observable variables, thus bringing to marketing rigor of thought and mathematical precision but losing substance and flexibility.

In a seminal book edited by Fuat Firat, Nikhilesh Dholakia and Richard Bagozzi (1987) called *Philosophical and Radical Thought in Marketing*, Richard Fullerton (1987), for example, sarcastically yet vividly described the traditional research style in marketing with an image of the marketing 'scientist' unreflectively aping 'hard' natural sciences in the hope of developing, from scanner data and quantitative virtuosity, 'eternal mathematical theorems' about marketing phenomena. Along the same lines, Morris Holbrook (1987a) argued that the conventional decision-oriented models are mainly applicable to that part of consumer behavior that is (1) easiest to explain (brand choice vs. product usage), (2) most important to practical marketing applications (market share vs. society's quality of life) and (3) most trivial in terms of human happiness (buying vs. consuming).

In general, the radical critics of mainstream marketing have tended to agree that the dominant logical-empiricist approach in marketing thought has inhibited both scholars' and practitioners' understanding of the full dimensions of marketing, contributing to 'marginalism and the cumulation of trivial findings' (Arndt, 1985: 20). Russell Belk (1987: 1), for example, in his ACR presidential address, provocatively declared that consumer researchers had, until then, specialized in doing 'petty, stupid or dull' studies on 'the dog-food level of things'.

Associated with this criticism, there was also a call for a thorough self-critical analysis of the political implications of the received working philosophy of mainstream marketing thought. John Sherry (1991), for example, called for a critical investigation of the power dynamics underwriting the ideology of consumption as well as its dysfunctional consequences that plague contemporary society. Influenced by critical theory, many of the early critics also argued that without a critical self-reflection of their received world-view and epistemological commitments, marketing scholars would become overly one-dimensional in the interests that they serve (Firat et al., 1987; Hirschman, 1993). Many tended to believe that the combination of philosophy with empirical investigation was of fundamental importance. Without it there was a danger that empirical study solidified and legitimized existing dogmas and prejudices.

Continuing this critique, the contemporary postmodern marketing scholars have called for more fundamental shifts in the modernist world-view and the 'established canons' of social sciences in general (Firat and Venkatesh, 1993, 1995; Joy and Venkatesh, 1994; Thompson, 1993). Particularly, postmodern critics have questioned critical theorists' reliance and confidence on the tradition of the Enlightenment, for example, their faith in applying the critical powers of reason to expose and eradicate contemporary forms of unreason, superstition and dogmatism.

On the whole, in the past the alternative interpretive approach to marketing and consumer research has constituted a heterogeneous body of literature grounded, perhaps, on a commitment to contest the prevalent logical-empiricist philosophy of mainstream marketing as well as on a shared view of the need for less reductionist ways of theorizing and studying consumer behavior, as well as on an advocacy of theoretical and methodological pluralism (Firat, 1997; Sherry, 1991). Here, however, discussing the historical and conceptual foundations of cultural marketing and consumer research we find it useful to distinguish the postmodern incredulity from the postpositivist critique.

Postpositivist critique – extending the domain

The early postpositivist critique of consumer research tended to revolve around issues related to extending the domain of consumer research, which had traditionally focused on purchase behavior at the individual level and, thus, on brand choice. Many critics shared the views of Holbrook (1987b: 131), who argued that 'there is a need to ground consumer research in a central preoccupation with consumption, independent of any relevance that subject might carry for marketing managers or [...] for any other external interests'. To gain a deeper understanding of different consumption-related experiences and activities, the critics also called for new theoretical and methodological approaches (Anderson, 1986). As Liisa Uusitalo and Jyrki Uusitalo argue:

> [New concepts and theories] essentially have to integrate existing knowledge from different research traditions. This integration work, at the same time, should be based on the motive of working out a methodology and philosophy of consumer research that dissociates itself from the research practice modeled on a purely positivistically understood idea of natural science. (1981: 562)

Particularly, multidisciplinary perspectives were advocated because neighboring disciplines were believed to harbor concepts, data and problem-solving strategies that expand horizons, heighten creativity and increase validity in consumer research (Wells, 1993). Accordingly, much of the postpositivist research on consumer behavior has been informed by the theoretical and methodological perspectives found in sociology and anthropology. As a consequence, a number of researchers have relied on the use of basic ethnographic methods and anthropological constructs such as 'rituals', 'rites of passage' or 'gift giving' in their attempts to understand consumption phenomena (Belk et al., 1989; Joy, 2001; Schouten, 1991; Wallendorf and Arnould, 1991).

This interest in multidisciplinary perspectives also produced an increased interest in understanding the role of symbols and symbolism in the marketplace and in the lives of consumers. *Structural symbolism*, and the work of anthropologist Claude Levi-Strauss for example, have been very influential in diffusing symbolic perspectives into interpretive marketing and consumer research (e.g., Levy, 1959, 1981). Similarly, the *symbolic anthropology* of Mary Douglas has played an important role in the development of the field in focusing attention on the symbolic and communicative dimensions of products and consumption activities (Douglas and Isherwood, 1996). *Semiotics*, in turn, has drawn attention to various aspects of popular culture and to the ways in which consumption symbols and signs play a role in mediating and creating culture (for a good overview, see Mick, 1986).

Moreover, symbolic interactionism, which is primarily concerned with the subjective aspects of social life, has been influential in focusing attention on the ways in which symbolic products are used to perform particular social roles in everyday settings for example (Solomon, 1983). While the studies that have drawn from symbolic anthropology have dealt primarily with the ways in which the use of symbolic products reflects and maintains a particular cultural order in particular settings, symbolic interactionists have studied people as more creative participants who actively construct their social worlds.

Postpositivist critiques have also drawn inspiration from phenomenology, existentialism and humanistic psychology, focusing on subjective experience and the overall patterns of subjective meaning associated with consumption (see Thompson, 1997; Thompson et al., 1989, 1994). In their seminal article 'The Experiential Aspects of Consumption: Consumer Fantasies, Feelings, and Fun', Morris Holbrook and Elizabeth Hirschman (1982), for example, presented a critique for the then-prevailing information processing model that presumes consumers as logical thinkers and problem-solvers. Drawing on phenomenology, their 'experiential view' turned attention to the ways in which symbolic meanings, hedonic responses and esthetic criteria play a role in consumption experiences.

Finally, some of the postpositivist critique of mainstream marketing thought has also been influenced by different versions of Marxist thought and critical theory. Many critics seem to believe that researchers can be liberated from the biases and errors of their thinking through critical self-reflection and rational thinking. Firat, Dholakia and Bagozzi, for example, have argued that:

> [t]oday marketing needs a thorough deconstruction. Through a process of criticism and self-criticism, it is possible to move to a novel reconstruction based on philosophical and analytical investigations into the assumptions, premises, and proclaimed truths that we have taken for granted for so long ... To be radical means to go to the roots and seek essential realities (relationships, processes, or dimensions) which are not necessarily apparent or reflected at the surface. (Firat et al., 1987: xvii)

Although the postpositivist critique of consumer research would seem to have much to offer for research on consumer behavior, its reliance on and faith in the 'humanist' subject as a political agent is not necessarily without problems, as we have discussed earlier. As the postmodern critics of mainstream marketing thought have emphasized, the prevailing views and implicit assumptions about subjectivity and agency need to be reflected upon and reconsidered.

Poststructuralism and postmodern incredulity

More recently, the critique of mainstream marketing and consumer research has taken a poststructuralist and/or postmodern turn. The postmodern thinkers, influenced by poststructuralism, tend to continue the self-critical work of the post-positivist and radical marketing thinkers, focusing on the narrow, dogmatic and unidimensional working philosophy of marketing and consumer research, and arguing that owing to its modernist assumptions it is unable to tap into the richness and complexity of human experience and social behavior (Firat and Venkatesh, 1993, 1995; Holt, 1997; Joy and Venkatesh, 1994; Thompson, 1993). However, as Alladi Venkatesh, John Sherry and Fuat Firat (1993: 217) have pointed out, postmodern critics emphasize that although the earlier debates on postpositivism and interpretivism are relevant, they cannot offer fundamental shifts in the word-view of marketing thought because they fall within the generally accepted paradigms of modernism and the established canons of social sciences. Therefore, they call for a radical modification of the basic distinctions, assumptions and ideals of the discipline.

Postmodern marketing research refers to a rather small and heterogeneous body of radical marketing literature, which tends to openly contest the modernist, Enlightenment-inspired metaphysics of mainstream marketing and consumer research. Postmodern marketing scholars tend to argue that in marketing and consumer research the taken-for-granted notions related to the consumer, consumption, markets and consumer culture rest largely on certain cultural and philosophical foundations that are found in the general historical framework known as modernism. The modernist framework usually refers to the philosophical and cultural ideas and conditions that have marked the period of modernity, which is usually viewed as starting from the French Enlightenment and lasting up until the present. Modernism and the Enlightenment philosophy have been generally characterized as based on a strong faith in human reason, as well as on the belief that progress in science and technology would be accompanied by progress in politics and morality. It was believed that the problems of both individuals and societies could be solved if the forces of intelligence and virtue could be made to prevail over ignorance and wickedness (Thompson, 1993).

Hence, much of the postmodern critique has addressed the philosophical legacy of the Enlightenment philosophy in marketing thought, deconstructing and contesting its epistemological positions and presenting alternative conceptualizations and theoretical positions. In the main, it is emphasized that postmodernism is a philosophy with its own epistemological assumptions and methodology, and that postmodern thinking advocates a complete rethinking of science in general. On the whole, however, the discussion of postmodernism in marketing and social sciences in general involves a rather perplexing and multi-faceted, even paradoxical critique of 'modernity' and modernist theory that revolves around a number of theoretical issues, cultural developments and conditions (for a review, see Brown, 1997).

Here, however, it would seem necessary to distinguish between three discursive domains to which the term postmodern generally refers: culture, history and theory (Grossberg, 1996). First, in the context of cultural texts, the term 'postmodern' refers to certain developments in architecture, literature, film and art in general. Second, the term 'postmodern' is also used to refer to some cultural changes in contemporary life and to the specificity of the contemporary historical formation or social condition that represents a radical break from modernity. This notion of 'postmodernity', referred to as the 'postmodern time' and 'postmodern era', characterized by fragmentation and uncertainty that arises from the lack of traditional religious and moral norms for example, appears to be a somewhat controversial issue. We personally tend to share the views of Stuart Hall (1996: 133), who argues that although there are some very perplexing features to contemporary culture that tend to outrun the critical and the theoretical concepts generated in the early modernist period, there hardly is 'any such absolutely novel and unified thing as the postmodern condition'. Third, at the level of theory the term refers to postmodern thinking or philosophy with particular views of the nature of knowledge and academic activity for example.[8] Among other things, it rejects the views of knowledge as accurate representation of some external reality and truth as correspondence to that reality, arguing that knowledge is perspectival and therefore there can be no 'totalizing metanarratives' or knowledge that captures the objective character of the world. It is this sense of the term, postmodern as a theoretical or philosophical perspective or mood, that is mainly of interest here.

Nevertheless, the postmodern turn in radical marketing thought arguably offers valuably perspicacious criticism and a number of fresh ideas for reconstructing marketing and consumer theory. Especially the issues raised by the advocates of a postmodern deconstruction of marketing philosophy seem potentially constructive here. Particularly, it would seem fruitful to consider the ideas of the postmodern critics (Firat and Venkatesh, 1993, 1995; Joy and Venkatesh, 1994; Thompson, 1993; Venkatesh et al., 1993) who have been inspired by recent poststructuralist thought and called for:

- rejecting the metanarrative of scientific truth;
- recognizing the textuality and discursive nature of culture, identity, consumption and representation;
- rejecting the transcendent, centered subject, and
- reflecting on the role of marketing and business activities in society and in the production of contemporary consumer culture in particular.

A central feature of this postmodern mood in marketing and consumer research is an incredulity toward 'metanarratives', which refers to doubt, skepticism, uncertainty and critical self-reflection concerning the prevailing ('modernist') transcendental subject assumptions and universal theories designed to explain social behavior and phenomena (e.g., Firat and Venkatesh, 1993, 1995; Thompson, 1993). Postmodernists question the spirit of modernity that aspires to master such frameworks or metanarratives for verifying and systematizing knowledge, and more broadly, for rationally organizing social life (Thompson, 1993). Rather, postmodern critics view many of the modernist narratives as time-bound cultural and historical constructions. Accordingly, as Firat and Venkatesh (1995) have observed, postmodern marketing thought questions the universal and transcendental status accorded to such categories as reason, truth, science, knowledge, rationality, progress and the like.

These 'postmodern' and poststructuralist views also inform the cultural perspective that we have taken on qualitative methodology in this book.

Notes

1   These shortcomings in methodological sophistication may arise from the fact that the prevalent disciplinary matrix, particularly in the United States, with its 'positivistic' narrative conventions, concerns and standards of rigor, have placed limits on researchers' interpretive horizons and truncated the range of theoretical questions that can be explored, as Craig Thompson (2002: 143) has argued.

2   In specifying the methodological perspective to cultural marketing and consumer research that we discuss in this book, we draw significantly from the 'analytics of interpretive practice' proposed by Jaber Gubrium and James Holstein (2003a) and also from Huber Dreyfus and Paul Rabinow's (1983) analysis of Michel Foucault's 'interpretive analytics'. We however have chosen to refer to the methodological perspective that we discuss in this book as 'analytics of *cultural* practice' to emphasize that the analytic focus in this approach lies strictly on cultural practices – not on the personalized meanings, values and experience of individual members of a culture.

3   The terms that different scholars use when referring to the discursive resources or interpretive frameworks that people use to construct meaning vary, to some extent, depending on the theoretical aspects emphasized in different approaches to discourse analysis. The term 'discourse', however, has arguably become a fairly widely adopted general term that refers to these interpretive frameworks. Some scholars prefer to use their own, specifically designed concepts, such as 'interpretive repertoires' (Potter, 1996) or 'conceptual repertoires' (Davies and Harré, 1990) when discussing the discursive production of meaning.

4   Although Saussure's work has been most influential for cultural theories in many ways, in particular in advancing the idea of arbitrary and relational meanings, we also consider it important to acknowledge and be aware of the diversity of theories of language that underlie and guide the work of distinctive cultural authors. The work of Mary Douglas, for example, draws inspiration from the socio-linguistics of Basil Bernstein (Atkinson, 1985) that highlights the variety of ways language may be used in different social contexts. This idea lies behind the Douglasian view of context-dependent nature of meanings.

5   We wish to point out here, however, that what is often referred to as 'humanism' – much like post-structuralism or postmodernism – is not a coherent theoretical and philosophical position. There coexist a number of different and often incommensurable 'humanisms', and 'humanists' frequently hold opposing philosophical or theoretical positions (Homer, 2000). Therefore, there are in fact multiple humanist subjects: the Sartrean, the Heideggerian and the positivist subjects, for example.

6   Essentialism, here, refers to the belief that people and/or phenomena have an underlying and unchanging essence, for example, either biologically (physiological, genetic) or socio-culturally determined fundamental or inherent character, nature or predisposition.

7   Gergen (1998: 43), for example, argues that individualist conceptualizations and tendencies should be rejected because they sustain 'a deeply flawed tradition of self-contained individualism'. Instead, he and many other constructionist scholars advocate an emphasis on community (interdependence, negotiation, dialogue) as the site of moral and political action.

8   Postmodern philosophy is characterized particularly by anti-foundationalism, anti-essentialism, and anti-realism.

FURTHER READING

For more details about the historical underpinnings and theoretical legacies of cultural marketing and consumer research we recommend the texts by Stuart Hall and Joost van Loon. They map the different streams of cultural studies and ethnography and discuss the basic philosophical and political tensions between the different approaches.

(Continued)

(Continued)

- Hall, Stuart (1980) 'Cultural Studies: Two Paradigms', *Media, Culture, and Society*, 2: 57–72.
- Hall, Stuart (1992) 'Cultural Studies and its Theoretical Legacies', in L. Grossberg et al. (eds), *Cultural Studies*. New York: Routledge. pp. 277–94. (Marxism/critical theory, postmodernism and cultural research)
- Van Loon, Joost (2001) 'Ethnography: Critical Turn in Cultural Studies', in P. Atkinson, A. Coffey, S. Delamont, J. Lofland and L. Lofland (eds), *Handbook of Ethnography*. London, Sage. pp. 273–84.

To learn more about marketing as a technology of government and about the ways in which marketers and marketing research are engaged in the cultural construction of consumer subjectivities we recommend that you read the seminal article 'Mobilizing the Consumer' by Nikolas Rose and Peter Miller. Their article is based on a set of interesting case studies, which focus on the different ways in which the individual has been linked to the act of consumption and to the object of consumption by means of 'psy' expertise.

- Miller, Peter and Rose, Nikolas (1997) 'Mobilizing the Consumer: Assembling the Subject of Consumption', *Theory, Culture and Society*, 14: 1–36.

Judith Butler provides an interesting poststructuralist account of subjectivity in her theorization of gender as a performative identity. In her later work, which is also cited in this book, she continues this theoretical development but *Gender Trouble* serves as a good introduction to the argument.

- Butler, Judith (1990) *Gender Trouble: Feminism and the Subversion of Identity*. London: Routledge.

Margaret Wetherell provides a good account of the contemporary methodological debates in discourse research, elaborating particularly on differences in evaluative criteria between two different streams of discourse analysis, conversation analysis and poststructuralist discourse analysis.

- Wetherell, Margaret (1998) 'Positioning and Interpretative Repertoires: Conversation Analysis and Post-structuralism in Dialogue', *Discourse & Society*, 9 (3): 387–412.

References

Alasuutari, Pertti (1995) *Researching Culture: Qualitative Method and Cultural Studies.* London: Sage.

Alasuutari, Pertti (1996) 'Theorizing in Qualitative Research: A Cultural Studies Perspective', *Qualitative Inquiry*, 2 (4): 371–84.

Anderson, Paul (1986) 'On Method in Consumer Research: A Critical Relativist Perspective', *Journal of Consumer Research*, (Sept.) 13: 155–73.

Appadurai, Arjun (1996) *Modernity at Large: Cultural Dimensions of Globalisation.* Minneapolis, MN: University of Minneapolis Press.

Arndt, Johan (1985) 'On Making Marketing Science More Scientific: Role of Orientations, Paradigms, Metaphors, and Puzzle Solving', *Journal of Marketing*, 49: 11–23.

Arnold, Stephen J. and Fischer, Eileen (1994) 'Hermeneutics and Consumer Research', *Journal of Consumer Research*, 21 (June): 55–70.

Arnould, Eric J. and Thompson, Craig J. (2005) 'Consumer Culture Theory (CCT): Twenty Years of Research', *Journal of Consumer Research*, 31 (March): 868–82.

Arnould, Eric J. and Price, Linda J. (1993) 'River Magic: Hedonic Consumption and the Extended Service Encounter', *Journal of Consumer Research*, 20 (June): 24–45.

Arnould, Eric J. and Wallendorf, Melanie (1994) 'Market-Oriented Ethnography: Interpretation Building and Marketing Strategy Formulation', *Journal of Marketing Research*, 31 (Nov.): 484–504.

Arnould, Eric, Price, Linda and Zinkhan, George (2002) *Consumers.* New York: McGraw–Hill.

Atkinson, Paul (1985) *Language, Structure, and Reproduction: An Introduction to the Sociology of Basil Bernstein.* London: Methuen.

Atkinson, Paul and Coffey, Amanda (1997) 'Analyzing Documentary Realities', in D. Silverman (ed.), *Qualitative Research: Theory, Method, and Practice.* London: Sage. pp. 45–62.

Atkinson, Paul and Silverman, David (1997) 'Kundera's Immortality: The Interview Society and the Invention of the Self', *Qualitative Inquiry*, 3 (3): 304–25.

Atkinson, Paul, Coffey, Amanda and Delamont, Sara (2001a) 'A Debate about Our Canon', *Qualitative Research*, 1 (1): 5–21.

Atkinson, Paul, Coffey, Amanda, Delamont, Sara Lofland, John and Lofland, Lyn (eds) (2001b) *Handbook of Ethnography.* London: Sage.

Ball, Michael S. and Smith, Gregory W.H. (1992) *Analyzing Visual Data.* Qualitative Research Methods, Vol. 24. Newbury Park, CA: Sage.

Banks, Marcus (1995) 'Visual Research Methods', *Social Research Update*, Social Research Update, Issue 11, Department of Sociology, University of Surrey, available online at: http://www.soc.surrey.ac.uk./sru/SRU11/SRU11.html.

Barbour, Rosaline S. and Kitzinger, Jenny (1999) *Developing Focus Group Research. Politics, Theory and Practice.* London: Sage.

Barter, Christine and Renold, Emma (1999) 'The Use of Vignettes in Qualitative Research', *Social Research Update*, Issue 25, Department of Sociology, University of Surrey, available online at: http://www.soc.surrey.ac.uk/sru/SRU25.html.

Bateman, Anthony and Holmes, Jeremy (1995) *Introduction to Psychoanalysis: Contemporary Theory and Practice*. London and New York: Routledge.

Beckmann, Suzanne C. and Elliot, Richard (2000) *Interpretive Consumer Research: Paradigms, Methodologies, and Applications*. Copenhagen: Copenhagen Business School Press.

Belk, Russell W. (1987) 'ACR Presidential Address: Happy Thought', in M. Wallendorf and P. Anderson (eds), *Advances of Consumer Research*, No. 14. Provo, UT: Association for Consumer Research. pp. 1–4.

Belk, Russell W. (1988) 'Possessions and the Extended Self', *Journal of Consumer Research*, 15 (Sept.): 139–68.

Belk, Russell W. (ed.) (1991) *Highways and Buyways: Naturalistic Research from the Consumer Behavior Odyssey*. Provo, UT: Association for Consumer Research.

Belk, Russell W., Ger, Güliz and Askegaard, Søren (1997) 'Consumer Desire in Three Cultures: Results from Projective Research', *Advances in Consumer Research*, 24: 24–8.

Belk, Russell W., Ger, Güliz and Askegaard, Søren (2003) 'The Fire of Desire: A Multisited Inquiry into Consumer Passion', *Journal of Consumer Research*, 30 (Dec.): 326–49.

Belk, Russell W., Wallendorf, Melanie and Sherry, John F. (1988) 'A Naturalistic Inquiry into Buyer and Seller Behavior at a Swap Meet', *Journal of Consumer Research*, 14 (March): 449–70.

Belk, Russell W., Wallendorf, Melanie and Sherry, John F. (1989) 'The Sacred and the Profane in Consumer Behavior: Theodicy on the Odyssey', *Journal of Consumer Research*, 16 (June): 1–38.

Bitner, Mary Jo (1992) 'Servicescapes: The Impact of Physical Surroundings on Customers and Employees', *Journal of Marketing*, 56 (April): 57–71.

Braidotti, Rosi (1994) *Nomadic Subjects: Embodiment and Sexual Difference in Contemporary Feminist Theory*. New York: Columbia University Press.

Branthwaite, Alan and Lunn, Tony (1985) 'Projective Techniques in Social and Market Research', in R. Walker (ed.), *Applied Qualitative Research*. Aldershot: Gower. pp. 101–21.

Bristor, Julia M. and Fischer, Eileen (1993) 'Feminist Thought: Implications for Consumer Research', *Journal of Consumer Research*, 19 (March): 518–36.

Brown, Stephen (1995) *Postmodern Marketing*. London and New York: Routledge.

Brown, Stephen (1997) 'Marketing Science in a Postmodern World: Introduction to a Special Issue', *European Journal of Marketing*, 31 (3/4): 167–82.

Brown, Stephen (1999) 'Marketing and Literature: The Anxiety of Academic Influence', *Journal of Marketing*, 63 (Jan.): 1–15.

Brown, Stephen, Hirschman, Elizabeth and Maclaran, Pauline (2001) 'Always Historicize! Researching Marketing History in a Post-historical Epoch', *Marketing Theory*, 1 (1): 49–89.

Brown, Stephen, Kozinets, Robert W. and Sherry, John F. Jr (2003) 'Teaching Old Brands New Tricks: Retro Branding and the Revival of Brand Meaning', *Journal of Marketing*, 67 (July): 19–33.

Burkitt, Ian (1998) 'Relations, Communication and Power', in I. Velody and R. Williams (eds), *The Politics of Constructionism*. London: Sage. pp. 121–31.

Butler, Judith (1993) *Bodies that Matter: On the Discursive Limits of 'Sex'*. New York: Routledge.

Butler, Judith (1997) *The Psychic Life of Power: Theories in Subjection*. Stanford, CA: Stanford University Press.

Butler, Judith (1990) *Gender Trouble: Feminism and the Subversion of Identity*. London: Routledge.

Clifford, James and Marcus, George E. (1986) *Writing Culture: The Poetics and Politics of Ethnography*. Berkeley, CA: University of California Press.

Coffey, Amanda (1999) *The Ethnographic Self: Fieldwork and the Representation of Identity*. London: Sage.

Coffey, Amanda and Atkinson, Paul (1996) *Making Sense of Qualitative Data: Complementary Research Strategies*. Thousand Oaks, CA: Sage.

Conroy, Marianne (1998) 'Factory Outlet Malls, Consumption, and the Performance of Middle-Class Identity', *Social Text*, 54 (1): 63–83.

Cova, Bernard and Cova, Veronique (2002) 'Tribal Marketing: The Tribalisation of Society and Its Impact on the Conduct of Marketing', *European Journal of Marketing*, 36 (5/6): 595–620.

Crabtree, James, Nathan, Max and Roberts, Simon (2003) *Mobile UK – Mobile Phones and Everyday Life*. The Work Foundation/iSociety, London: Peter Runge House.

Culler, Jonathan ([1981] 2001) *The Pursuit of Signs*. London and New York: Routledge.

Currie, Dawn H. (1997) 'Decoding Femininity: Advertisements and Their Teenage Readers', *Gender & Society*, 11 (4): 453–77.

Czarniawska, Barbara (2004) 'On Time, Space, and Action Nets', *Organization*, 11 (6): 773–88.

Davies, Bronwyn and Harré, Rom (1990) 'Positioning: The Discursive Production of Selves', *Journal for the Theory of Social Behavior*, 20: 43–63.

Davis, Murray S. (1971) 'That's Interesting! Towards a Phenomenology of Sociology and a Sociology of Phenomenology', *Philosophy of Social Sciences*, 1: 309–44.

De Saussure, Ferdinand (1983) *Course in General Linguistics*. London: Duckworth.

Dean, Mitchell (1999) *Governmentality: Power and Rule in Modern Society*. London: Sage.

Denzin, Norman K. (2001a) 'The Seventh Moment: Qualitative Inquiry and the Practices of a More Radical Consumer Research', *Journal of Consumer Research*, 28 (Sept.): 324–30.

Denzin, Norman K. (2001b) 'The Reflexive Interview and a Performative Social Science', *Qualitative Research*, 1 (1): 23–46.

Denzin, Norman K. and Lincoln, Yvonna S. (eds) (2002) *The Qualitative Inquiry Reader*. Thousand Oaks, CA: Sage.

Denzin, Norman K. and Lincoln, Yvonna S. (2003) 'Introduction: The Discipline and Practice of Qualitative Research', in N.K. Denzin and N.S. Lincoln (eds), *The Landscape of Qualitative Research*. London: Sage. pp. 1–45.

DiMaggio, Paul (1995) 'Comments on "What Theory is *Not*"', *Administrative Science Quarterly*, 40: 391–7.

Dougherty, Deborah Jane (1988) 'Understanding New Markets for New Products', *Strategic Management Journal*, 11: 59–78.

Douglas, Mary (2002) *Purity and Danger: An Analysis of the Concepts of Pollution and Taboo*. London and New York: Routledge.

Douglas, Mary and Baron Isherwood (1996) *The World of Goods: Towards an Anthropology of Consumption*. London: Routledge.

Dreyfus, Hubert L. and Rabinow, Paul (1983) *Michel Foucault: Beyond Structuralism and Hermeneutics*. Chicago: University of Chicago Press.

du Gay, Paul, Hall, Stuart, Janes, Linda, Mackay, Hugh and Negus, Keith (1997) *Doing Cultural Studies: The Story of the Sony Walkman*. London: Sage.

Dyer, W. Gibb and Wilkins, Alan L. (1989) 'Better Stories, Not Better Constructs, to Generate Better Theory: A Rejoinder to Eisenhardt', *Academy of Management Review*, 14 (4): 613–19.

Eisenhardt, Kathleen M. (1989) 'Building Theories from Case Study Research', *Academy of Management Review*, 14 (4): 532–50.

Ellis, Carolyn and Bochner, Arthur P. (2000) 'Autoethnography, Personal Narrative, Reflexivity: Researcher as Subject', in N.K. Denzin and Y.S. Lincoln (eds), *Handbook of Qualitative Research*. London: Sage. pp. 733–68.

Elster, Jon (1989) *Nuts and Bolts for the Social Sciences*. Cambridge: Cambridge University Press.

Emerson, Robert M., Fretz, Rachel I. and Shaw, Linda L. (1995) *Writing Ethnographic Fieldnotes*. Chicago: University of Chicago Press.

Emmison, Michael and Smith, Philip (2002) *Researching the Visual: Images, Objects, Contexts and Interactions in Social and Cultural Inquiry*. London: Sage.

Falzon, Christopher (1998) *Foucault and Social Dialogue: Beyond fragmentation*. London and New York: Routledge.

Fine, Mark A. and Kurdek, Lawrence A. (1993) 'Reflections on Determining Authorship Credit and Authorship Order on Faculty–Student Collaborations', *American Psychologist*, 48 (11): 1141–7.

Firat, Fuat A. (1997) 'Welcome to CMC', *Consumption, Markets and Culture*, 1, 1–6.

Firat, Fuat A. (1999) 'Rethinking Consumption', *Consumption, Markets & Culture*, 3 (4): 283–376.

Firat, Fuat A. (2001) 'Consumer Research for (the Benefit) of Consumers', *Journal of Research for Consumers*, issue 1, at www.jrconsumers.com.

Firat, Fuat A. and Dholakia, Nikhilesh (1998) *Consuming People: From Political Economy to Theatres of Consumption*. London: Routledge.

Firat, Fuat A. and Venkatesh, Alladi (1993) 'Postmodernity: The Age of Marketing', *International Journal of Research in Marketing*, 10: 227–49.

Firat, Fuat A. and Venkatesh, Alladi (1995) 'Liberatory Postmodernism and the Reenchantment of Consumption', *Journal of Consumer Research*, 22 (Dec.): 239–67.

Firat, Fuat A., Dholakia, Nikhilesh and Bagozzi, Richard (1987) 'Introduction: Breaking the Mold', in Fuat A. Firat, Nikhilesh Dholakia and Richard Bagozzi (eds), *Philosophical and Radical Thought in Marketing*. Lexington, MA: Lexington Books. pp. xiii–xxi.

Fischer, Eileen and Bristor, Julia (1994) 'A Feminist Post-structuralist Analysis of the Rhetoric of Marketing', *International Journal of Research in Marketing*, 11 (4): 317–31.

Foley, Douglas and Valenzuela, Angela (2005) 'Critical Ethnography: The Politics of Collaboration', in N.K. Denzin and Y.S. Lincoln (eds), *Handbook of Qualitative Research*. London: Sage. pp. 217–34.

Foucault, Michel (1972) *The Archaeology of Knowledge*. London: Tavistock Publications.

Foucault, Michel (1977) *Discipline and Punish: The Birth of the Prison*. New York: Vintage/Random House.

Foucault, Michel (1978) *The History of Sexuality, Vol. 1: The Will to Knowledge*. New York: Pantheon Books.

Foucault, Michel (1980) *Power/Knowledge: Selected Interviews and Other Writings, 1972–1977*. Brighton: Harvester.

Foucault, Michel (1983) 'The Subject and Power', in H. Dreyfus, and P. Rabinov (eds), *Michel Foucault: Beyond Structuralism and Hermeneutics*. Chicago: Chicago University Press. pp. 214–32.

Foucault, Michel (1986) *The History of Sexuality, Vol. 2: The Use of Pleasure*. New York: Viking.

Foucault, Michel (1991) 'Governmentality', in G. Burchell, C. Gordon and P. Miller (eds), *The Foucault Effect: Studies in Governmentality*. Chicago: University of Chicago Press. pp. 87–104.

Fournier, Susan (1998) 'Consumers and their Brands: Developing Relationship Theory in Consumer Research', *Journal of Consumer Research*, 24 (March): 343–73.

Frow, John and Morris, Meaghan (2003) 'Cultural Studies', in N.K. Denzin and Y.S. Lincoln (eds), *The Landscape of Qualitative Research: Theories and Issues*. London: Sage. pp. 489–539.

Fullerton, Richard A. (1987) 'The Poverty of Ahistorical Analysis: Present Weakness and Future Cure in US Marketing thought', in Fuat A. Firat, Nikhilesh Dholakia and Richard Bagozzi (eds), *Philosophical and Radical Thought in Marketing*. Lexington, MA: Lexington Books. pp. 97–116.

Gadamer, Hans-George (1989) *Truth and Method*. New York: Crossroad.

Geertz, Clifford (1973) *The Interpretation of Cultures*. New York: Basic Books.

Gergen, Kenneth J. (1997) 'The Place of the Psyche in a Constructed World', *Theory and Psychology*, 7: 723–46.

Gergen, Kenneth J. (1998) 'Constructionist Dialogues and the Vicissitudes of the Political', in I. Velody and R. Williams (eds), *The Politics of Constructionism*. London: Sage. pp. 33–48.

Gergen, Mary M. and Gergen, Kenneth J. (2003) 'Qualitative Inquiry: Tensions and Transformations', N.K. Denzin and N.S. Lincoln (eds), *The Landscape of Qualitative Research*. London: Sage. pp. 575–610.

Gergen, Kenneth J. and Thatchenkery, Tojo J. (1997) 'Organizational Science in a Postmodern Context', *Journal of Behavioral Science*, 32: 356–77.

Glaser, Barney G. and Strauss, Anselm L. (1967) *The Discovery of Grounded Theory*. Chicago: Aldine.

Goffman, Erving (1979) *Gender Advertisements*. New York: Harper & Row.

Goldman, Robert and Papson, Stepen (2004) *Nike Culture: The Sign of the Swoosh*. London: Sage.

Gould, Stephen, J. (1995) 'Researcher Introspection as a Method in Consumer Research: Applications, Issues, and Implications', *Journal of Consumer Research,* 21 (March): 719–22.

Green, Eileen and Adams, Alison (eds) (2001) *Technology, Consumption and Identity*. London: Routledge.

Grossberg, Lawrence ([1986] 1996) 'History, Politics and Postmodernism: Stuart Hall and Cultural Studies', in D. Morley and K-H. Chen (eds), *Stuart Hall: Critical Dialogues in Cultural Studies*. London: Routledge. pp. 151–73 [*Journal of Communication Inquiry*, 10 (2): 61–77].

Gubrium, Jaber F. and Holstein, James A. (2003a) 'Analyzing Interpretive Practice', in N.K. Denzin and Y.S. Lincoln (eds), *Strategies of Qualitative Inquiry*. London: Sage. pp. 214–48.

Gubrium, Jaber F. and Holstein, James A. (2003b) 'From the Individual Interview to the Interview Society', in J.F. Gubrium and J. Holstein (eds), *Postmodern Interviewing*. London: Sage.

Guion, Lisa (2002) 'Establishing the Validity of Qualitative Studies', Publication FCS6014 of the Department of Family, Youth and Community Sciences, Florida Cooperative Extension Service, Institute of Food and Agricultural Sciences, University of Florida (available online at: http://edis.ifas.ufl.edu/pdffiles/FY/FY39400.pdf).

Hacking, Ian (1999) *The Social Construction of What?* Cambridge, MA: Harvard University Press.

Hacking, Ian (2004) 'Between Michel Foucault and Erving Goffman: Between Discourse in the Abstract and Face-to-Face Interaction', *Economy and Society*, 33 (3): 277–302.

Hall, Stuart (1980) 'Cultural Studies: Two Paradigms', *Media, Culture, and Society*, 2: 57–72.

Hall, Stuart (1992a) 'The West and the Rest: Discourse and Power', in S. Hall and B. Gieben (eds), *Formations of Modernity*. London: Sage/The Open University. pp. 275–320.

Hall, Stuart (1992b) 'The Question of Cultural Identity', in S. Hall et al. (eds), *Modernity and Its Futures*. London: Sage/ The Open University. pp. 273–316.

Hall, Stuart (1996) 'The Meaning of New Times', in D. Morley and K-H. Chen (eds), *Stuart Hall: Critical Dialogues in Cultural Studies*. London: Routledge. pp. 223–37.

Hall, Stuart (1997a) 'The Work of Representation', in S. Hall (ed.), *Representation: Cultural Representations and Signifying Processes*, pp. 13–74.

Hall, Stuart (1997b) 'The Spectacle of the Other', in S. Hall (ed.), *Representation: Cultural Representations and Signifying Processes*, London: Sage. pp. 223–79.

Hammersley, Martyn (1987) 'Some Notes on the Terms 'Validity' and 'Reliability', *British Educational Research Journal,* 13 (1): 73–81.

Hammersley, Martyn and Atkinson, Paul (1995) *Ethnography: Principles in Practice*, 2nd edn. London: Routledge.

Hammersley, Martyn (2003) 'Conversation Analysis and Discourse Analysis: Methods or Paradigms', *Discourse and Society*, 14 (6): 751–81.

Harper, Douglas (2000) 'Reimagining Visual Methods', in N.K. Denzin and Yvonna S. Lincoln (eds), *Handbook of Qualitative Research*. London: Sage. pp. 717–32.

Hazel, Neal (1995) 'Elicitation Techniques with Young People', *Social Research Update*, Issue 12, Department of Sociology, University of Surrey, http://www.soc.surrey.ac.uk/sru/SRU12.html.

Heisley, Deborah D. and Levy, Sidney J. (1991) 'Autodriving: A Photoelicitation Technique', *Journal of Consumer Research*, 18 (Dec.): 257–72.

Helliwell, Christine and Barry Hindess '"Culture", "society" and the figure of man', *History Of The Human Sciences*, 12 (4): 1–20.

Hetrick, William P. and Lozada, Héctor R. (1994) 'Consuming the Critical Imagination: Comments and Necessary Diversions', *Journal of Consumer Research*, 21 (Dec.): 548–58.

Hine, Christine (2000) *Virtual Ethnography*. London: Sage.

Hirschman, Elizabeth C. (1985) 'Scientific Style and the Conduct of Consumer Research', *Journal of Consumer Research,* 12 (Sept.): 225–39.

Hirschman, Elizabeth C. (1986) 'Humanistic Inquiry in Marketing Research: Philosophy, Method, and Criteria', *Journal of Marketing Research*, 23: 237–49.

Hirschman, Elizabeth C. (ed.) (1989) *Interpretive Consumer Research*. Provo, UT: Association for Consumer Research.

Hirschman, Elizabeth C. (1993) 'Ideology in Consumer Research, 1980 and 1990: A Marxist and Feminist Critique', *Journal of Consumer Research,* 19 (March): 537–55.

Holbrook, Morris B. (1987a) '"Oh Consumer, How You've Changed": Some Radical Reflections on the Roots of Consumption', in Fuat A. Firat, Nikhilesh Dholakia and Richard Bagozzi (eds), *Philosophical and Radical Thought in Marketing*. Lexington, MA: Lexington Books. pp.156–77.

Holbrook, Morris B. (1987b) 'What is Consumer Research?', *Journal of Consumer Research*, 14, 128–32.

Holbrook, Morris B. and Hirschman, Elisabeth C. (1982) 'The Experiential Aspects of Consumption: Consumer Fantasies, Feelings and Fun', *Journal of Consumer Research*, 9 (Sept.): 132–40.

Holbrook, Morris B. and Hirschman, Elisabeth C. (1993) *The Semiotics of Consumption: Interpreting Symbolic Consumer Behavior in Popular Culture and Works of Art*. Berlin: de Gruyter.

Hollander, Jocelyn A. (2004) 'The Social Context of Focus Groups', *Journal of Contemporary Ethnography,* 33 (5): 602–37.

Holt, Douglas B. (1991) 'Rashomon Visits Consumer Behavior: An Interpretive Critique of Naturalistic Inquiry', *Advances in Consumer Research*, 18: 57–62.

Holt, Douglas B. (1997) 'Poststructuralist Lifestyle Analysis: Conceptualizing the Social Patterning of Consumption in Postmodernity', *Journal of Consumer Research*, 23 (March): 326–50.

Holt, Douglas B. (2002) 'Why Do Brands Cause Trouble? A Dialectical Theory of Consumer Culture and Branding', *Journal of Consumer Research*, 29 (June): 387–412.

Holt, Douglas B. (2003) 'What Becomes an Icon Most?', *Harvard Business Review*, 81 (3): 43–9.

Holt, Douglas B. and Thompson, Craig J. (2004) 'Man-of-Action Heroes: The Pursuit of Heroic Masculinity in Everyday Consumption', *Journal of Consumer Research*, 31 (Sept.): 425–40.

Homer, Sean (2000) 'Mapping the Terrain of Theoretical Anti-Humanism', *Free Associations*, 7 (4): 29–51.

Howarth, David (2000) *Discourse*. Buckingham: Open University Press.

Hughes, Rhidian (1998) 'Considering the Vignette Technique and Its Application to a Study of Drug Injecting and HIV Risk and Safer Behaviour', *Sociology of Health and Illness*, 20 (3): 381–400.

Hunt, Shelby D. (1983) *Marketing Theory: The Philosophy of Marketing Science*. Homewood, IL: Richard D. Irwin Inc.

Hurworth, Rosalind (2003) 'Photo-Interviewing for Research', *Social Research Update*, Issue 40, Department of Sociology, University of Surrey, available online at: http://www.soc.surrey.ac.uk./sru/SRU40.html.

Hussey, Michael and Duncombe, Nicola (1999) 'Projecting the Right Image: Using Projective Techniques to Measure Brand Image', *Qualitative Market Research*, 2 (1): 22–30.

Jones, Steve (ed.) (1999) *Doing Internet Research: Critical Issues and Methods for Examining the Net*. Thousand Oaks, CA: Sage.

Joy, Annamma (2001) 'Gift Giving in Hong Kong and the Continuum of Social Ties', *Journal of Consumer Research*, 28 (Sept.): 239–56.

Joy, Annamma and Venkatesh, Alladi (1994) 'Postmodernism, Feminism, and the Body: The Visible and the Invisible in Consumer Research', *International Journal of Research in Marketing*, 11: 333–57.

Karjalainen, Toni-Matti (2004) *Semantic Transformation in Design: Communicating Strategic Brand Identity through Product References*. University of Art and Design Helsinki, A-48. Helsinki: Ilmari Design Publications.

Kassarjian, Harold H. (1987) 'How We Spent Our Summer Vacation: A Preliminary Report on the 1986 Consumer Behavior Odyssey' in M. Wallendorf and P. Anderson (eds), *Advances in Consumer Research*, 14. Provo, UT: Association for Consumer Research. pp. 376–7.

Katila, Saija and Meriläinen, Susan (1999) 'A Serious Researcher or Just Another Nice Girl?: Doing Gender in a Male-Dominated Scientific Community', *Gender, Work and Organization*, 6 (3): 163–73.

Kellner, Douglas (2002) 'Critical Perspectives on Visual Imagery in Media and Cyberculture', *Journal of Visual Literacy*, 1: 81–90.

Kendall, Gavin and Wickham, Gary (1999) *Using Foucault's Methods*. London: Sage.

Kirk, Jerome and Miller, Mark (1986) *Reliability and Validity in Qualitative Research*. Qualitative Research Methods, Vol. 1. Newbury Park, CA: Sage.

Kitcher, Philip (2002) 'The Third Way: Reflections on Helen Longino's *The Fate of Knowledge*', *Philosophy of Science*, 69: 549–59.

Kitzinger, Jenny and Farquhar, Clare (1999) 'The Analytical Potential of "Sensitive Moments" in Focus Group Discussions', in R.S. Barbour and J. Kitzinger (eds), *Developing Focus Group Research. Politics, Theory and Practice,* Thousand Oaks, CA: Sage. pp. 156–72.

Kjeldgaard, Dannie (2002) 'Youth Identities and Consumer Culture: Navigating Local Landscapes of Global Symbols', *Advances in Consumer Research*, 29: 387–92.

Kozinets, Robert V. (2001) 'Utopian Enterprise: Articulating the Meanings of Star Trek's Culture of Consumption', *Journal of Consumer Research*, 28 (June): 67–88.

Kozinets, Robert V. (2002a) 'Can Consumers Escape the Market? Emancipatory Illuminations from Burning Man', *Journal of Consumer Research*, 29 (June): 20–38.

Kozinets, Robert V. (2002b) 'The Field Behind the Screen: Using Netnography for Marketing Research in Online Communities', *Journal of Marketing Research*, 39 (1): 61–72.

Lakoff, George and Johnson, Mark (1980) *Metaphors We Live By*. Chicago and London: University of Chicago Press.

Leiss, William, Kline, Stephen and Jhally, Sut (1986) *Social Communication in Advertising*. New York: Methuen Publications.

Levy, David A. (1997) *Tools of Critical Thinking: Metathoughts for Psychology*. Boston, MA: Allyn and Bacon.

Levy, Sidney J. (1959) 'Symbols for Sale', *Harvard Business Review*, 37 (July): 117–29.

Levy, Sidney J. (1981) 'Interpreting Consumer Mythology: A Structural Approach to Consumer Behavior', *Journal of Marketing*, 45 (Summer): 49–61.

Lewis, Justin (1997) 'What Counts in Cultural Studies?', *Media, Culture & Society*, 19: 83–97.

Lincoln, Yvonna S. and Guba, Egon G. (1985) *Naturalistic Inquiry*. Beverly Hills, CA: Sage.

Lincoln, Yvonna S. and Guba, Egon G. (2003) 'Paradigmatic Controversies, Contradictions, and Emerging Confluences', in N.K. Denzin and N.S. Lincoln (eds), *The Landscape of Qualitative Research*. London: Sage. pp. 253–91.

Lofland, John and Lofland, Lyn H. (1984) *Analyzing Social Settings. A Guide to Observation and Analysis*. Belmont, CA: Wadsworth.

Longino, Helen E. (1995) 'Gender, Politics and the Theoretical Virtues', *Synthese*, 104 (3): 383–97.

Longino, Helen E. (1996) 'Subjects, Power, and Knowledge: Description and Prescription in Feminist Philosophies of Science', in E. Fox Keller and H.E. Longino (eds), *Feminism and Science*. New York: Oxford University Press. pp. 264–79.

Longino, Helen E. (2002) *The Fate of Knowledge*. Princeton, NJ: Princeton University Press.

Macbeth, Douglas (2001) 'On "Reflexivity" in Qualitative Research: Two Readings and a Third', *Qualitative Inquiry*, 7 (1): 35–68.

Mackay, Hugh (ed.) (1997) *Consumption and Everyday Life*. London: Sage.

MacLaren, Pauline and Catterall, Miriam (2002) 'Researching the Social Web: Marketing Information from Virtual Communities', *Marketing Intelligence and Planning*, 20 (6): 319–26.

Madriz, Esther (2000) 'Focus Groups in Feminist Research', in N.K. Denzin and Y.S. Lincoln (eds), *Handbook of Qualitative Research*. Thousand Oaks, CA: Sage. pp. 835–51.

Marcus, George E. and Fischer Michael M.J. (1999) *Anthropology as Cultural Critique*, 2nd edn. Chicago: University of Chicago Press.

McCracken, Grant (1986) 'Culture and Consumption: A Theoretical Account of the Structure and Movement of the Cultural Meaning of Consumer Goods', *Journal of Consumer Research*, 13 (June): 71–85.

McCracken, Grant (1988) *The Long Interview*. Newbury Park, CA: Sage.

McQuarrie, Edward F. and Mick, David G. (1999) 'Visual Rhetoric in Advertising: Text-Interpretive, Experimental, and Reader–Response Analyses', *Journal of Consumer Research*, 26 (June): 37–54.

Mick, David G. (1986) 'Consumer Research and Semiotics: Exploring the Morphology of Signs, Symbols, and Significance', *Journal of Consumer Research*, 13 (Sept.): 196–213.

Mick, David G. and Buhl, Claus (1992) 'A Meaning-Based Model of Advertising Experiences', *Journal of Consumer Research,* 19 (Dec.): 317–38.

Miller, Daniel (1995) 'Consumption and Commodities', *Annual Review of Anthropology*, 24: 141–61.

Miller, Daniel (1997) 'Consumption and Its Consequences', in H. Mackay (ed.), *Consumption and Everyday Life*. London: Sage. pp. 13–54.

Miller, Daniel (1998) *A Theory of Shopping*. Cambridge: Polity Press.

Miller, Gale (1997) 'Building Bridges: The Possibility of Analytic Dialogue Between Ethnography, Conversation Analysis and Foucault', in D. Silverman (ed.), *Qualitative Research: Theory, Method and Practice*. London: Sage. pp. 24–44.

Miller, Peter and Rose, Nikolas (1997) 'Mobilizing the Consumer: Assembling the Subject of Consumption', *Theory, Culture and Society*, 14 (1): 1–36.

Mills C. Wright (2000) *The Sociological Imagination*. New York: Oxford University Press.

Moisander, Johanna (2000a) 'Gender and Green Consumerism: Analyzing a Case of Domestication of Women – the Green Cleaners of the Planet', in J. Schroeder and C. Otnes (eds), *Gender, Marketing, and Consumer Behavior. Proceedings of the 5th Conference*, Urbana, IL: University of Illinois Printing Services. pp. 193–204.

Moisander, Johanna (2000b) 'Group Identity, Personal Ethics, and Sustainable Development: Suggesting New Directions for Social Marketing Research', in E. Jochem et al. (eds), *Society, Behaviour, and Climate Change Mitigation*. Dordrecht: Kluwer Academic Publishers. pp. 127–56.

Moisander, Johanna (2001) 'Representation of Green Consumerism: a Constructionist Critique', Acta Universitatis Oeconomicae Helsingesis, A-185. Helsinki: Helsinki School of Economics /HeSE Print.

Moisander, Johanna and Pesonen, Sinikka (2002) 'Narratives of Sustainable Ways of Living: Constructing the Self and the Other as a Green Consumer', *Management Decision*, 40 (4): 329–42.

Moisander, Johanna and Valtonen, Anu (2005) 'Cultural Marketing and Consumer Research: Analytics of Cultural Practice', *European Advances in Consumer Research*, 7.

Morgan, David L. (1993) *Successful Focus Groups: Advancing the State of the Art*. Newbury Park, CA: Sage.

Muniz, Albert M., Jr and O'Guinn, Thomas C. (2001) 'Brand Community', *Journal of Consumer Research*, 27 (March): 412–31.

Murray, Jeff B. and Ozanne, Julie L. (1991) 'The Critical Imagination: Emancipatory Interests in Consumer Research', *Journal of Consumer Research*, 18 (Sept.): 129–44.

Murray, Jeff B., Ozanne, Julie L. and Shapiro, Jon M. (1994) 'Revitalizing the Critical Imagination: Unleashing the Crouched Tiger', *Journal of Consumer Research*, 21 (Dec.): 559–65.

Negus, Keith (2002) 'The Work of Cultural Intermediaries and the Enduring Distance between Production and Consumption', *Cultural Studies*, 16 (4): 501–15.

Oksala, Johanna (2004) 'Anarchic Bodies: Foucault and the Feminist Question of Experience', *Hypatia*, 19 (4): 97–119.

Peñaloza, Lisa (1994) 'Atravesando Fronteras/Border Crossings: a Critical Ethnographic Exploration of the Consumer Acculturation of Mexican Immigrants', *Journal of Consumer Research*, 21 (June): 32–54.

Peñaloza, Lisa (1998) 'Just Doing It: A Visual Ethnographic Study of Spectacular Consumption Behavior at Nike Town', *Consumption, Markets and Culture*, 2 (4): 337–400.

Peñaloza, Lisa (2000) 'The Commodification of the American West: Marketer's Production of Cultural Meanings at the Trade Show', *Journal of Marketing*, 64 (Oct.): 82–109.

Peñaloza, Lisa (2001) 'Consuming the American West: Animating Cultural Meaning and Memory at a Stock Show and Rodeo', *Journal of Consumer Research*, 28 (Dec.): 369–98.

Peñaloza, Lisa and Gilly, Mary C. (1999) 'Marketer Acculturation: the Changer and the Changed', *Journal of Marketing*, 6 (July): 84–104.

Peräkylä, Anssi (1997) 'Reality and Validity in Research Based on Tapes and Transcripts', in D. Silverman (ed.), *Qualitative Research: Theory, Method and Practice*. London: Sage. pp. 201–20.

Pink, Sarah (2001) *Doing Visual Ethnography*. London: Sage.

Potter, Jonathan (1996) *Representing Reality: Discourse, Rhetoric and Social Construction*. London: Sage.

Potter, Jonathan (1997) 'Discourse Analysis as a Way of Analysing Naturally Occurring Talk', in D. Silverman (ed.), *Qualitative Research: Theory, Method and Practice*. London: Sage. pp. 144–60.

Potter, Jonathan (2003) 'Discursive Psychology: Between Method and Paradigm', *Discourse and Society*, 14 (6): 783–94.

Potter, Jonathan and Wetherell, Margaret (1987) *Discourse and Social Psychology: Beyond, Attitudes and Behavior*. London: Sage.

Puchta, Claudia and Potter, Jonathan (2002) 'Manufacturing Individual Opinions: Market Research Focus Groups and the Discursive Psychology of Evaluation', *British Journal of Social Psychology*, 41: 345–63.

Puchta, Claudia and Potter, Jonathan (2004) *Focus Group Practice*. London: Sage.

Pulkkinen, Tuija (2000) *The Postmodern and Political Agency*. Jyväskylä: SoPhi.

Richardson, Laurel (1990) *Writing Strategies: Reaching Diverse Audiences*. Newbury Park, CA: Sage.

Richardson, Laurel (2000) 'Writing: A Method of Inquiry', in N.K. Denzin and Y.S. Lincoln (eds), *Handbook of Qualitative Research*. London: Sage. pp. 932–48.

Riessman, Catherine (1993) *Narrative Analysis*. Qualitative Research Methods, Vol. 30. Newbury Park, CA: Sage.

Ritson, Mark and Elliott, Richard (1999) 'The Social Uses of Advertising: An Ethnographic Study of Adolescent Advertising Audiences', *Journal of Consumer Research*, 26 (Dec.): 260–77.

Rogers, Carl R. (1961) *On Becoming a Person: A Therapist View of Psychotherapy*. London: Constable.

Rolin, Kristina (1999) 'Can Gender Ideologies Influence the Practice of the Physical Sciences?', *Perspectives on Science*, 7 (4): 510–33.

Rolin, Kristina (2002) 'Gender and Trust in Science', *Hypatia*, 17 (4): 95–118.

Rook, Dennis W. (1988) 'Researching Consumer Fantasy', in E. Hirschman and J.N. Sheth (eds), *Research in Consumer Behavior: A Research Annual*, Vol. 3. Greenwich, CT: JAI Press.

Rosaldo, Renato (1989) *Culture and Truth: The Remaking of Social Analysis*. Boston, MA: Beacon Press.

Rose, Gillian (2001) *Visual Methodologies*. London: Sage.

Rose, Nikolas (1999) *Powers of Freedom: Reframing Political Thought*. Cambridge: Cambridge University Press.

Sawicki, Jana (1994) 'Foucault, Feminism, and Questions of Identity', in G. Gutting (ed.), *The Cambridge Companion to Foucault*. Cambridge: Cambridge University Press. pp. 286–313.

Schau, Hope Jensen and Gilly, Mary C. (2003) 'We Are What We Post? Self-Presentation in Personal Web Space', *Journal of Consumer Research*, 30 (Dec.): 385–404.

Schouten, John (1991) 'Selves in Transition: Symbolic Consumption in Personal Rites of Passage and Identity Reconstruction', *Journal of Consumer Research*, 17 (March): 412–25.

Schouten, John W. and McAlexander, James H. (1995) 'Subcultures of Consumption: An Ethnography of New Bikers', *Journal of Consumer Research*, 22 (June): 43–61.

Schroeder, Jonathan E. (2002) *Visual Consumption*. London: Routledge.

Schroeder, Jonathan and Borgerson, Janet L. (1998) 'Marketing Images of Gender: A Visual Analysis', *Consumption, Markets and Culture*, 2 (2): 161–201.

Schwandt, Thomas A. (1996) 'Farewell to Criteology', *Qualitative Inquiry*, 2: 58–72.

Schwandt, Thomas A. (2003) 'Three Epistemological Stances for Qualitative Inquiry: Interpretivism, Hermeneutics, and Social Constructionism', in N.K. Denzin and N.S. Lincoln (eds), *The Landscape of Qualitative Research*. London: Sage. pp. 292–331.

Scott, Joan W. (1992) 'Experience', in J. Butler and J.W. Scott (eds), *Feminists Theorize the Political*. New York: Routledge. pp. 22–40.

Scott, Linda M. (1994) 'Images in Advertising: The Need for a Theory of Visual Rhetoric', *Journal of Consumer Research*, 21 (Sept.): 252–74.

Sherry, John F., Jr (1991) 'Postmodern Alternatives: The Interpretative Turn in Consumer Research', in T.S. Robertson and H.H. Kassarjian (eds), *Handbook of Consumer Behavior*. Englewood Cliffs. NJ: Prentice-Hall. pp. 548–91.

Sherry, John F., Jr. (1998) *ServiceScapes: The Concept of Place in Contemporary Markets*. Chicago: NTC Business Books.

Sherry, John F., Jr. and Schouten, John W. (2002) 'A Role for Poetry in Consumer Research', *Journal of Consumer Research*, 29 (Sept.): 218–34.

Silverman, David (1993) *Interpreting Qualitative Data: Methods for Analysing Talk, Text and Interaction*. London: Sage.

Silverman, David (1998) 'The Quality of Qualitative Health Research: The Open-Ended Interview and Its Alternatives', *Social Sciences in Health*, 4 (2): 104–18.

Silverman, David (2000) *Doing Qualitative Research: A Practical Handbook*. London: Sage.

Smith, John K. and Deemer, Deborah (2003) 'The Problem of Criteria in the Age of Relativism', in N.K. Denzin and N.S. Lincoln (eds), *Collecting and Interpreting Qualitative Materials*. London: Sage. pp. 427–57.

Solomon, Michael R. (2003) *Conquering Consumerspace*. New York: AMACOM.

Solomon, Michael R. (1983) 'The Role of Products as Social Stimuli: A Symbolic Interactionism Perspective', *Journal of Consumer Research*, 10 (Dec.): 319–29.

Spiggle, Susan (1994) 'Analysis and Interpretation of Qualitative Data in Consumer Research. Journal of Consumer Research', *Journal of Consumer Research*, 21 (Dec): 491–504.

Stake, Robert E. (1995) *The Art of Case Study Research*. London: Sage.

Stake, Robert E. (2003) 'Case Studies' in N.K. Denzin and N.S. Lincoln (eds), *Strategies of Qualitative Inquiry*. London: Sage. pp. 134–64.

Stake, Robert E. and Trumbull, Deborah J. (1982) 'Naturalistic Generalizations', *Review Journal of Philosophy and Social Science*, 7: 1–12.

Stern, Barbara B. (1993) 'Feminist Literary Criticism and the Deconstruction of Ads: a Postmodern View of Advertising and Consumer Responses', *Journal of Consumer Research*, 19 (March): 556–65.

Stern, Barbara B. (1996) 'Deconstructive Strategy and Consumer Research: Concepts and Illustrative Exemplar', *Journal of Consumer Research*, 23 (Sept.): 136–47.

Taylor, Stephanie (2000) 'Locating and Conducting Discourse Analytic Research, in M. Wetherell, S. Taylor and S. Yates (eds), *Discourse as Data*. London: Sage. pp. 5–48.

Tedlock, Barbara (2003) 'Ethnography and Ethnographic Representation', in N.K. Denzin and Y.S. Lincoln (eds), *Strategies of Qualitative Inquiry*. London: Sage. pp. 165–213.

Thomas, Jim (1993) *Doing Critical Ethnography*, Qualitative Research Methods Series, Vol. 26. Newbury Park, CA: Sage.

Thompson, Craig J. (1993) 'Modern Truth and Postmodern Incredulity: a hermeneutic Deconstruction of the Metanarrative of "Scientific Truth" in Marketing Research', *International Journal of Research in Marketing*, 10: 325–38.

Thompson, Craig J. (1997) 'Interpreting Consumers: a Hermeneutical Framework for Deriving Marketing Insights from the Texts of Consumers Consumption Stories', *Journal of Marketing Research*, 34: 438–55.

Thompson, Craig J. (2002) 'A Re-Inquiry on Re-Inquiries: A Postmodern Proposal for a Critical-Reflexive Approach', *Journal of Consumer Research*, 29 (June): 142–5.

Thompson, Craig J. (2004) 'Marketplace Mythology and Discourses of Power', *Journal of Consumer Research*, 31 (June): 162–80.

Thompson, Craig J. and Haytko, Diana L. (1997) 'Speaking of Fashion: Consumers' Uses of Fashion Discourses and the Appropriation of Countervailing Cultural Meanings', *Journal of Consumer Research*, 24 (June): 15–42.

Thompson, Craig J. and Hirschman, Elisabeth (1995) 'Understanding the Socialized Body: A Poststructuralist Analysis of Consumers' Self-Conceptions, Body Images, and Self-Care Practices', *Journal of Consumer Research*, 22 (Sept.): 139–52.

Thompson, Craig J. and Troester, Maura (2002) 'Consumer Value Systems in the Age of Postmodern Fragmentation', *Journal of Consumer Research*, 28 (March): 550–71.

Thompson, Craig J. Locander, William B. and Pollio, Howard R. (1989) 'Putting Consumer Experience into Consumer Research', *Journal of Consumer Research*, 16 (Sept.): 133–47.

Thomson, Craig J., Locander, William B. and Pollio, Howard R. (1994) 'The Spoken and the Unspoken; A Hermeneutic Approach to Understanding the Cultural Viewpoints that Underlie Consumers' Expressed Meanings', *Journal of Consumer Research*, 21 (Dec.): 432–52.

Thompson, Craig J., Stern, Barbara and Arnould, Eric J. (1998) 'Writing the Differences: Poststructuralist Pluralism, Retextualization and the Construction of Reflexive Ethnographic Narratives in Consumption and Market Research', *Consumption, Markets & Culture*, 2 (1): 105–231.

Turner, Graeme (1990) *British Cultural Studies: An Introduction*. New York and London: Routledge.

Uusitalo, Liisa and Uusitalo, Jyrki (1981) 'Scientific Progress and Research Traditions in Consumer Research', in K.B. Monroe *Advances in Consumer Research*, Vol. 8. Ann Arbor, MI: Association for Consumer Research. pp. 559–63.

Valtonen, Anu (2004a) 'Rethinking Free Time: A Study on Boundaries, Disorders, and Symbolic Goods', Acta Universitatis Oeconomicae Helsingiensis, A–236, (Helsinki: Helsinki School of Economics HeSE Print).

Valtonen, Anu (2004b) '"You Should Wear High-Heels": An Autoethnographic Account of Gendered Body Height Ideals', a paper presented at the 7th ACR Conference on Gender, Marketing Consumer Behavior, Madison, WI, 24–27 June 2004.

van Loon, Joost (2001) 'Ethnography: a Critical Turn in Cultural Studies', in P. Atkinson, A. Coffey, S. Delamont, J. Lofland and L. Lofland (eds), *Handbook of Ethnography*. London: Sage. pp. 273–84.

Van Maanen, John (1988) *Tales of the Field: On Writing Ethnography*. Chicago: University of Chicago Press.

Veijola, Soile and Jokinen, Eeva (1994) 'The Body in Tourism', *Theory, Culture & Society*, 11 (3): 125–51.

Venkataramani, Sita Johar, Holbrook, Morris B. and Stern, Barbara (2001) 'The Role of Myth in Creative Advertising Design: Theory, Process and Outcome', *Journal of Advertising*, 30 (20): 1–25.

Venkatesh, Alladi Sherry, John F. and Firat A. Fuat (1993) 'Postmodernism and the Marketing Imaginary', *International Journal of Research in Marketing*, 19: 215–23.

Vidich, Arthur J. and Lyman, Stanford M. (2003) 'Qualitative Methods: Their History in Sociology and Anthropology', in Y.S. Lincoln (eds), *Strategies of Qualitative Inquiry*. London: Sage. pp. 55–129.

Wallendorf, Melanie and Arnould, Eric J. (1991) 'We Gather Together: Consumption Rituals of Thanksgiving Day', *Journal of Consumer Research*, 18 (June): 13–31.

Wells, William D. (1993) 'Discovery-oriented Consumer Research', *Journal of Consumer Research*, 19 (March): 489–504.

Wetherell, Margaret (2001) 'Debates in Discourse Research', in M. Wetherell et al. (eds), *Discourse Theory and Practice*. London: Sage. pp. 380–99.

Wetherell, Margaret and Maybin, Janet (1996) 'The Distributed Self: A Social Constructionist Perspective', in R. Stevens (ed.), *Understanding the Self*. London: Sage. pp. 219–79.

Williamson, Judith (1978) *Decoding Advertisements: Ideology and Meaning in Advertising*. London: Marion Boyars.

Winter, Glyn (2000) 'A Comparative Discussion of the Notion of "Validity" in Qualitative and Quantitative Research', *The Qualitative Report* [On-line serial], 4 (3/4); available at: http://www.nova.edu/ssss/QR/QR4-3/winter.html.

Wolcott, Harry F. (1990) *Writing Up Qualitative Research*. Newbury Park, CA: Sage.

Woodward, Kathryn (1997) 'Concepts of Identity and Difference', in Kathryn Woodward (ed.), *Identity and Difference*. London: Sage. pp. 7–62.

Yin, Robert K. (1989) *Case Study Research: Design and Methods*. Newbury Park, CA: Sage.

Zaltman, Gerald (2003) *How Customers Think: Essential Insights into the Mind of the Market*. Harvard, MA: Harvard Business School Press.

Zaltman, Gerald and Coulter, Robin Higie (1995) 'Seeing the Voice of the Customer: Metaphor-based Advertising Research', *Journal of Advertising Research*, 35 (July/August): 35–51.

Index